WHEN THE LIGHTS WENT OUT

HOW ONE BRAWL ENDED HOCKEY'S COLD WAR AND CHANGED THE GAME

GARE JOYCE

ANCHOR CANADA

To Ellen, Laura, and Susan

Library and Archives Canada Cataloguing in Publication

Joyce, Gare
    When the lights went out : how one brawl ended hockey's cold war and changed the game / Gare Joyce.

Includes index.
ISBN 978-0-385-66275-8

    1. World Junior Championships (Hockey). 2. Hockey—Tournaments—Canada. 3. Hockey—Tournaments—Soviet Union. 4. Hockey—Tournaments—Czechoslovakia. I. Title.

GV847.7.J69 2007   796.962'62094373   C2007-903775-5

Cover image: Jiri Kolis/Spectrum Pictures
Cover design: CS Richardson
Printed and bound in Canada

Published in Canada by
Anchor Canada, a division of
Random House of Canada Limited

Visit Random House of Canada Limited's website: www.randomhouse.ca

TRANS   10   9   8   7   6   5   4   3   2   1

CONTENTS

ACKNOWLEDGEMENTS

This book is the product of more than 100 interviews over the course of the year. Almost everybody I contacted generously gave their time and best recollection of events 20 years in the past. What was remarkable wasn't that so much was forgotten—but rather that so much was remembered in vivid detail. I won't thank all by name here, but I will reserve special mention for a few: Pat Burns, who spent a morning hearing me out during his recovery from cancer; Sandy Templeton, who put into full perspective her late husband's life and accomplishments (no truly bad man could win the love and devotion of a woman so kind); Jim Cressman, whose authority and years of service to the game are the stuff I can only aspire to; Sherry Bassin, who, on Piestany as on everything else, was never at a loss for words and good humour; Shawn Simpson, who answered every call; Everett Sanipass and his father Joe, who dodged no questions; Alexander Mogilny, who can be as entertaining in an interview as he ever was on the ice; Professor Robert Edelman, who held my hand as he walked me through the history of Soviet sport; and Dennis McDonald, who scheduled his interview around his wife's medical treatments. These people went above and beyond and for that I am forever thankful.

Many people who were not quoted here played crucial roles in helping me research this book: George Milkov at *ESPN The Magazine* provided the translation for the interviews with the Soviet coaches; Artem Telepin Nicholaevich, Sergei Samoilev and Todd Diamond dug up numbers for contacts in Russia; and Tim Campbell ran down contacts in Winnipeg. For their sundry roles I must thank Paul Romanuk in London, UK, Dave Langford of London, Ont., Jim Kelley in Buffalo (the London of Western New York), Mike Sands of the Calgary Flames, Craig Button of the Toronto Maple Leafs, Tom Harrington of the CBC, sports librarian Dave Pal, thinking man's goaltender Seamus Kotyk, Stan Butler of the Brampton Battalion, Brian Kilrea of the Ottawa 67's, Mark

Giles at *ESPN The Magazine*, Derek Finkle of the much-missed *Toro* magazine, Ken Campbell of *The Hockey News*, Terry Koshan of the Toronto *Sun*, Canadian matinee idol Doug Bell, and Brad Pascal and Andre Brin of Hockey Canada. NHL media relations folk who bailed me out include John Hahn in Detroit, Zack Hill in Philly, Peter Hanlon in Calgary and Michael Gilbert in Buffalo.

A few journalists and historians must be acknowledged here. While everybody had the story of the fall-out from Piestany, Jim Cressman's work in the London *Free Press* was the definitive account of the tournament itself. And CBC's coverage of the game remains riveting stuff all these years later, with Don Wittman, Sherry Bassin and Fred Walker doing yeoman work. The best accounts of the 1986 WJC appeared in *The Hamilton Spectator*. The best profile of Bert Templeton was written by William Houston in *The Globe and Mail* a few years after Piestany. The Canadian Press detailed all the bench-clearings in and around the time of Piestany. The definitive history of Soviet sport is Professor Edelman's *Serious Fun*. There are dozens of sources for the history of Canada and the Soviets in the bygone era of the game, but a favorite of mine is the late Scott Young's *War on Ice*.

This book would have remained a foggy notion if I hadn't been aided and abetted by two consummate professionals: my agent Rick Broadhead, who will not only take my call but answer my email on a Sunday (at 2 a.m.), and my editor at Doubleday Canada, Nick Massey-Garrison, who suffered my quick, rough draft and, oh, about eight macro- and micro-edits.

Finally, I'd like to thank my daughters Ellen and Laura for their patience and support. (Ellen at age seven showed real upside as a hockey journalist by asking Cliff Fletcher why the Leafs practiced on ice. For her part, Laura is still stung by the fact that I wrote about a Canadian junior team that Darcy Tucker didn't play on.) And I'd like to thank my partner in life and words, Susan Bourette. I promise, I'll only ask you to read this *one* more time.

PROLOGUE—VANCOUVER
Remembering and Trying to Forget

Fortysomethings who were once national sports heroes are milling around a conference room at the Westin Hotel, a study in vintage testosterone. Those who once knew glory are now staring down middle age. But the next best thing to playing a championship season is replaying it. Reading the old clippings, leafing through the photographs and telling stories told many times over the years: a poor second to the original act, but still the next best thing. Hockey Canada has invited members of the 1982 and 1985 Canadian under-20 teams to the 2006 World Junior Championship in Vancouver, a reunion of the first Canadian squads to win the WJC, back when Canadian hockey fans were discovering the tournament. It has taken no time for the former teammates to pick up where they left off. They're transported back to a time before their hairlines started to recede. Back to a time before some of them made millions and before others realized they wouldn't.

Hockey Canada officials are all smiles. The reunion is a big success. Reporters are chasing the former players before they're bused off to their exhibition shinny game. Making small talk with the Hockey Canada officials, I suggest they should consider a reunion of the 1987 team. After all, I say, that 1987 team had lost only one game at the WJC, and it was the most successful Team Canada ever if the measure is how many players made it to the NHL. Just a few weeks before, one alumnus of that '87 Canadian team passed 500 NHL goals, while another is approaching 600. A key player on the 1987 team went on to become a key player on the 1989 Stanley Cup champions. One of his linemates at the world juniors that year went on to win Stanley Cups with three different clubs. Add in a couple of Olympic gold medals. The 1987 squad was a team of winners.

An uncomfortable silence follows. The Hockey Canada officials look at me as if I've just announced that I have a bomb strapped to my chest. Initial reaction: slack-jawed disbelief. Subsequent reaction: the wincing smile produced by a joke in bad taste. "I don't think so," says one guy wearing his Hockey Canada lapel pin. He looks around the room to see if any cameras are trained on him—if he is being punked or pranked. This is how Hockey Canada feels about 1987.

———

The game between that never-to-be-reunited Canadian team and the Soviet squad at the 1987 World Junior Championships is one of the most famous and infamous in hockey history. One poll rated it the fourth most famous game in international hockey history, the only junior game in the top ten. Yet if you trust the record book, it never happened. If you look up the final standings at the 1987 WJC, the International Ice Hockey Federation's under-20 tournament, you'll find the final standings: gold to Finland, silver to Czechoslovakia, bronze to Sweden. If you look for

Canada and the Soviet Union, you won't find them. The IIHF officials kicked those two teams out of the tournament. The Canadians who had won the tournament in 1982 and 1985. The Soviets who had won seven championships in the tournament's ten-year history. Canada and the USSR, DQed. The results of their games, voided, wiped. The IIHF handed victory to a Finnish team and medals to the others by executive decision, a vote, rather than the sum of all games on the ice. It's the sort of rewriting of history that evokes Soviets revisionism, doctoring photographs to remove discredited politicians. The Canadians and the Soviets, the players on both sides, came away with nothing more than stamps in their passports, asterisks, and memories of a few weeks together.

Casual hockey fans might not be able to place it if you mention the year, the tournament and the teams. Other details will trigger memories, though. Describe the bench-clearing and many will dial in. If that fails, refer to "the game when they turned the lights out" that will draw knowing nods. Others tie it to the site of the game: Piestany, a spa town in the former Czechoslovakia. "The Punch-Out In Piestany."

I have friends who covered the great Canada–Soviet games from bygone days, whether it was the Summit Series, the Canadiens–Red Army game on New Year's Eve, the 1976 Canada Cup. I've listened to them talk about greatness. And yet it's Piestany and those two junior teams I keep coming back to. It wasn't the best game in hockey history, or even tournament history. And those were far from the best teams that the two nations ever sent to the world juniors. Fact is, though, these two teams played a game that was unlike any other. "Sometimes you win, sometimes you lose and sometimes you're rained out," goes the expression. But Canada vs. the Soviet Union at the 1987 WJC ended up as none of the above. In that sense, this game stands alone in the history of sport.

True, it's not the only story of international competition turning into a theatre of gothic violence. There was another game too awful to finish: the Soviet Union's water polo contest against the Hungarians at the 1956 Olympics in Melbourne. Most people wrongly presume that water polo is a benign game. This contest was as friendly as a bullfight, and it left the pool just a little less red than the sand at the matador's feet. The game was called with a minute or so remaining and Hungary being credited with a 4–0 victory. Poetic justice: Hungary went on to become Olympic champions of 1956, weeks after the Hungarians watched Soviet tanks and 200,000 troops roll into their country to snuff out a democratic revolution.

Even junior hockey, at least Canadian junior hockey, had its own story of a championship that ended ambiguously, without resolution or satisfaction. The 1971 Memorial Cup Eastern final between Guy Lafleur's Quebec Remparts and Marcel Dionne's St. Catharines Black Hawks was spoiled, unfinished. The rowdy fans at the Colisée in Quebec threw batteries or knives or golf balls at the players, depending on which account you believe. They rocked the visitors' bus and knocked out the windows. When the Black Hawks refused to make a return trip to Quebec because the safety of their players couldn't be assured, major junior officials declared the series forfeited. The Remparts skated away with the Memorial Cup, however devalued it might have been. The Black Hawks still had the Ontario junior title, not bad as far as consolation prizes go.

Yet Piestany eclipsed the precedents.

Piestany was more vicious. The violence of the water polo game between the Hungarians and the Soviets was submerged—befitting the Cold War, it was like an iceberg, seven-eights underwater. You couldn't have seen the worst of it. In contrast, the violence in Piestany was in plain view. You didn't have to strain to see it. Just the opposite—you might have wanted to look away.

Piestany was more unjust. The St. Catharines Black Hawks of old deserved better, but ultimately it was *their* decision not to go to Quebec, not to take the ice. In contrast, the Canadian juniors were told that they couldn't come out of the dressing room. They were screwed over by a bunch of international hockey executives they never met and wouldn't have recognized.

All stories are about justice in some form, of things working out one way or another. But for the players who suited up in Piestany, that has never happened. They've never had their just deserts. They've never received their due. And that injustice has stuck with me.

The teams, too, were fascinating, both on paper and on the ice. The squads that the two nations sent to the world juniors that year rate as two of the strangest to represent hockey's dominant nations.

The Canadians' roster was a twenty-piece puzzle that didn't quite fit: a first-overall draft pick who barely played; two players passed over in the draft who were first-liners; a captain who barely talked; a seventeen-year-old under-ager who only stopped talking so that he could write a column for a newspaper back home; and so on down the line. The inconsistency carried over to the bench: a head coach who would never get a shot at the NHL and an assistant coach who would have his name engraved on the Stanley Cup.

The Soviets were twenty pieces that fit together to make up a picture you couldn't recognize. Canadians presumed European players would back down from a fight; these Soviet juniors didn't cower, didn't back down, not for a second. Whether they were merely willing participants in the most famous brawl in hockey history, or in fact instigators is a matter of opinion; that one Soviet player's actions, leaving the bench during a five-on-five brawl, incited a bench clearing that ended up with the teams' disqualification is a matter beyond dispute.

And, yes, then there was that disqualification. The IIHF officials voted to stop play; the result was twenty years of replays. They wanted to make an embarrassing moment go away; with the disqualification they made sure it would never go away. They didn't even consider a middle ground; a team that lost a single game at the tournament was sent home without a handshake. The IIHF executives capped it off by telling the Canadians they were still invited to the post-tournament banquet; and of course they were offended when the Canadians told them that they had lost their appetites.

———

Over years of covering hockey, I sought out those who played or at least played a role in that game. The two best known alumni from the Canadian class of '87 are Theoren Fleury and Brendan Shanahan. Both were one-of-a-kind: Fleury was the NHL's shortest impact player and its most tightly wired; Shanahan was a 50-goal-scorer who did a lot of his best work after he dropped his gloves.

I asked them: is there anything you wouldn't do to win a game, any line you wouldn't cross? It was, on its face, not a question about Piestany. It's another way of inquiring about the disposability of conscience in the biggest games, when victory is at hand. Both read the question in the context of Bobby Clarke's slash on Valeri Kharlamov in the Summit Series. Their answers revealed something about the players, and perhaps as much about the game of hockey.

The time seemed right for a question about conscience. I posed it to Fleury and Shanahan before the deciding game of the World Cup in 1996. You could have charged a car battery with the nervous energy given off the Canadian team in the dressing room at the Molson Centre. The Gretzky- and Messier-led troupe had been less than overpowering during the tournament and often there had been a country-club feel to the team cobbled together and coached by Glen Sather—perqs, ego maintenance, and low, low fire. Not for Shanahan and Fleury, though. They might have been the best Canadians on the ice in the team's overtime semi-final victory over Sweden.

"It depends on what kind of guy you are," Fleury said. "I know we have guys in this dressing room who are like that, guys who would be willing to do whatever it takes. I don't know if I'm that kind of player."

It sounded like a honest answer. It didn't sound like bullshit tough talk by a guy covering inner softness. It didn't sound like self-denial of a sociopath who would stop at nothing and leave the rationalizing for later. Then again, opponents couldn't know if he was that type of player. They presumed that he wasn't that type of player and assumed the risks. Or they presumed he was and played with apprehension.

Shanahan went a different direction. He made it sound like he had a conscience but occasionally played without it. "Standing here in my dress shoes and dress pants I can tell you that I hope there are some things I wouldn't do on the ice. But in the past, once I get on the ice, I've done some things I've felt bad about afterwards. I was raised around hockey and that Bobby Clarke story, that's our history. There's a pressure on us to be an example to young kids, to play the game with respect for the other guys. The real danger is that you have to be able to leave that stuff on the ice. You can't do what we do anywhere else in society. We've been raised in a game that values toughness."

Shanahan admitted—or maybe professed—to be capable of getting lost in the moment. He said that it had happened before and that he felt remorse and regret—because he thought the game was not a privilege so much as a trust. It's not a game but our history.

Piestany never came up in their answers but their answers can be read into Piestany. For Fleury, no one could have known what he'd do in the crucible. He didn't know himself. For Shanahan, many might have been shocked at what he'd do in a big game. Lost in the moment, he did things that rattled him afterward. What Fleury and Shanahan said had to ring true for other players in other games and on both benches. Hockey is not a neat and orderly pastime. When consciences and what passes for good judgment lapse, a game can descend into chaos. Even when it's a championship game. Even when it's the biggest game of players' young lives.

———

I've spent ten New Year's Eves on the road, covering Hockey Canada's teenage heroes. I've seen a bunch of Canada-Russia games up close. I've seen many more games featuring Canadian juniors up against other nations' best, and some of them have been memorable. But none had the same tension as a Canada-Russia showdown. The other games were "friendlies" even if there were medals on the line. Like Brendan Shanahan, those who put on Team Canada sweaters are aware of hockey history, "our history." They're too young to have watched games against the former Soviet Union and they might not know the names of the stars or the famous games, but they know there is history. It means something to them simply because they know it means more to the generations who went before them. And I'm sure that it cuts the other way too—that young Russians look to a game against Canada with pressures self-imposed and otherwise, freighted with history and expectations.

Not all Canada-Russia games that I've seen look or feel the same. A few times the nations' best teenagers played in front of no more than a few hundred fans. In Boston in 1996, Canada narrowly beat the Russians on the inspired play of nineteen-year-old Jarome Iginla. In

Hämeenlinna, Finland in 1998, Maxim Afinogenov clinically finished off a two-on-one nine minutes into overtime to put Russia into the semifinals and end Canada's run of seven gold medals in eight years.

Other times the Canada-Russia showdowns at the WJC played to packed arenas. At the Luzhniki Arena in Moscow at the 2001 tournament, Ilya Kovalchuk whooped and hollered and showboated on an empty-net breakaway to cap a Russian win in the preliminary round. At the University of North Dakota's home rink in 2005, Canada smoked Russia after Sidney Crosby caught Alexander Ovechkin with his head down and separated his shoulder in the final.

The CHA had heralded every championship as irrefutable proof of the robust health of the game in the country. Maybe every championship had been just that. But when the Canadian juniors had fallen short—as they did in seven straight world junior tournaments from 1998 to 2004 inclusive—different messages had supposedly been delivered. The WJC was "a tough tournament to win." The WJC wasn't "all about winning." Dozens of variations on "winning isn't everything." It was like that when Canadian teams had to take consolation in wearing silver medals after a loss in the finals, or in playing for a bronze medal, or in losing to Kazakhstan and plunging to eighth place in 1998.

It's hard to reconcile the party line that "it's not whether you win or lose" with the idea that only champions deserve reunion tributes. No matter. Hockey Canada was going to celebrate its champions and pass over those who wore the maple leaf but didn't come home with gold medals.

———

Wandering around the gala at the Westin in Vancouver, I catch up to Sherry Bassin. The general manager of the two teams reunited here, Bassin is holding court, talking about a motivational stunt that he pulled back in '82. It has the richness of detail and unhesitating delivery of a story often, even regularly, retold.

"Back in '82 we needed a tie in our last game against the Czechs to win the gold, so I came into the room after the second period with one of the gold medals," says Bassin, a gentleman whose raspy voice, boundless energy and antic delivery are those of an old-school stand-up comic. "Took it from where they were holding the medals. No one was looking. I walked around the dressing room and held the medal up, showed it to the players. I told them, 'This is what it's about. This is what you're playing for. Look at it. Look at it! *Look at it!*' And then I brought it real close to one of the players, waved it right in his face. He went to touch it and I pulled it away. 'You can't touch it. Not yet. If you win, yeah. Then you're a champion. But till then you can't touch it. And if you don't win you'll never touch it.' Those kids were on fire. You woulda had to scrape them off the ceiling."

Across the room, Jim Sandlak is catching up with friends from a team that had bonded long ago and is renewing those bonds instantly. Sandlak was a useful forward who played on both the championship team in 1985 and the Canadian squad that won a silver medal at the world juniors a year later. I ask him to compare the teams and the experiences—did losing make his second turn at the WJC an afterthought?

This is like setting up an umbrella stand on the parade route, but Sandlak gives the question more thought and time than I expected. His memories of '86 are no less vivid. "Of course it's easier and more fun to look back on a tournament that you won [rather than] the one you come up short the next year," Sandlak says. "And maybe I learned more from coming up short that second year than I did from the first. It came to us versus the Soviets [in '86]. If we beat them then we'd have won the gold medal. We lost 4–1 to them, but unless you could go back and look at it real close, you would have no idea how close we were to winning the gold. All the guys on that '86 team, including a couple of other guys here, know that the game could have gone either way. A couple of calls. A post. A bounce. They [the Soviets] were a great team, don't get me wrong. But we were a great team too. The line between winning and losing . . . it's a real fine line so many times."

———

After the reception I look at my notes.

" . . . you can't touch it . . ."

" . . . and if you don't win you'll never touch it . . ."

" . . . go back and look at it real close, you would have no idea how close we were to winning the gold . . ."

" . . . the line between winning and losing . . . it's a real fine line so many times . . ."

" . . . maybe I learned more from coming up short . . ."

Idealists believe sport isn't simply winning and losing but learning, a way to self-knowledge. The lessons from "coming up short" in Piestany were a crash course in the occasional cruelty of fate. Shit Happens 101. These were the most improbable circumstances ever. Not a fine line between winning and losing—there was no line, just some blurry smudge left by an official's eraser. How close to winning the gold: it's a distance usually measured by a win or loss, by a goal or two, by minutes or even seconds, but the Canadian juniors were not denied by a game nor a bounce nor ticks of a clock. No, their shot at a gold—in fact, their shot at any medal—came down to a vote. Never mind not being able to touch a gold medal. A team that might have been deserving winners of the gold yet the players weren't even allowed to see the tournament medal presentations. A team that was just minutes away from a triumph over the Soviet Union and . . . Well, there's no knowning.

What if your watershed moment is a cheat, a fix, a scandal? What if you're punished for something you've been taught you have to do? Does that build character or break character? What are you prepared to do and what will you refuse to do when a game matters most? Opening the histories and mysteries of Piestany had to yield a more interesting and valuable story in the human condition than the reunion of champions, the formula for nostalgia.

The first step, it seems, is to find a video copy of this piece of hockey history. The shelves of video stores are lined with official releases of classic games of international hockey. Loaded with extras. The entire Summit Series of 1972 has been a staple on the DVD market for several years. It conjures up baby boomers' memories of where they were when Paul Henderson scored his goal: sitting in high-school assemblies or phoning in sick to work or figuring out some way to take in that historic Game Eight. The '72 Summit Series has appealed to those who love country and nostalgia more than the game's aesthetics. A more recent release, the thirtieth-anniversary edition of the inaugural Canada Cup, offers fans a better look at a game played at perhaps its highest level ever, a Canadian team featuring two legends who were denied their chance to meet the Soviets in 1972: Bobby Orr and Bobby Hull. They will have a chance to see their boyhood heroes in their primes: Bobby Clarke, Denis Potvin, Guy Lafleur, Bob Gainey and others.

I find these items, and a variety of team histories. *Slap Shot. Les Boys.* But the 1987 world juniors—N/A. Nothing listed for ordering.

So I Google "Piestany hockey junior Canada 1987," thinking I might at least read a reprinted account of the game, or an article published in the years after that shines some light on the game in Piestany. The search produces 415 hits, most from fans who have listed every video in their personal hockey library—or who are searching for video copies of the game. A few links to sites with commentaries, Don Cherry saying that what "the Canadian team did was right."

A page on TSN's site left a vast expanse for interpretation, plenty of room for the middle ground, by describing it as "either the best or worst moment in Canadian hockey."

I narrow the search: "Piestany DVD hockey junior Canada 1987." This produces almost 200 hits. One of the first listed is the website of an outfit that sells DVDs of famous games. I sort through famous games (the Montreal Canadiens vs. Central Red Army, New Year's Eve 1975), and others that have a memorable result but which few have seen (USA vs. USSR at the 1960 Olympics in Squaw Valley). For hockey fans who would seek out this site, there is little need to explain the significance of these games, each a reminder of the occasional transcendence of a game played with sticks and skates. Then I sort through far too many hockey-fight collections to list. It is enough to list, say, "1984 playoffs, Montreal and Quebec"; the packages have to be shilled like upcoming pro wrestling matches ("chaos . . . bench-clearing brawls at the end of the second and start of the third"). On balance, violence trumps excellence. There isn't, say, a Best of Bob Gainey, but there are several Best of Bob Probert collections—some co-starring Joey Kocur. A Toronto Maple Leaf collection, headlined by the complete Game Six of the 1967 Stanley Cup finals, is padded by "Leaf fights 1971–1991, featuring Tiger Williams, Dave Dunn and Wendel Clark" and a Wendel Clark highlight package that lists fights with Probert, Marty McSorley and Rick Tocchet, but no game-winning goals.

The catalogue isn't listed chronologically. It doesn't differentiate between international games and NHL contests. A complete mixed bag. Then, at the foot of one page, a simple notation: "1987 world junior brawl game . . . Team Canada vs. USSR." It is described as "an awesome game featuring many young future NHLers like Shanahan, Fedorov, Fleury and many others . . . a huge brawl begins and the wimpy international refs [sic] don't know what to do to squelch it so they shut all the lights off in the packed arena . . . the players fight in the dark . . . unbelievable footage . . . $25.99 US." Black market? Grey market? Licensed? Not really clear. Not that it matters. Since 1987 those Canadian players might as well have been dissidents in the eyes of Hockey Canada; they were, are, and forever will be the shunned; their exploits are glossed over the in organization's official histories. This DVD is hockey *samizdat*. I add it to my shopping cart. And when my order is placed and its tracking number listed, I feel closer to the truth about teams, and a game played twenty years ago.

SHAWN SIMPSON GOALTENDER SAULT STE. MARIE GREYHOUNDS

BORN: Aug. 10, 1968 Gloucester, Ontario
HEIGHT: 5'11" WEIGHT: 157 SHOOTS: Right
NHL DRAFT: Washington Capitals — 3rd Round — 1986 Draft

YEAR	TEAM	GP	MIN	GA	SO	AVE
1985-1986	Sault Ste. Marie Greyhounds OHL	42	2233	219	1	5.88
1984-1985	Gloucester Midgets	30	1350	35	12	1.16
1983-1984	Gloucester Midgets	22	990	36	8	1.65

JIMMY WAITE GOALTENDER CHICOUTIMI SAGUENEENS

BORN: April 15, 1969 Sherbrooke, Quebec
HEIGHT: 5'11" WEIGHT: 162 SHOOTS: Left
NHL DRAFT: Available for 1987 — N.H.L. Draft

YEAR	TEAM	GP	MIN	GA	SO	AVE
1985-1986	Cantonniers de l'est Midget		NOT AVAILABLE			
1984-1985	Castors de Sherbrooke Bantam		NOT AVAILABLE			
1983-1984	Castors de Sherbrooke Bantam		NOT AVAILABLE			

GREG HAWGOOD DEFENCE KAMLOOPS BLAZERS

August 10, 1968 St. Albert, Alberta
HEIGHT: 5'9" WEIGHT: 185 SHOOTS: Left
NHL DRAFT: Boston Bruins — 10th Round — 1986 Draft

YEAR	TEAM	GP	G	A	PTS	PIM
1985-1986	Kamloops Blazers WHL	71	34	85	119	86
1984-1985	Kamloops Blazers WHL	66	25	40	65	72
1983-1984	Kamloops Blazers WHL	49	10	23	33	39

KERRY HUFFMAN DEFENCE GUELPH PLATERS

BORN: Jan. 3, 1968 Peterborough, Ontario
HEIGHT: 6'02" WEIGHT: 185 SHOOTS: Left
NHL DRAFT: Philadelphia Flyers — 1st Round, 1986 Draft

YEAR	TEAM	GP	G	A	PTS	PIM
1985-1986	Guelph Platers OHL	56	3	24	27	37
1984-1985	Peterborough Jr. "B"	24	2	5	7	53
1983-1984	Peterborough Midgets		NOT AVAILABLE			

CHRIS JOSEPH DEFENCE SEATTLE THUNDERBIRDS

September 10, 1969 Burnaby, B.C.
HEIGHT: 6'02" WEIGHT: 194 SHOOTS: Right
NHL DRAFT: Available for 1987 Draft

YEAR	TEAM	GP	G	A	PTS	PIM
1985-1986	Seattle Thunderbirds WHL	72	4	8	12	50
1984-1985	Burnaby Midgets	52	18	48	66	52

LUKE RICHARDSON   DEFENCE   PETERBOROUGH PETES
BORN: March 26, 1969   Ottawa, Ontario
HEIGHT: 6'03"   WEIGHT: 197   SHOOTS: Left
NHL DRAFT: Available for 1987 Draft

YEAR	TEAM	GP	G	A	PTS	PIM
1985-1986	Peterborough Petes OHL	63	6	18	24	57
1984-1985	Ottawa West Jr. B	35	5	26	31	72

GLEN WESLEY   DEFENCE   PORTLAND WINTER HAWKS
BORN: Oct. 2, 1968   Red Deer, Alberta
HEIGHT: 6'01"   WEIGHT: 192   SHOOTS: Left
NHL DRAFT: Available for 1987 Draft

YEAR	TEAM	GP	G	A	PTS	PIM
1985-1986	Portland Winter Hawks WHL	69	16	75	91	96
1984-1985	Portland Winter Hawks WHL	67	16	52	68	76
1983-1984	Red Deer Rustlers AJHL	57	9	20	29	40

THEOREN FLEURY   CENTRE   MOOSE JAW WARRIORS
BORN: June 29, 1968   Russell, Manitoba
HEIGHT: 5'10"   WEIGHT: 160   SHOOTS: Right
NHL DRAFT: Not Drafted — Free Agent

YEAR	TEAM	GP	G	A	PTS	PIM
1985-1986	Moose Jaw Warriors WHL	72	43	65	108	124
1984-1985	Moose Jaw Warriors WHL	71	29	46	75	82
1983-1984	St. James Canadians Midget	22	33	31	64	88

DAVE McLLWAIN   CENTRE   NORTH BAY CENTENNIALS
BORN: June 9, 1967   Seaforth, Ontario
HEIGHT: 6'00"   WEIGHT: 176   SHOOTS: Left
NHL DRAFT: Pittsburgh Penguins — 9th Round — 1986 Draft

YEAR	TEAM	GP	G	A	PTS	PIM
1985-1986	North Bay Centennials OHL	64	37	35	72	37
1984-1985	Kitchener Rangers OHL	61	13	21	34	29
1983-1984	Seaforth Jr. B	33	42	36	78	30

YVON CORRIVEAU   LEFT WING   WASHINGTON CAPITALS
BORN: Feb. 8, 1967   Welland, Ontario
HEIGHT: 6'01"   WEIGHT: 200   SHOOTS: Left
NHL DRAFT: Washington Capitals 1st Round — 1985 Draft

YEAR	TEAM	GP	G	A	PTS	PIM
1985-1986	Toronto Marlboros OHL	59	54	37	91	75
1984-1985	Toronto Marlboros OHL	59	21	29	50	98
1983-1984	Welland Cougars Jr B	35	19	20	39	46

DAVID LATTA   LEFT WING   KITCHENER RANGERS
BORN: Jan. 3, 1967   Thunder Bay, Ontario
HEIGHT: 6'00"   WEIGHT: 187   SHOOTS: Left
NHL DRAFT: Quebec Nordiques — 1st Round — 1985 Draft

YEAR	TEAM	GP	G	A	PTS	PIM
1985-1986	Kitchener Rangers OHL	52	36	34	70	60
1984-1985	Kitchener Rangers OHL	54	38	30	68	26
1983-1984	Kitchener Rangers OHL	62	17	26	43	54
1982-1983	Orilva Travelways Jr. A	43	16	25	41	26

SCOTT METCALFE   LEFT WING   KINGSTON CANADIANS
BORN: Jan. 6, 1967   Mississauga, Ontario
HEIGHT: 6'00"   WEIGHT: 192   SHOOTS: Left
NHL DRAFT: Edmonton Oilers — 1st Round — 1985 Draft

YEAR	TEAM	GP	G	A	PTS	PIM
1985-1986	Kingston Canadians OHL	66	36	44	80	211
1984-1985	Kingston Canadians OHL	58	27	33	60	100
1983-1984	Kingston Canadians OHL	68	25	49	74	154
1982-1983	Toronto Young Nats Midgets	39	22	43	65	74

STEPHANE ROY   LEFT WING   GRANBY BISONS
BORN: June 29, 1967   Cap Rouge, Quebec
HEIGHT: 6'00"   WEIGHT: 182   SHOOTS: Left
NHL DRAFT: Minnesota North Stars — 3rd Round — 1985 Draft

YEAR	TEAM	GP	G	A	PTS	PIM
1985-1986	Granby Bisons QMJHL	58	33	52	85	26
1984-1985	Granby Bisons QMJHL	72	28	54	82	34
1983-1984	Chicoutimi Sagueneens QMJHL	68	15	33	48	25

EVERETT SANIPASS   LEFT WING   VERDUN JR. CANADIANS
BORN: Feb. 13, 1968   Moncton, N.B.
HEIGHT: 6'02"   WEIGHT: 198   SHOOTS: Left
NHL DRAFT: Chicago Black Hawks — 1st Round — 1986 Draft

YEAR	TEAM	GP	G	A	PTS	PIM
1985-1986	Verdun Jr. Canadians QMJHL	67	28	66	94	320
1984-1985	Verdun Jr. Canadians QMJHL	38	8	11	19	84
1983-1984	Moncton Midget "AA"	50	44	77	121	79

PIERRE TURGEON   CENTRE   GRANBY BISONS
BORN: Aug. 28, 1969   Rouyn, Quebec
HEIGHT: 6'01"   WEIGHT: 204   SHOOTS: Left
NHL DRAFT: Available for 1987 Draft

YEAR	TEAM	GP	G	A	PTS	PIM
1985-1986	Granby Bisons QMJHL	69	47	67	114	31
1984-1985	Angevins de Bourassa AAA		NOT AVAILABLE			

PAT ELYNUIK   **RIGHT WING**   **PRINCE ALBERT RAIDERS**
BORN: Oct. 30, 1967   Foam Lake, Saskatchewan
HEIGHT: 6'00"   WEIGHT: 181   SHOOTS: Right
NHL DRAFT: Winnipeg Jets — 1st Round — 1986 Draft

YEAR	TEAM	GP	G	A	PTS	PIM
1985-1986	Prince Albert Raiders WHL	68	53	53	106	62
1984-1985	Prince Albert Raiders WHL	70	23	20	43	54
1983-1984	P.A. Midget Raiders SAHA	26	33	30	63	54

MIKE KEANE   **RIGHT WING**   **MOOSE JAW WARRIORS**
BORN: May 29, 1967   Winnipeg, Manitoba
WEIGHT: 5'10"   WEIGHT: 179   SHOOTS: Right
NHL DRAFT: Signed as a Free Agent on the Montreal Canadians

YEAR	TEAM	GP	G	A	PTS	PIM
1985-1986	Moose Jaw Warriors WHL	67	34	49	83	162
1984-1985	Moose Jaw Warriors WHL	65	17	26	43	141
1983-1984	Winnipeg Monarchs Midget	21	17	19	36	59

BRENDAN SHANAHAN   **RIGHT WING**   **LONDON KNIGHTS**
BORN: Jan. 23, 1969   Mimico, Ontario
HEIGHT: 6'03"   WEIGHT: 206   SHOOTS: Right
NHL DRAFT: Available for 1987 Draft

YEAR	TEAM	GP	G	A	PTS	PIM
1985-1986	London Knights OHL	59	28	34	62	70
1984-1985	Mississauga Reds Midgets	36	20	21	41	26
1983-1984	Young Nationals Bantams	NOT AVAILABLE				

PART I

WHEN THE LIGHTS WENT OUT:
The History of a Hockey War

HISTORY, n., An account mostly false, of events mostly
unimportant, which are brought about by rulers
mostly knaves, and soldiers mostly fools.

WAR, n., A byproduct of the arts of peace.

—From Ambrose Bierce's *The Devil's Dictionary*

Playing and Replaying

nsert the disk. Press play.

Look at Shawn Simpson. He's there at centre ice, in his goalie equipment, sitting on the chest of Vadim Privalov, pounding the bigger goaltender, driving his blocker, stiff as an ironing board, into Privalov's face. Simpson has pulled Privalov's white sweater over his head. The letters on the front of Privalov's sweater, CCCP, cover his eyes. Simpson has Privalov in hockey's version of a straitjacket. Two, three, four punches, all with bad intentions. Privalov doesn't have a clue what to do. He barely gets his hands up. Only after eating Simpson's blocker does he try to wrestle his way back up onto his skates. The camera dwells on them. They flop around. It looks like a pair of Michelin Men sumo wrestling, like two fat men fighting over a bar of soap on a shower floor. Just a few minutes before, the camera caught Simpson on the bench—though he's nineteen he looks like he's fifteen. He's all of 155 pounds, and maybe three or four of that seems to be a red super-mullet. Simpson vs. Privalov. It's the most unforgettable image from this game, two backup goaltenders fighting against their equipment as much as each other.

Listen to Don Wittman and Sherry Bassin, the guys in the mustard-yellow CBC jackets. They're straining to be heard over the crowd's whistling. Just seconds ago, when the network was coming out of a commercial, Wittman described a little pushing and shoving and wrestling in front of the Soviet net as "a real skirmish." He says that it all started when "Sanipass and Shesterikov collided." But then again, it has been coming since the opening face-off this day, thirty-four minutes earlier on the game clock. And it has been coming for almost forty years on the ice. The "skirmish" has escalated into something much more serious than that.

Wittman: I've never seen this in international play.

Bassin: This is unbelievable.

Wittman: The goaltenders are now fighting . . . Shawn Simpson has the Soviet goaltender down. . . . There's no way to restore order . . . they don't know how to deal with a situation like this.

Just keep watching the screen and let it play out. It's not just a fight between these two goaltenders but this "situation," a skirmish that descends into chaos.

Just keep watching an event that will take its place in hockey lore. Canada versus the USSR at the 1987 World Junior Championship. A crowd of three thousand sees it in the arena. Almost all are fans from Piestany and nearby towns. There are a few clusters of team officials, a handful of scouts, a television crew, the parents of one player, and one newspaper reporter, but really that's about it. It's a small-scale sports event by those measures. It's much more a television event. A hundred thousand or so are watching CBC's original broadcast live on an early Saturday afternoon; hundreds of thousands more will see clips of it on the evening news. The footage is a little dark, a little blurry, like all the television broadcasts that came out from behind the Iron Curtain, back when there still was an Iron Curtain. This is January 4, 1987, and the broadcast originates in a country that will cease to exist in just a few years: Czechoslovakia.

Try to look away. You can't. You can't for the same reason they couldn't look away at the Roman Colosseum. For the same reason that people slow down at car crashes and can't resist train wrecks. The camera pulls back. Fights all over the ice. Imagine two bags of ball bearings ripping open and spreading over a floor—that's what it looks like: fights from one end of the ice to the other, fights in every corner, fights in front of the nets. There's enough equipment, sticks, gloves, helmets and sweaters, to stock a sporting goods store. Forty players, and there must be thirty-six of them fighting. One-on-one wars. Two-on-one gang-ups. It looks like a parody of a hockey fight, a scene for a movie. But not even *Slap Shot* was like this. Each scrap like the barroom scene in *Shane*, minus the breakaway chairs. Punches. Everett Sanipass, a big, tough Native kid from New Brunswick, lands the best punch, a right hand that drops one Russian before he can grab Sanipass's sweater. Kicks. Stephane Roy takes the worst one when he's down, one guy serving as the holder and the other hoofing an extra point. There is only one head-butt you can pick out, but it's a classic. Vladimir Konstantinov drives the top of his head into the face of Greg Hawgood, who falls to the ice, his nose broken, his head spinning, blood pooling up on the ice.

Listen to Wittman and Bassin again.

Wittman: Smirnov just knees a Canadian player. . . . This is terrible . . .

Bassin: There is two guys on a Canadian player here, two guys on him. . . . There's pandemonium here.

Let the disk play. Wittman and Bassin are shouting just to be heard over the whistling and the booing, shouting over each other because they can't hear each other. Two voices become one. "I don't know how they're going to be

able to continue the game. . . . This is far from over . . .
Sanipass is ready to go with anybody . . . he's hitting anybody around . . ."

Hit pause.

———

Find the scoring summary from that game. Never has a
summary summarzied so little.

JANUARY 4
CANADA 4 SOVIET UNION 2

First period
   1. Canada, Fleury (Keane, Sanipass) 4:34
   2. Soviet Union, Shesterikov (Zelepukin) 4:45
   3. Canada, Latta (Hawgood) 15:32
   4. Canada, Fleury (unassisted)

Penalties: Fleury (Canada) 9:05; Wesley (Canada) &
Davydov (Soviet Union) 15:55

Second period
   5. Soviet Union, Kostichkin (Tsygurov) 11:13
   6. Canada, Nemeth (unassisted) 12:08

Penalties: Malakhov (Soviet Union) 0:47; Popov
(Soviet Union) 3:02; Popov, Monaeckov (Soviet Union)
& Sanipass, Fleury (Canada) 6:04; Davydov (Soviet
Union) 7:25; Hawgood (Canada) 9:15; Latta (Canada)
& Davydov (Soviet Union) 10:52

Shots on goal—(unknown)
   Goaltenders
   Canada: Waite
   Soviet Union: Ivannikov

That's how it appeared in newspapers in Canada on January 5, 1987. It never appeared in the IIHF record books. The game report is nowhere to be found in the IIHF archive, so says the IIHF's media liaison. Maybe that game report was crumpled up into a ball on January 4, 1987. It never made it into the books.

Look at the roster of the Canadian team:

Steve Chiasson
Yvon Corriveau
Pat Elynuik
Theoren Fleury
Greg Hawgood
Kerry Huffman
Chris Joseph
Mike Keane
David Latta
Dave McLlwain
Scott Metcalfe
Steve Nemeth
Luke Richardson
Stephane Roy
Everett Sanipass
Brendan Shanahan
Shawn Simpson
Pierre Turgeon
Jimmy Waite
Glen Wesley

Check these names against the 2006–07 NHL record book. All but one of the players from the Canadian team has played in the league: Shawn Simpson.

Check these names against the draft lists from 1986 and 1987. All but one of them is drafted by a NHL club. The one undrafted is impossible not to notice. He's all over the screen, all over the ice, throwing a hundred punches: Mike Keane.

Look at the NHL draft list from June 1987. Pierre Turgeon is at the top of the list, a pick by the Buffalo Sabres. Can't spot him during the fight. The second name is Brendan Shanahan's. He's easy to pick out during the scrap.

Check the Soviet Union's roster from the game.

Evgeni Davydov
Sergei Fedorov
Alexander Galcheniuk
Valeri Ivannikov
Alexander Kerch
Vladimir Konstantinov
Pavel Kostichkin
Vladimir Malakhov
Dmitri Medvedev
Alexander Mogilny
Igor Monaenkov
Vadim Musatov
Sergei Osipov
Valeri Popov
Vadim Privalov
Sergei Shesterikov
Andrei Smirnov
Dmitri Tsygurov
Anton Zagorodny
Valeri Zelepukin

Check the NHL record books from back in 1987. Count the Russian-born players in the league at the time. Zero.

Count them in the history of the league up to 1987. One. Viktor Nechayev played three games for the Los Angeles Kings in the early '80s and scored one goal before being sent down to play for minor-league teams in Saginaw and New Haven.

Check the names on the roster against those engraved on the Stanley Cup twenty seasons later. Fedorov, three times: Konstantinov, once; Mogilny, once; Malakhov, once; Zelepukin, once.

Remind yourself of one fact. Back in January of 1987, the Iron Curtain was not yet drawn and the NHL didn't have free access to Soviet talent—not yet, anyway. Players on this Soviet junior team will be the first to make their way from the motherland to the NHL while still in their primes. Mogilny defected a couple of years after this game in Piestany. Konstantinov was similarly spirited away from a Soviet team at a tournament. Fedorov waited until he was able to go through official channels, but he didn't have to wait long.

———

Hit slow search. Go back to the start of the fight. Hit play. Look for the referee. You don't see Hans Rønning. You see the linesmen, Peter Pomoell of Finland and Julian Gorski of Poland. But not the guy with the whistle, the one who's supposed to be in charge. The executives at the world junior hockey championship assigned the referee from Norway to work the last game, a contest between Canada and the Soviet Union with the gold medal hanging in the balance. He started the game. He does not stick around for the end. He skates off the ice—the only one in the game who surrenders.

Let it roll and keep looking for Rønning. A guy in black and white stripes shouldn't be that hard to pick out, but because of the melee it's like playing Where's Waldo? There he is, talking to the penalty timekeeper. The body language is plainer than any signal he has given during the game, more telling than any call he has made. He looks stunned. He looks helpless. He looks shaken, even impotent. He must wish he could blend into the background, but it's hard to do in referee's stripes. He wishes he were a chameleon, not a zebra.

Look into the stands. The fans are in deep shadow. Earlier in the game the cameras were focused on young Czechoslovakian fans wearing Maple Leaf pins and holding Canadian flags. They were cheering the Canadians in this game. The fans at this tournament cheered the Canadians almost as loudly as they cheered the Czechoslovaks. The cheers for the Canadians were a not-so-subtle protest against Soviet hegemony.

Listen to the whistling while the fights rage. It's white noise—high-pitched, ear-piercing, as if the audio is being scrambled by officials who want to suppress the broadcast. That's not it, though. No, it's whistling, the European equivalent of the Bronx cheer. You can't make out any of the 5,000 fans in the hard wooden seats. There are no crowd shots once the fights start. You can only guess what they are thinking—some are whistling because they just want to see a hockey game, others because they see something sinister in the Soviets clearing their bench.

Visualize clusters of teenage hockey players in their national team jackets sitting in the back rows of the arena. The Finns, the Swedes, the Americans, the host Czechs. A camera caught them in one quick shot earlier in the broadcast. They came here for the closing ceremonies and medal presentations that are supposed to come after the buzzer at the end of the third period, after the anthem of the winning team is supposed to be played on the tinny PA system. The Finns know that the Canadians need a five-goal victory over the Soviets to win the gold—anything less and Finland will win its first World Junior Championship. The Finns and everyone else think that "anything less" would be: a) a close Canadian victory; b) a tie; or c) a Soviet win. Even as the fight on the ice unfolds in front of them, the Finns or anyone else can't imagine that "anything less" will be d) none of the above. The other teams in the World Junior

Championship have no idea what will come to pass. When the fight breaks out, they have no idea how it will affect the tournament's outcome.

Find Jack and Audrey McLlwain in the stands. They're trying to pick out their son Dave on the ice. They were waving the Maple Leaf earlier in the game. Now Audrey is clutching the flag with white knuckles. Their son has never been a fighter—that was never his game. Now he has no choice.

Now consider what should be done about this game and about this bench-clearing brawl, with the World Junior Championship of 1987 hanging in the balance. The top officials in international hockey are in attendance, including the International Ice Hockey Federation president Gunther Sabetzki. You can't see them, but you know that they occupy the choice seats, a few rows up at centre ice. They're not whistling. They had been warned about the game getting out of hand, but thought a bench-clearing impossible. Now they're huddling, trying to figure out a way to end the tournament and save face. The American manager takes his Canadian counterpart aside to offer support, but that support is tempered with political pragmaticism: if it comes down to a close vote, he'll do what he can to help the Canadians, but he'll offer no guarantees. It amounts to, "I'm with you through thick, but not thin."

Look at the players again. The ones still standing are too arm-weary, too exhausted, to keep punching. They stagger around, drunk with fatigue. The whistling reaches a crescendo.

Pause the DVD once more. The screen is half black, like a partial eclipse of the sun. There were technical problems, glitches, all game long. But this isn't somebody spilling coffee on the control board.

Let the DVD run. "They're trying to turn the lights off . . ." Wittman begins. Bassin jumps in: "They're trying to control the play." Wittman finishes what he's saying:

". . . but that doesn't solve anything . . ." And then everything cuts to black. It's not the television feed going down. No, the lights in the arena have been turned off. The cameramen want to show that it's not the power going out or the cable being cut. They focus the cameras on the skylight on the other side of the rink. People walk about against that backdrop, silhouetted figures that give a spectral effect. Then the camera is trained on the scoreboard, still lit, still showing the score

2 . . . 4

and the time

13:53

and the period

II

and the teams in block letters

USSR—CANADA

Another number briefly flashes on the screen:

5:00

on the Canadian side of the scoreboard. There's no knowing what the official operating the scoreboard intends by this, and maybe it's just a slip. It is, however, unintentionally prescient: Canada will incur a major penalty in a very short time and the Soviets will emerge with wrists slapped. What you can't see on the screen is that the fights still rage. Only those in attendance, including the officials in the stands, can make it out; the referee in the runway to the

dressing rooms, the broadcasters, the scouts, a player's parents and a reporter can detect something else. Something
that was never seen before in international hockey, or even
international sport. Something that will never come to pass
again. Walking—not skating—out into this orgy of violence are soldiers. Carrying guns. At the Zamboni gate,
German shepherds, foaming at their mouths, staring at
their leashes.

Wait for the lights to turn on again. Players mill
about. They have no idea what to do. Or at least most
don't: Greg Hawgood skates off the ice and heads for the
dressing room to receive treatment for his broken nose.
But the referee and linesmen aren't around to hand out
penalties or direct players to the penalty box or the bench
or the exits. Equipment litters the ice and the players loi-
ter. Fred Walker, a reporter for the CBC, flags down
Everett Sanipass. He has never backed down from a fight
and he doesn't back down from the interview request.
Though he has thrown the biggest punches on the ice
before the lights went out, it's clear when the camera
focuses on Sanipass that he's still waiting to shave for the
first time. He has the face of a schoolboy. Walker puts the
microphone in front of Sanipass. Walker says: "Everett
Sanipass, you were the first one involved in that fracas on
the other side of the ice. What happened?" Sanipass is
breathing hard but otherwise is no worse for wear. His
black hair is hanging in front of his eyes. Maybe it's
fatigue, or maybe it's a case of nervousness, but Sanipass
seems confused. His syntax is scrambled. His words have
a faint French-Canadian accent. He tries to remain calm.
He opts for understatement. "A bit too aggressive," he
begins, and Walker's expression doesn't change. Sanipass
continues: "They been on us all through the game. I don't
think . . . I think we took a bit too much. I was gonna settle it down a bit. I wasn't expecting for the other guys to
do it. I really didn't expect that at all. . . . They were

stickin' us and everyt'ing." By the end of the interview, Sanipass looks puzzled, overwhelmed, and, yes, downhearted.

Press pause.

———

I replay this sequence for Fred Walker twenty years later, hit pause, ask him about his interview with Sanipass. "Just a couple of minutes after that interview, off camera, a trainer comes up to me in the hallway and tells me that Everett is in the dressing room, bawling his eyes out. The trainer tells me that Everett thinks that I blamed him—that I fingered him—for the brawl. That wasn't my intent. I went into the dressing room. I go in the dressing room and here is this tough kid, just inconsolable, weeping. I tell him that I wasn't trying to blame him, nor is that the impression the public would take from the interview. Everett can't even speak. He just nods."

———

Piestany was fast-tracked into hockey's lore. The funny thing is, for such a famous moment involving so many soon-to-be famous players, there's a secret history to Canada vs. the Soviet Union in Piestany in 1987. Secret *histories*, really.

The story of Fred Walker's trip to the dressing room to console Everett Sanipass is instructive. So much happened out of view of the cameras. So much wasn't told that day, or in the aftermath. Not even in the twenty years that have followed. It was an emotional maelstrom, but the video record of the game shows only anger, desperation and even hatred. There was so much more, including regret, sorrow, compassion and forgiveness. Some things didn't come out at the time—some things that the participants won't know about even twenty years later. Maybe because it dates back to an era before instant information. Maybe because things happened so fast.

No one knew that this would be the last battle in hockey's Cold War. *Perestroika* was something everyone had heard about, but almost nobody knew the consequences. A political scientist or two might have been able to predict how the Soviet Union would be reshaped in the coming months. How things collapsed and those things that didn't collapse were torn down. In fact, things were already changing behind the scenes, more than anyone in the West knew.

The DVD opens many questions and answers only a few. It doesn't fully explain how the battle starts, and its outcome takes place off camera. It doesn't even begin to explain how Piestany will touch lives and even change the game.

History and Hypotheticals

Telling the story of Piestany requires context. Not just about how the Canadians and the Soviets reached that final game at the 1987 WJC. No, the whole backstory is needed, the arc of history. The place of these nations in the game of hockey in the late 1980s. The emergence of the WJC as the second most significant international fixture on the sport's calendar.

Skip the prehistory, the stuff of sepia-toned photographs, those days when Canada had challengers but no rivals. Start with the arrival of the Soviet Union on the scene in the late '40s. The Soviets ushered in the game's modern era. Legions of Canadians didn't recognize the looming threat to their presumed ownership of the game. The Soviets had strange names. They had strange-looking equipment, as if designed by Rube Goldberg. Players wore bicycle helmets and even boxing headgear. Strange approaches to the game, soccer-style buildup, offences built on intricate webs of passes. Strange approaches to player development, training off the ice—they developed dry-land training, stuff that looked like it belonged in gym class, not an elite hockey program, because they didn't have a rink with artificial ice in the late '40s and the early '50s.

The Soviets were too unconventional, too alien, for Canadians to take seriously. Even Canada's first loss to the Soviets in the world championships—the East York Lyndhursts, a Senior B team sponsored by a car dealership, lost to the USSR 7–2 back in 1954—became fodder not for anguish, but rationalization. Canada sent less than their best—*way less*. "We could send a good hockey team to that so-called world tournament in Stockholm and run the Russians right out of the rink," the *Toronto Star*'s Milt Dunnell wrote. "It wouldn't be anything to brag about." Dunnell's words echoed widely-held sentiments, maybe even understated them.

A year later, the Penticton Vees did exactly what Dunnell claimed a good Canadian team would do: the Vees ran the Soviets right out of the rink, routing them 5–0 at the 1955 world championships and hammering Vsevolod Bobrov, the player who passed for the USSR's Rocket Richard. Radio broadcasts of the game reached what was then Canada's largest-ever radio audience and was effectively streamed into the national consciousness. And in Penticton, the local newspaper's headline voiced a sentiment that reached far beyond its circulation: Thousands Greet Vees as Title Comes "Home."

At the 1956 Winter Olympics, though, Canadians again took up the refrain of "if only we'd sent our best," though perhaps less full-throated. The Soviet Union's hockey club won gold in its first trip to the Olympics; the Canadian side, the Allan Cup–winning Kitchener-Waterloo Dutchmen, gave the USSR its only tight contest but lost 2–0. Canadian flag-wavers noted that the Canadians had once again sent a respectable side but the Soviets had never had to contend with *les Canadiens* or the Red Wings. Credit to the champions began to trickle in, some grudging, some prophetic. "If the Russians improve as much over the next four years as in the last 365 days, we'll have to annex them as the 11th province to get the shiny bauble back," Dunnell wrote. The Canadian coach, Bobby Bauer, was not so stingy with praise. "When you play your best game, what is there to say? They amazed us with the precision of their plays. Russia has arrived as a world power."

Each subsequent Canadian title in world champi-onships—the Whitby Dunlops in 1958, the Belleville McFarlands a year later and the Trail Smoke Eaters in 1961—was less a win over the world than a smiting of the Soviets. The idea that our victory was less important than their defeat gained currency when Canadians took some comfort in the U.S. capturing the Olympic gold in Squaw Valley in 1960. But by the '60s and into the early '70s the Soviets' domination of international amateur play was complete.

Nothing will ever eclipse the Summit Series of '72 in Canadian sports history. It was the rare sporting moment when the height of occasion meets the height of drama. But even here, even in the wake of Paul Henderson's goal, were qualifiers. Some still tried to spin it: *If only Bobby Orr hadn't been injured . . . if only they had taken Bobby Hull . . . if only they had taken the Soviets seriously from the get-go and shown up in shape. . . .* Any one of those components falling into place would have yielded an easier win. All of them, an emphatic win. Not that the theories could get tested quickly. Too easy to write off the Russians' wins over the World Hockey Association's stars in '74 as a win over a better bunch of Dunlops, McFarlands and Vees. Too easy to discount the Russian club teams' impressive showings against NHL clubs in exhibition play later as, well, something less than our best versus their best.

The triumph at the Canada Cup in '76 was arguably the highest level the game ever reached. Canada iced its strongest squad ever. The stars aligned astrologically: Orr in his last hurrah; Hull out of exile; the Canadiens contingent featuring Lafleur, Gainey, Robinson, Savard and Lapointe; the feral Bobby Clarke, among others. Canada's sublime victory was all the proof the true believers required. Canadian supremacy was well established and safe. For three years, anyway.

Then the Soviets whacked the NHL all-stars 6–0 at Madison Square Garden in the deciding game of the Challenge Cup. "Just a better team," Bobby Clarke conceded. The Soviets went on to dominate the 1979 world championships as the tournament had never been dominated before: Two victories over the Czechs by a combined score of 17–2, two victories over the Swedes by a combined score of 20–6, two wins over Canada by a combined score of 14–4. The Soviets were running everybody out of the rink.

Thus the result from the 1980 Olympics was not surprising so much as inconceivable. Hollywood appropriated the Miracle on Ice, the American amateurs' victory over the Soviets at the Lake Placid Olympics, for a couple of movies of dubious merit. It's easy to think of the Americans' 4–3 victory over the Soviet Union at the 1980 Olympics as an "upset." It's easy to think "miracle" is so much stars-and-stripes hype. Do that and you fail to appreciate the accomplishments of the Soviet team the previous season. The idea of college players beating this Soviet team in a medal-round game seemed to be pure fantasy. Rumours circulated—the Soviets tanked the game to assure that the Americans would attend the 1980 Olympics in Moscow. "Something less explicit would have been more likely," says Robert Edelman, a University of California historian who specializes in Soviet culture and sport. "The players could have been balking at [the coaching style of] Viktor Tikhonov. They could have been angry about the benching of [goaltender Vladislav] Tretiak." But whether they threw the game (and why bench Tretiak in a big game?) or were playing to embarrass their coach, this Soviet loss stands as an unimaginable anomaly in the record of the Big Red Machine.

The Soviets came back the following season with a team that was at least the equal of the '79 squad. They were motivated by the loss to the U.S. and by the death of Valeri Kharlamov in a car accident. They thumped Team Canada 8–1 in the game for the Canada Cup. The Soviets didn't lose another international amateur game through three world championships and the 1984 Olympic Games. They lost two games, against Edmonton and Calgary, in a six-game series against NHL clubs. The most memorable of the four wins was the Soviets' 5–0 rout of the Canadiens at the Forum. The Habitants' fans were cheering the visitors by the end of the game.

Signs of vulnerability started to show at the 1984 worlds: a narrow loss to the host Czechs, the eventual champions, and another to the Canadians. The Canadians hadn't pulled off a win against the Soviets in this tournament for a generation. They had only really threatened a couple of times at the worlds since '61. The signs of a waning dynasty showed that fall, when Canada beat the USSR in the final game of the Canada Cup. Any victory was almost enough to erase from the collective Canadian memory the resounding defeats in 1979 and 1981. Doug Wilson's goal to tie the game late in the third period and Mike Bossy's seeing-eye overtime winner were the footnotes. Canada once again triumphant, (almost) always triumphant: that was the story at this highest level of the game. Canada's narrow victories in dramatic fashion were given weight equal to the Soviets' resounding routs. At least by Canadian hockey fans.

———

During the Soviets' run through amateur hockey in the '70s, the IIHF launched the world under-20 tournament.

There was no great fanfare when the Soviets hosted the inaugural tournament in Leningrad in 1974. It was a little six-team affair, and the Peterborough Petes, with Doug Jarvis leading the way and Roger Neilson behind the bench, finished third.

The Soviets' dominance in the first few under-20 championships was admired in hockey circles, but fans hardly noticed. The world juniors were played exclusively in Europe. It flew under the media radar. The Canadian Amateur Hockey Association and the major junior leagues made the tournament no priority at all. They attended, but weren't committed. Canada sent junior club teams in the early years: the Petes, third-place finishers in 1974; a Western league all-star squad led by Bryan Trottier, second in 1975; the Sherbrooke Beavers, second in 1976; and the St. Catharines Fincups, coached by Bert Templeton and led by Dale McCourt, second in 1977. These teams didn't get much credit at the time. Their results seem more impressive now. Today, club teams from the Canadian junior leagues would be outmatched against the Russian or Czech or American national sides. In retrospect, they were positioned for failure to a worse extent than the East York Lyndhursts and the Kitchener-Waterloo Dutchmen back in the '50s. Not that anyone in Canada would have paid much attention. You had to look hard to find any coverage in the media. Canadians were able to overlook or discount or completely miss the Soviets' ascendancy. Eventually they were going to become familiar with the names on those Soviet rosters in the '70s: Fetisov, Larionov, Krutov, Makarov. They'd form the core of the Soviet team that mopped the floor with the Canadians—Gretzky, Lafleur, Clarke and a class of Hall of Famers—in '81.

"Understand that those were great, great Soviet teams," says Sherry Bassin, general manager of Canadian junior squads in the early '80s. "The first five years, the Soviet juniors not only won every game they played, they never trailed in any game. As dominant as the Big Red Machine, the national team, was back in international and Olympic play in the '60s and '70s it just looked like they were playing another game entirely. A lot of people probably thought they might never lose a game, the way they were playing."

The world juniors first grabbed headlines in Canada in 1978 when it came to North America. With Montreal hosting the tournament, Bobby Smith of the Ottawa 67's and sixteen-year-old Wayne Gretzky of the Soo Greyhounds led a nationwide all-star team. The world juniors went from a footnote in sports sections to a topic of conversation among hockey fans. Gretzky and the under-20s first skated into the national spotlight together. Hockey fans were amazed by Gretzky, who made the tournament, like so many things he would touch, his own.

Or almost his own. A trick of memory. The images replayed in all the tributes to Number 99—Gretzky spinning, weaving through defencemen, making an elite international game look like driveway ball hockey—eclipse a larger truth. Though Gretzky, the youngest player at the world juniors, was voted the tournament's top forward, he did not lead Canada to a gold medal. Not even a silver. The Soviets won their fifth consecutive gold, undefeated once more. The Czechs took the silver and Canada the bronze.

The Canadian program went back to its club-team approach in subsequent tournaments. Only after a desultory finish by the Cornwall Royals in 1981 did the CAHA and the Canadian junior leagues give the tournament a top priority. A familiar mindset ("We could be better") was overtaken by a pragmatic one ("We have to be better"). The CAHA and the junior leagues acknowledged that a club team, even a Memorial Cup champion, wasn't going to be good enough to compete in the world juniors. They assembled an all-star team to send to the '82 under-20s in Minnesota. This provided an image as memorable as

Gretzky's sensational dekes. More memorable, even. Canada won its first-ever gold, an event so unlikely that the organizers didn't have the Canadian anthem on hand for the medal presentation. The Canadian players put their arms around each others' shoulders. They belted out a version of "O Canada" as if it was a rugby song: long on heart, oblivious to tunelessness.

Looking back on that 1982 tournament, it was a remarkable feat for a Canadian team composed of future NHL journeymen Scott Arniel, Troy Murray, James Patrick and others whose hockey cards go for a nickel. They ran up a 7–0 score against the previously dominant Soviets before securing the gold with a tie in the final game of the round-robin against Czechoslovakia.

Dave Morrison, the son of a NHLer from bygone days, Joe Morrison, was a member of that Canadian team. He has spent the last decade as an NHL scout. His take on Soviet hockey in the '80s is based on what he saw as a player and scout. "Back in 1982, it was like the Soviets and Canadians were playing different games," Morrison said. "It wasn't just that they were pass-first and we were shoot-first. They played a game in circles. We played in straight lines. But even within a few years, after [we beat them in] Minnesota, you could see the Soviets' game changing—they didn't use the dump and chase like we did, but they used it occasionally. They'd chip the puck off the glass. We had no misconceptions about it, though. The Russians were great players . . . a lot of skill."

But Canada didn't snap the Soviets' championship streak in '82. No, the Swedes had won gold in '81. That suggested the world was already catching up to the Soviets. That the Soviets had good years and bad years like everyone else—they didn't have a factory where they turned out players like so much sausage.

The Canadian squad that was sent to the 1985 WJC in Finland had a lot more star quality than the gold-medal winners from '82. The lineup was loaded with future NHLers; four would have their names engraved on the Stanley Cup: Claude Lemieux, Stephane Richer, Jeff Beukeboom and Shayne Corson. Another would have his name chanted by fans of the Toronto Maple Leafs: Wendel Clark. The Canadians' run through the tournament resembled that of '82: a 5–0 shutout win over the Soviets early on and a presentation of gold medals after a 2–2 tie with Czechoslovakia in the last game.

That victory only raised expectations the next winter, expectations of Canada winning the WJC at home. The Canada–Soviet Union game at the 1986 world juniors was one for the ages, a 4–1 Soviet win at Hamilton's Copps Coliseum. "I played on both [the '85 and '86] teams," Jim Sandlak says, "and there wasn't any difference between them. The '86 Soviet team was much better than the one the year before. You had to give [the Soviets] credit. They played in a tough place to play. They played on a smaller ice surface than they were used to. And they beat us when they had to."

Selmar Odelein says the Soviets' system was more memorable than its components. "They just came at us in waves," says Odelein, a defenceman with both the 1985 and '86 teams. "There was no way that you could send your checking line out to shut one line or one player down. You couldn't really tell which was their first line and which was their fourth. You didn't get their numbers because you couldn't tell them apart. Guys like Valeri Kamensky played great against us, but it's not fair to name one and not the others. They had skilled guys going from the top to the bottom of their roster. They showed us a game that we hadn't seen back in our junior league. They could skate and pass the puck better than anyone we had played against. Though they didn't go for big hits, they were mean. Maybe you had to be on the ice to understand that, but the stickwork was also something we'd never seen."

Status Quo and Sea Changes

For baby boomers it might not seem like so long ago. It might seem like just yesterday when it's a number on paper: 1987. It might seem like the recent rather than the distant past when you consider that so many players in the 1987 WJC are still playing today. And it seems like just yesterday if you watched the Canada–Soviet Union game at Piestany in the world junior tournament.

Only when you look at the touchstones, only when you catalogue the watershed moments, does it become clear that this is *yesterday* and *history.* Nineteen eighty-seven: Ronald Reagan had called the Soviet Union "the evil empire" only three years before. That didn't quite call détente dead and closed, but close. Mikhail Gorbachev had moved into the corner office at the Kremlin in 1985. He didn't look like the standard-issue Politburo apparatchik, but no one trusted appearances. Reagan was looking into the Star Wars missile system, waiting for the ultimate plot twist, a Soviet attack. Gorbachev was looking at tearing down the homeland's status quo before it fell down, going for reform with *perestroika,* opening a closed society with *glasnost*, realizing all the potential for a progressive, socialist state. In the West there was still the backwash of dread and fear of the Red Menace. In the USSR the "evil empire" was presumed to be Imperial America. There was still the residue of decades of demonization of everything on the other side of the Iron Curtain, looking East, looking West.

The chilling of the Cold War coincided with the Soviets' arrival on the international sport scene in the 1950s. They joined the Olympic movement in 1952. The values in a Canadian hockey dressing room hadn't changed much in the time between the East York Lyndhursts and the Gretzky-Lemieux era. Prior to that, they had hardly changed since Howie Morenz. Traditional, anachronistic, primitive: take your pick. The Canadian juniors in 1987 weren't old enough to remember 1972. They were only four or five years old when the Summit Series was played. It didn't matter. That stuff went right into their collective subconscious. It was written into their genetic code. They saw the highlights and they were versed in the history. They knew about Paul Henderson's winning goal, about Bobby Clarke's two-handed slash on Valeri Kharlamov. And in the years since, they'd seen the showdown games between Canada and the Soviet Union. When the players on the 1987 world junior team were in grade school they saw the Soviets drill NHL all-stars in the Challenge Cup and the 1981 Canada Cup. They knew players on the Canadian team that had lost to the Soviets in Hamilton in '86. They understood how hard it had been for them to listen to the Soviet national anthem at the world juniors, played in front of a Canadian crowd.

"Back then, they knew so little about the Soviets," Shawn Simpson says. "The names all sounded the same. The teams all played the same game. They were the Big Red Machine, just this faceless machine that ground up all the other teams. They were the dirty Commies to us. It wasn't that we were not as smart as the public. Everyone thought the same thing. We hated what we didn't know."

The press fanned the flames. The press's hatred was unimpeded by an almost wilful ignorance. John Robertson of the *Toronto Star* waved the Canadian flag and burned the Hammer and Sickle. He hammered anyone who admired anything about the Soviet game. He dismissed hockey commentator Howie Meeker as "shrill" for having the nerve to point out the beauty of the Soviets' passing game. He described the Soviet team as "a product of the same unending conveyor belt of human misery which churns out mindless millions of oppressed creatures at a cost no free country would pay." He also derided the players. He called them "born losers." To be a Soviet was to be defeated no matter what the score. "From the neck up, each is a robot; to be ever-exploited as a mindless vehicle of propaganda by the state; to be always watched; always guarded; to be forever denied the luxury of free speech, or the freedom to believe in any gospel but the gospel according to Lenin." It was overwrought and it was purple. It was knee-jerk patriotism and xenophobia. But it wasn't out of line with what the readers of the sports pages believed. For many, they were having their own opinions and prejudices bounced back to them.

The press didn't speak for all the players in the Canadian system, though. Many could put the politics aside when it came to the game. They didn't think of the Soviet players as "born losers." The players to a one also saw it Howie Meeker's way with regard to skill. Any hate, as far as it went, came with a chaser of grudging respect. "We knew nothing about the politics or history, other than the hockey history," Greg Hawgood says. "What we did know is that they could play. They were just incredible skaters, right through their lineup. They could pass the puck better than we could. Any Canadian team playing the Soviets knew they were up against it."

Those who took their swings at the Soviet game hadn't spent a lot of time in Canadian junior arenas. They hadn't noticed that the game at the junior level wasn't quite art. It wasn't even family entertainment. The scribes like John Robertson and commentators like Don Cherry took shots at Howie Meeker and others who despaired about the state of hockey at the grassroots in Canada. Our country's game: love it or leave it. Don't fix what isn't broken. We're still the world's best. We still play a beautiful game. We turned out Wayne Gretzky and Mario Lemieux.

Which was true, of course, but it was hardly a representative portrait of the game as it was played in the major junior leagues. Fighting was as hockey-fashionable as Cooperalls. Rodney Dangerfield cracked that he went to the fights and a hockey game broke out. Everybody laughed. Not because it was ridiculous, but because it hit close to home. The players on the Canadian junior team were just a fraction of the top one percent of their class, stretching from the Memorial Cup champs down to Junior C. It was hard even for the top juniors to aspire to be the Canadiens of the late '70s. Those heights were painfully out of reach for the bottom 99 percent. All those still had prospects, though. They heard about Philadelphia's Broad Street Bullies in the '70s and Cherry's Boston crew featuring John Wensink and Stan Jonathan. They saw Dave Semenko taking shifts with Wayne Gretzky. The NHL money was out there for players who were skilled or tough. Ninety-nine percent could only fantasize about skill. Toughness was immediately accessible. Skill was precious. Toughness was in stock.

"I think there were more fights in junior back then," Everett Sanipass says. "I'd bet that all of us on that Canadian team had played in games where fights had cleared the benches."

"There were guys who could play the game out there, but there were also a lot of knuckleheads," Shawn Simpson says.

Here is a just a sample of the bench-clearing brawls that resulted in suspensions of players and coaches in major junior and its feeder leagues in the twelve months before the 1987 WJC.

January 28, 1986: bench-clearing brawl between the Brandon Wheat Kings and the Lethbridge Broncos in a Western Hockey League game.

February 15, 1986: bench-clearing brawl between the Creighton Bombers and the Melville Millionaires during a Saskatchewan Junior Hockey League game.

March 27, 1986: bench-clearing brawl between the North Bay Centennials and the London Knights in the Ontario Hockey League playoffs. Bert Templeton was behind the bench for the Cents. Brendan Shanahan was on the ice for the Knights.

April 6, 1986: bench-clearing brawl between the Moncton Midland Hawks and the Summerside (PEI) Capitals in an Atlantic provincial Junior A playoff game.

September 30, 1986: bench-clearing brawl between the St. Boniface Saints and the St. James Canadiens in a Manitoba Junior Hockey League game.

November 2, 1986: bench-clearing brawl between the Oshawa Generals and the Peterborough Petes in an OHL game.

November 7, 1986: bench-clearing brawl between the Spokane Chiefs and the New Westminster Bruins in a WHL game.

November 23, 1986: bench-clearing brawl between the Pembroke Lumber Kings and the Hawkesbury Hawks in a provincial Junior A Central Ontario Hockey League game.

December 16, 1986: bench-clearing brawl between the Humboldt Broncos and the Yorkton Terriers in a Saskatchewan Junior Hockey League game. The referee suspended the game.

It's just a partial list. There is no counting them—not if you open it up to times when the benches held back but five or six fights took place on the ice simultaneously. Not if you open it up to include Junior B or Junior C, where lack of skill and desperation to make it to major junior threw gasoline on competitive fires.

"I'd be surprised if there was any one of us whose team had not been in a bench-clearing," Scott Metcalfe says. "I'm not saying it was a good thing, but it was just part of junior hockey at the time. The big rivalry was Belleville and Kingston in our part of the Ontario league. We'd been in two bench-clearings just with Belleville before I went to the world junior [tryouts]. We had a couple of others with a couple of other teams. I was always a tough guy, but we weren't a goon team. That was just how it was back then. If you're playing someone six or eight times in a season—if you know you're up against this one player all that time—you fought him at the start of the season just to send him a message or at the end of the season because you were sick and tired of him. It was pretty tough stuff, and I know that [Canadian junior hockey] was starting to lose more and more skilled players to U.S. college because the skilled guys just couldn't be bothered with the crap they'd have to take to stay in junior."

The mid- and late 1980s weren't the best of times in Canadian junior hockey. But they weren't the worst of times. Frank Bonello of NHL Central Scouting called the draft classes of '86 and '87 "decent but unexceptional," which might be generous. There were good players, even a Hall of Fame player or two. It was hard to call any of them transcendent, though. You couldn't say that they were players for the ages. They were players for the times.

And though they were proud to have been selected to play for Canada at the WJC, they weren't "mindless robots" any more than the Soviets were. They were teenagers. They were playing for themselves. They always had. That they were playing for the Canadian hockey system, that they were playing to uphold the Canadian brand of the game—these were leaps that others made. They weren't playing for validation of Canadian values. Not the way they saw it.

———

It's easy to forget that now. Now that some of the secrets have been spilled. Now that the documents have been released. Now that the inner workings of the Soviet regime—the *last* Soviet regime, as it turned out—are studied in university political science courses, and no longer simply speculated about by Kremlinologists in intelligence agencies. It was a closed society being opened. Not quickly. Wider than originally imagined. Not with bold declarations of reform most of the time, but rather with a framing that would reassure the old guard.

Those Kremlinologists made educated guesses. The rest of us just guessed. One thing we believed. One thing we were confident in: they weren't like us.

What wasn't coming undone in the Soviet Union in the late '80s was being reinvented. Rules that had been constant for decades were being reconsidered. What had remained unchanged going back to Lenin and Stalin was being changed overnight. One of the areas of change little talked about at the time was sport. It might have been missed because sportswriters in the West were more concerned about who won and who scored rather than which way the wind was blowing.

The Soviet Union's squads in international sport were part of the greater mystery. No one knew what to expect when its athletes showed up at the Olympic Games in 1952. The Soviets had thought about sending athletes to the Summer Games in 1948, but Stalin wanted to hold back until victory could be guaranteed across the board. Stalin's plan: use sports to inspire the masses; use athletes to demonstrate to the world, and their own people, the superiority of the Soviet system; use athletes to command international respect. Part of the plan: what's made in the USSR stays in the USSR. Soviet athletes were going to play in Soviet leagues, compete in Soviet competitions like the Spartakiads, a sort of domestic Olympics. They were going to make forays across the Iron Curtain only for major international competitions.

What we didn't know then we found out later. We didn't know about sports then because the Kremlinologists in the intelligence community had bigger things to worry about. They were worried about thermonuclear war, about spies in our midst. They weren't worried about teams running up the score, about athletes winning gold medals. Leonid Brezhnev's last days as Soviet leader were government's "period of stagnation," says historian Robert Edelman. Edelman says that the moribund leadership didn't reflect a quickly evolving society, that Brezhnev and the rest were almost oblivious to it. And one of the most fluid of the areas was sport.

Soviet sports leagues—the soccer league, the hockey league—made money. They paid out more to the Kremlin than the cost of their subsidies. It was that way with domestic play, and all the more true with events like the European championships in soccer or the Challenge Series and Canada Cups in hockey. The Soviets took home a piece of the gate and television money. The Soviet soccer program wasn't quite up there with its hockey program in the '80s, but it was an international power, a runner-up in the

European championship in 1986. Renat Daffayev was regarded as the world's top goalkeeper.

But *perestroika* brought opportunities and it brought demands. Other areas of society had first call on government resources. In a crumbling system sport was in a position to be choked off. Sports officials had to investigate going commercial and going professional, if they were going to keep playing. The soldier-athletes in soccer and hockey were amateurs in name only, and none of them had any illusions otherwise. They had played against the world and they certainly weren't amateurs in any meaningful sense. Olympic officials were opening the door to professionals. It was time to go out into the world and play with the world. Some mourned the old system: world champion pole vaulter Sergei Bubka was the loudest and most conspicuous proponent of the old way. Others said changes couldn't be fast enough or sweeping enough.

Teams in the Soviet soccer league were the first to go openly pro. Players started to transfer from one team to another not by order of bureaucrats, but rather by virtue of the highest bid. *Goskomsport* (the Ministry of Sport) started looking for commercial opportunities. The outfit started selling advertising for major Western corporations on team uniforms, on rinkboards and on stadium billboards. *Sovintersport*, a division of *Goskomsport,* opened for business: its product was Soviet muscle. It looked to move Soviet athletes to teams in Europe and North America in exchange for hard currency. *Sovintersport*'s first product line was soccer players. Teams took a piece of the transfer fees, and the rest found its way into the coffers of *Goskomsport* and the Kremlin. Basketball players were being flogged to teams in Finland and Spain. Soviet athletes could look West for the first time and do more than wonder "what if?"

The athletes chose up sides. Those who prospered under the old regime took Sergei Bubka's line. Viktor

Tikhonov had ascended to the top spots in Soviet hockey—
coach of the national team, coach of the stacked Red Army
team—in the late '70s. He had survived being "Miracled"
in Lake Placid in his first Olympic Games. He was one of
those who prospered. Above reproach. Though many
of our stereotypes were wrong, in Tikhonov, the stereotype
of the Soviet coach as a meglomaniacal disciplinarian,
the hard taskmaster, fit like a fur hat. The culture of the
national team program became *his* culture. The old regime
gave Tikhonov the hammer and he treated the national
team members and his Red Army players like nails. Veteran
players bristled under the despot. They had looked to the
West for years and wondered, "What if we could get away
from him?" They weren't robots, no matter what John
Robertson or other Canadian sportswriters said. They
weren't mindless and they weren't born losers. They knew
enough of the world through their travels to tournaments
to have some sort of idea about what they were missing.
They saw a window of opportunity opening for athletes in
other sports. Not surprisingly, they wanted to climb
through that window.

Though everything was changing *above* them, life
wasn't so very different for the elite players in the Soviet
junior program. They already had the benefit of a system of
grassroots player development that would collapse from a
lack of resources after they moved on. NHL scouts in
Europe thought the Soviet program was lagging behind the
standard that it had set in the mid- and late '70s; nonetheless, the consensus was that the Soviet class of '69 birthdays was likely its strongest ever. "Mogilny, Fedorov and
Pavel Bure were probably the world's best three players
born that year," scout Inge Hammarstrom says. "It's hard
to think of a year when the Soviets—or any country—ever
turned out three players of that quality."

These young players were the first generation of
teenage players who came along at the time of open

professionalism in the Soviet Union. They were the first generation of teenage players who saw their mentor teammates question the authority of Tikhonov and the others. They were the first generation of teenage players who saw other top Soviet athletes leave for Europe and North America, and they saw things differently.

"The Soviets were idealistic at some level about sport," professor Robert Edelman says. "They wanted victory. They also wanted to be better—to elevate the game and set higher standards. They wanted their sportsmen to serve as examples to the Soviet people . . . one reason that they had tried to distance themselves from the Canadian game. They thought that the Canadian game was a brutal one [and] brawling was bourgeois."

They weren't just idealists and ideologues, though. They were hockey men. They were fully able to pick up on the quality of the best Canadian squads—whether it was the '76 Canada Cup team or the Canadian sides at the 1982 and '85 WJCs. And they understood that the Canadian approach gave teams with less impressive talent a chance to compete. They paid the Canadians the highest compliment: imitation. "I heard on absolutely unquestionable authority that the Soviets were looking to play a more Canadian game," Sherry Bassin says. "Not that they wanted to give up their game . . . the skill part of it, the skating. Just that they wanted to bring in a physical toughness. They wanted their players to have more of a physical edge to their game and to play with more urgency. That's what coaches were demanding of their players at the junior tournaments [in the mid-'80s]. That was the direction they were going."

Lives and Times

By 1987 the world junior program was becoming a pressure cooker. It had started to build with that first win in 1982. It intensified with the win in '85 and the tense loss to the Soviets the next year at home. The fact that Canada had won before overshadowed the challenge in front of the team: they were expected to be the world's best junior team after having met each other just a few weeks before. Most were strangers to one another. Some had played against each other. A few players had crossed paths before. Theoren Fleury and Mike Keane were playing together in Moose Jaw. Kerry Huffman and Steve Chiasson had grown up in Peterborough and played together for years, right up to being on the blue line of the Guelph Platers. Most were the stars on their teams. They came to the tryouts with the hope of landing a spot in the lineup and not only representing their countries, but also representing their leagues, whether it was the Western Hockey League, the Ontario Hockey League or the Quebec Major Junior Hockey League. And they came with the hope of representing their respective teams back home.

They wore the maple leaf on the front of their sweaters, they wore red and white, but they all had their own teams, their own stories.

You might have thought their stories would all have been similar, or that hockey stardom follows some sort of template. You'd be wrong, though. Yes, they all played the same game and, yes, they were almost guaranteed to have started playing at a young age and to have enjoyed some success early on. And, yes, they went on to enjoy some level of celebrity while in their mid-teens, some sort of status as hometown heroes. But they might as well have been pulled at random from twenty high-school classes and street corners across the country.

It's true of every year, and it was true of this particular year. Back in 1986, when thirty young men reported to the tryout camp in Orleans, just outside of Ottawa, you had a bunch of young men who were going on to very different careers and very different lives. There was but one common thread: for three weeks, they were going to play together as hard as they ever had. As hard as they would ever play. And when it was done they were going to say goodbye, most of them forever. If they ever again crossed paths, it was going to be a wave, a handshake, maybe small talk. Too often sports is compared to war, but this was one sense where the analogy is accurate, an intimate brotherhood of young men who were previously strangers, an intense, communal dependence that all involved know will last a few weeks and then be gone.

It takes only a few of these players' life stories to underline how different their lives and circumstances were.

Take Brendan Shanahan. His life ran closest to the stock story of a young hockey player's life. He was the youngest of four brothers who grow up in Mimico, a little pocket of middle-class and working-class neighbourhoods in the west end of Toronto. His father, Donal, was a fireman, one who supposedly looked at Brendan as a candidate for the firehall. The Shanahan brothers were all athletes: hockey players and lacrosse players. Like them, he was a solid six foot two. The brothers were all in that range. By the time he arrived at the Canadian junior camp he was already a heralded player, projected to be one of the top two players selected in the first round of the NHL entry draft in June 1987. He was an estimable fighter, one who quickly established his talent with his stick and his ungloved fists in the Ontario Hockey League, one who became an instant favourite of the fans of his team, the London Knights.

It was nature *and* nurture. He would always say that he had to fight his brothers at every turn—it was a great story, the idea that he had to elbow older, larger brothers on either side of him at the dinner table just to get his fair share. If Frank McCourt could write a hockey player's story, it would surely read like this. The only snag is, it was not quite true. His brothers would roll their eyes for years when interviewed about the subject. He was our little brother, they said. We didn't beat him up. No, we protected him, they protested. It was his gag, his prank, that he put over on his brothers. Don't let the truth stand in the way of a good story: it's a rule that has served generations of Hibernian storytellers well. It was his guiding principle.

All the players in Piestany were chasing a shot at the NHL but for Shanahan the chase was more urgent. He wanted to make it in time for his father to see it—or more importantly to appreciate it. Donal Shanahan wasn't going to the firehall anymore because of early onset Alzheimer's. "I remember Brendan saying that his father could have been fire chief," says Jim Cressman, who covered Shanahan as a London Knight. "He was that high up in the fire department administration. It had to be so hard for a teenager to move away from home and deal with that." Adds Brendan's older brother Brian: "It was hard for all of us but especially for Brendan. He was just fifteen when our father was diagnosed. I really feel like he was robbed of having a father at all."

Take Theoren Fleury. His life was nothing like Shanahan's. There was love in his home, but there was serious trouble: dysfunction, neglect and abuse, at least in the form of substance abuse. He was a Métis, born in Russell, Manitoba. His father, Wally, was a hard drinker. He made it to a lot of Theoren's games, but would leave after a few minutes to make his way to a nearby bar. His mother rarely came to see him play. She was addicted to Valium. He defined himself by the game he played and the teams he played for. An arena, any arena, became his home, but teams were no substitute for a family. He said years later that he never had a friend on the youth-league teams he played for. He forever regarded his status as a lone wolf as a point of pride. "I wouldn't have become as tough and determined to play if I had a regular home life," he says. "I don't look back on [my youth] as a lonely or unhappy time. The game was always an escape from the bad things in my life." And whenever he was asked about his prospects— whether it was making the step up to junior, or playing for the world junior team, or playing in the NHL—he always said the same thing. "I've never been cut from a team I played for." It was his motto and his mantra. He would repeat it many times. In his words there was a fearsome resolve, in his demeanour, darkness.

Take Everett Sanipass. He might never have played the game except for the persistence of his father. The Sanipasses grew up on the Micmac reserve near Big Cove, New Brunswick. As a boy, Everett knew little of life off the reserve. "I was just a happy kid who liked to play pond hockey every day, hour after hour after school," he says. "I knew a lot more about the pond than all the other places." He was by his own estimation an innocent, never thinking ill of people.

He was disappointed that he wasn't able to play in the youth leagues off the reserve. Every season, it seemed like something would come up. One year, he tried to sign up too late. Another year the paperwork was lost after he applied. Everett thought these were coincidences. His father, Joe Sanipass, knew better. He knew that the league didn't have any use for a Native kid. There weren't any in the league. Joe Sanipass wasn't taking up something as a cause—not right away, anyway. He wasn't fighting to get Native kids into the league. If that's what it came to, it would be great. But the first thing was to make sure that the league officials let *his* Native kid play. If the league officials thought that Joe Sanipass was going to go away if they ignored him, they were cured of that notion when they received a letter from a lawyer he had hired. "The lawyer's message was pretty basic," Joe Sanipass says. "Either this Native kid is on the ice when the league starts, or *nobody* is." That's how Everett Sanipass became the first Native kid to play in the local league. That's how he got off the reserve. That's how he got off the pond.

It was a tougher thing when Joe had a decision to make when Everett turned thirteen. His game was too good for the pond and, by then, too good for the local league. He needed a challenge if he was going to improve. And the only place for it was in Moncton—in the bantam league there. Which meant that Everett was going to have to leave the reserve. Which meant that he was going to have to be billeted by another family.

"It was tough to do, but my father thought I could get a better education off the reserve and maybe get a college scholarship if I played in the league in Moncton," he says. Three seasons away from the reserve. Everett Sanipass thought he had seen it all when he made it to Moncton. And then his team made a trip to Europe. "All over the place, Sweden, Finland, Denmark, and everywhere we went we were the people's favourite team," he says. "We were like heroes. I thought it would never get better. I thought that I had already done everything I could in hockey."

An innocent. No idea. No idea that there were people looking at him. No idea that scouts from the Quebec major junior league were looking at him. And when he finally heard about it—Joe let everyone know that Everett had gone as far as he wanted to go: Moncton. On a trip with Moncton midgets, that was fine. But Everett wasn't going to be moving away.

That was the story when the Verdun Junior Canadiens drafted him. That was the story they stuck to when Verdun offered to fly him to Montreal—not to play for them, just to watch a practice, they told him, just to show him what he was missing. Everett and Joe flew to Montreal. The team told him there were tickets waiting for him for the Canadiens game at the Forum that night—but watch practice first. Everett got an eyeful at practice, and the general manager asked him: "Think you can play with these guys?" Everett said he didn't see why he couldn't. The general manager asked him if he wanted to skate with them in practice. Everett said he didn't have his skates or equipment. We'll find something, the general manager said. Fifteen minutes later, Everett Sanipass stepped onto the ice in skates he was wearing for the first time. His first junior practice.

An hour later, he stepped back onto the ice after getting stitches in his face from his first junior practice. Afterward, the general manager cornered Sanipass and told him that the team had a game Sunday afternoon—did he want to play? Everett Sanipass looked at Joe. Sure, Everett said, "but do I still get to go to the Forum tonight?" The next afternoon, Everett Sanipass took a regular shift with the Verdun Junior Canadiens.

Take the warden's son. If someone had told you that one of the players went to a prison on Career Day, that one young man went with his family for Christmas dinner with inmates, you'd have picked Mike Keane out of the lineup. Ferally tough, Keane was the son of a guy who knew how to handle tough cases. "A type-A personality," Theoren

Fleury says. "In more than twenty years I've never played with anybody who was as competitive as him. I think I was lucky to have had a chance to play with him early in my career. I learned a lot from him." He looked like Huck Finn, maybe Opie from the wrong side of the tracks. He sounded like Joe Friday—he never said anything more than needed to be said. He used this to-the-point approach as cover—he had a slight speech impediment, a stutter. But if anyone—*anyone*—looked at him sideways, it was trouble.

Take the army brat. Well, not quite an army brat. Shawn Simpson seemed dialled into everything that was happening on the team. He grew up in an Ottawa suburb, son of an administrator in the Department of National Defence. He grew up just around the corner from Dennis McDonald, the manager of the Canadian team. Simpson's home was closer to the rink than the hotel where the Canadian juniors bunked during the tryouts. His friends and family came to the practices—within a few days they knew as much about the players on the squad as the CAHA staff. Simpson had his file on everybody. He had his work-up and he told his family all about his teammates. On every roster you'll find one of those players, one who knows somebody on every team, who keeps track of all the gossip and rumours, who doesn't need a little black book because he has everything logged away in memory.

Take the one player that never imagined he'd be any-where near a spotlight. Dave McLlwain was playing Junior D in his hometown of Seaforth, population 1,600, down near Sarnia, just eighteen months before the 1987 WJC. OHL teams didn't draft him, though hundreds of others were selected. He was spotted at a tryout for a Junior B team in Kingston, sent to Kitchener for a look, later traded to North Bay, and selected for this world junior team. "I wasn't surprised that I wasn't drafted into the Ontario league," McLlwain says. "I never really thought about playing at the next level, never mind the NHL." Said

Dave Draper, the chief scout for the Canadian juniors: "Dave McLlwain was probably the last guy to make the cut. He was a surprise to make that team just because he had almost no reputation. You might think he was lucky to get noticed but the fact is he turned out to be suited to European hockey."

It was hard to think of some of them as teenagers or kids. A couple of players *weren't* kids, at least in the sense that they had already made the NHL, that they had already been on *Hockey Night in Canada*. The Detroit Red Wings sent Steve Chiasson to the junior program. The Washington Capitals did the same with Yvon Corriveau. Chiasson seemed older than everyone else on the team—not by anything he said, not that he said much. He did his business with a look that said he wasn't impressed, wasn't surprised. He had a been-there, done-that air, confidence that in someone older might be seen as world-weariness. "Steve was just this quiet and intense guy who everyone respected," Scott Metcalfe says. "He had no fear. Most of the time you didn't know what he was thinking, but he only talked when he had something to say." No stammer like Keane though. He was the easy and obvious pick as the team captain.

What seemed intense at the time seemed darker and edgier to others, especially to those who had come to know Chiasson in his brief time in Detroit. "Steve was a good kid and a talented one, but it was clear early on that he played hard on the ice and he played hard off the ice," says Jim Devellano, then the general manager of the Red Wings. "We had more than a few players you could say that about, like a lot of teams in the league." Hard to imagine that the Canadian team's coaches and managers knew this when they appointed Chiasson captain. Easy to presume that the players didn't think anything was out of the ordinary with the guy wearing the C.

Four defencemen had played in the national junior championships the year before. Chiasson and Kerry

Huffman were on the Memorial Cup champion Guelph Platers. Chiasson was the tournament's MVP. Huffman won the award as the most sportsmanlike player. Greg Hawgood was the top defenceman on the Kamloops Blazers, the WHL champs. Glen Wesley took the same role for the Portland Winter Hawks, the tournament's hosts.

Some were growing up in the spotlight. Most were highly-touted prospects coming up through bantam and midget. No one was rated higher than Pierre Turgeon, who was supposed to be the pocket version of Mario Lemieux, if the scouts were to be believed. But Turgeon lacked anything resembling Lemieux's self-possession. Turgeon was the talent who would never speak in a crowded room. He could barely carry on a conversation in private. "I remember interviewing him at his billets' home that season," says Jim Kelley, a hockey writer then of the *Buffalo News*. "Here was a guy who'd only ever gone out with one girl, is sitting there at a kitchen table drinking milk. He puts on some song—like the lightest AM pop stuff—and he's looking like he's frozen. It seemed like he had no idea what to do or why I was talking to him."

Two teenage members of Canada's Olympic program took a pass on playing in Czechoslovakia with the junior nationals. Team officials had hoped goaltender Sean Burke and defenceman Zarley Zalapski would join on with the team. They had especially hoped to bring in Burke, who was regarded as the game's next great goaltender, the next Ken Dryden. But Burke and Zalapski flew home after playing at the Soviet Izvestia tournament. The third nineteen-year-old in the Olympic program, forward Steve Nemeth, joined the Canadian juniors in Switzerland, where they stopped for a couple of exhibition games en route to Czechoslovakia.

———

To outsiders, the Soviets' 1987 junior team looked more homogeneous than the Canadians'. "Most of us knew each other very well before Piestany," Pavel Kostichkin says. "[Each of us] would have a friend or two or more on that junior team. The players for that junior team came from only a few teams in the Soviet league, and we had all played against each other in tournaments. Many of us knew others from other teams because we trained together. For instance, Andrei Smirnov was my friend even though we played on different teams in Moscow. That was typical. There was no one who you could really call 'unknown.'"

Yet they came from all over the USSR. Vladimir Konstantinov played on a frozen river in Murmansk. Alexander Mogilny travelled even farther, from China's northern border. In a sense, though, the Soviets were at least as ethnically diverse as the Canadians: Alexander Kerch grew up in Latvia, Alexander Galcheniuk in Ukraine, Pavel Kostichkin in Belarus. But most of the players, including Sergei Fedorov, grew up in Moscow or outlying industrial towns. And all of them had been recruited in their early teens by the state hockey academy in the Soviet capital. They stayed in residence at the academy and trained there for eleven months of the year. Mogilny, for one, didn't see his parents for two years. "It's hard, but the way that we saw it, it had to be done," Mogilny says. "It's an opportunity that thousands try for. All of us cared about our game and about our team. That was something that we didn't need to be told about. I think the Russians are a very proud people— we didn't need to be told to be proud about playing. It came from inside us, not from above."

They were Soviet teenagers of a certain time, and Venedict Eroyev's novel *Moscow Circles* was set in that time. It was a day-in-the-life, stream-of-(semi-)consciousness study of an alcoholic ne'er-do-well who wants to see the Kremlin but can't find it, making endless loops of Moscow on its subways and trains. The protagonist hates all things—except vodka—but reserves a special contempt for Soviet youth. "Honestly I can't respect the younger generation. They inspire in me horror and revulsion . . . I'm not saying that when we were their age everything was holy, very little was holy, but there were so many things for which we did care a damn. They don't care a damn about anything."

It reads like John Robertson's writings about young Soviets, but Eroyev intended satire. The young were the ones whose hope wasn't extinguished by experience. The players in the Soviet junior lineup had hope and did care about things. They hadn't surrendered like the author's drunken, train-riding protagonist or Robertson's "mindless robots." There wasn't unanimity about those hopes, dreams and expectations. All to do with ambitions. All to do with beliefs in the system and doubts about it.

Take Vladimir Konstantinov. He would have stepped forward and volunteered, before you had a chance to take him. He was a young man but an old soul, old at nineteen. They said it even then. Nickname: *Dyada*, Russian for Gramps. It was a joke about his appearance—you could see his five o'clock shadow fill in during practice, as if in time-lapse photography. It was also a joke about his manner—he was serious-minded. He had a character, a game and a set of features that seemed to be hardened by playing on frozen ponds in his hometown of Murmansk, north of the Arctic Circle, where his father was a merchant sailor. Easy to see an influence in his son's life. The father's sense of discipline came across in the son's dedication and determination in training. The father's respect for rank and orders came across in the son's ready acceptance of coaching, the willingness when a coach asked him to give up a promising soccer career to play hockey full time, or when he was moved from centre to the blue line after he made the elite league. The father's sense of service came across in the son's commitment to Red Army, signing up for a twenty-five-year hitch while others looked for easy outs and soft landings and no-show postings. Maybe the father needed something stable when back home. Maybe the son just came by it on his own.

Vladimir looked older but was really just a kid when he met a girl, Irina. He married her when his teammates were still interested in chasing skirts. Early in their marriage they had a daughter. Serious, committed, tough and skilled, he was an easy, even automatic choice for the 1987 Soviet junior team. He was already in the good graces of Viktor Tikhonov. He had already skated for the Soviet national team at the world championships. Tikhonov had a plan for him. He played at centre for the national team and Tikhonov planned to convert him from a blueliner to a physical, checking forward. Konstantinov was the good soldier; he went along.

"He was the quiet man," Igor Larionov says. "Vladi always was there for you. He was so steady and so reliable that sometimes people missed how talented he was offensively. He was proud but he had no ego in his game or in his life. He cared about others, his teammates and the other people in his life." He and Irina dared to think about the West—not to live there, just to imagine it. Irina probably dreamed more about the West. She picked up a fair bit of English on her own. She even read a book in English as a teenager—not a classic piece of literature, but *Wheels*, by Arthur Hailey, a pulpy bestseller about Detroit and the auto industry. Vladimir Konstantinov thought about playing on the other side of the Iron Curtain, but he always envisioned it would be with a CCCP on his sweater.

Take Sergei Fedorov. He would have gone quietly had you taken him. Like Konstantinov, he was a favourite of Viktor Tikhonov. The coach said that Fedorov, Alexander Mogilny and Pavel Bure were to be the future of the Soviet team, the heirs to Igor Larionov, Sergei Makarov and Vladimir Krutov—the KLM Line. Tikhonov anointed the three young players but favoured Fedorov over Mogilny and Bure. All three had the goods on the ice. Hard to pick between them. But Tikhonov liked Fedorov more off the ice than the others. Valeri Matveev was a journalist for *Pravda* who befriended Fedorov. "He was quiet, worked hard and was big and strong," Matveev said. "He fit right in." To Tikhonov, Fedorov seemed more malleable. He seemed less individualistic—or at least less independently minded. He seemed less likely to bristle under the old Soviet system. He seemed less likely to buy into the traditions—that the best players from the national team form the core of Tikhonov's Red Army team; that the Red Army players hold down positions in the military, like Fetisov ranked a major and Larionov a captain. It was easier to picture Fedorov in that role than Mogilny, who seemed to have his eyes to the horizon, or Bure, who seemed little more than a boy.

It was easier to picture Fedorov getting with the program because his father, Viktor, worked in the higher echelons of the Soviets' sports ministry. Tikhonov recognized that Sergei was a legacy—what Tikhonov couldn't reach, Viktor would.

Tikhonov had his domino theory—Sergei Fedorov would sign up and play along and then Mogilny and Bure would follow. Fedorov knew from his father that Tikhonov marginalized others who were talented because they tried to stand alone. He knew the cautionary tales. He had heard about Helmut Balderis, the Latvian who was one of the greatest talents in Soviet hockey and certainly the greatest to be regularly passed over when the national team was selected. Balderis had feuded with Tikhonov going back to the coach's days before being promoted to the national team. Tikhonov had nailed Balderis to the bench when the Soviets lost to the U.S. in Lake Placid. Balderis went home and joined his club team in Riga and was screwed around by Tikhonov and the national team's program, left off the roster even though he led the elite league in scoring. There's only one winner when the coach is a tyrant—you can win with him, you can't win against him. Talent is not enough, not without compliance. Viktor Fedorov knew that much. He told his son exactly that.

Take Alexander Mogilny. He wouldn't have let you take him. He didn't let *them*, either. He was among them, but never quite one of them. He did well by the system but was never part of the system.

Mogilny grew up in Khabarovsk, a city of 500,000, near the border with China. He grew up in a city that little resembled the western Soviet Union. Khabarovsk was a fraction of the size of Leningrad in population, yet it was spread over an area about the same size. Some Soviets longed to leave the country, but Khabarovsk, improbably, had an illegal immigration problem. Many Chinese workers were permitted into the region as labourers; others slipped in without the paperwork and found either legitimate work or a life of crime.

Mogilny grew up thinking of Moscow as the other side of the world. He grew up closer to Alaska than to Moscow. He grew up closer to Beijing than to Moscow. Moscow was the power behind his life, but it was a city he never thought he was going to even visit.

It stayed that remote until he was in his early teens, until his family got a call one day. He didn't know how it happened. Someone—it might have been an official, it might have been a coach—saw him play hockey in a tournament. Or maybe even just on a frozen pond. Someone found out somehow. That was how it was back then. The Soviet sports establishment had an amazing facility not only for finding talent but for finding it without ever seeming to look for it. Mogilny was asked—or rather, *told*—to come to Moscow to enter the elite sports academy. He never went to a tryout; he was just called.

His whole world had been contained within his city, within his family and within the game that he played. His father worked as a train repairman, and the job afforded them a humble existence, but one that looked better when compared to other townspeople. Alexander Mogilny wasn't trying to escape. He didn't try to transcend. He just played and goals were at either end of the rink—goals in the other sense, career objectives, didn't crowd his thoughts. He lived—and played—in the moment.

He was an outsider when he went to Moscow. Fedorov, the son of an official; Pavel Bure, son of an Olympic athlete—they were connected. Mogilny seemed to have dropped out of the sky. Alone from his town in that sports program. Alone from his area. Alone from his time zone. But he excelled. "Mogilny was difficult to coach but genius is always a challenge," says Igor Kuperman, a former Soviet hockey journalist. "The others, Bure and Fedorov, were excellent too, but Mogilny was excellent and *different*." He was proud in a way that outsiders are proud, thinking that he didn't just have to show his talent but defend it. He was resigned in a way that outsiders are resigned, thinking that he could earn his place but never feel comfortable or confident in it. He looked at Moscow as if he was still outside it.

He was precocious on the ice and off. Others saw only the game. He noticed other things. He was aware of society because it was new to him. Life in Moscow wasn't just new but also evolving, changing almost daily. He didn't know what to think of the men who came and went in the Kremlin. He did notice other things. "I started to see more people with more things from the West," he says. "They were allowed to have clothes from the West. They were allowed to have other things as well. I saw that. I heard about people being allowed to travel. People weren't free to travel even inside the Soviet Union. By '85 or '86 there were people travelling to the West." He saw them travelling outside the Soviet Union but he didn't think that he might go west and stay there. He didn't dream about going to the National Hockey League or playing pro. "It was the farthest thing from mind," he says. "I lived each day for the day." He didn't think about where the game was going to take him, not until it was taking him there. He didn't think about where playing for the national junior team would take him until he was packing his bags for Piestany. He wasn't impressed by the prospect. "It wasn't that far to travel," he says. "I'd already travelled a lot farther just to get to Moscow."

Take the player who only jokes. Evgeni Davydov could have been sitting beside the drunk on the subway train in *Moscow Circles*—not drunk, perhaps, but egging him on. Davydov was a spectacularly gifted player—a teenager mentioned in the same breath as Kharlamov. But he couldn't be urged or ordered to make the most of his game. "He didn't have the attitude to be a great player, maybe," says Alexander Semak, a Soviet international who played with Davydov. "He had the talent to be a player . . . he almost couldn't help it . . . but he didn't want the responsibility that went with being a great player." He didn't want the pressure. And he was soft. He played scared a lot of the time—a normal reaction for the player going half or three-quarter speed, the player doing just enough to get by. Afterwards he would laugh and mock, knowing that he had gotten away with it again. "He wasn't grown up," Igor Kuperman says. "The idea [in North America] is that the Soviet sports programs forced athletes to be tough and to grow up fast, but this wasn't always the case. It was like everywhere else—some grow up, some don't. And the hockey program forced some to grow up. Hockey allowed Davydov to stay like a boy."

Take the player the coaches always look to. Valeri Zelepukin was that player. The most loyal one. He never cheated on effort. A coach only had to look at him to know whether he had pushed a team too hard in practice. He was as talented as Fedorov or Mogilny or even Davydov, but he was that important complementary player. He had a future in the Soviet program, though not a role as big as the one drawn up for Fedorov and Mogilny, the one Davydov had no taste for.

Mentoring and Badgering

The obituary appeared in December 2003.

Hockey 'lifer' had passion for game
Templeton a mentor to junior players
Legendary OHL coach, 63, battles to the very end

It was delicately phrased. Recurring themes were suggested, floated. It's a balancing act—saying something respectful, implying something darker.

"Templeton's public persona could be abrasive and unapologetic, and it gave him a reputation for being difficult to deal with by the media . . .

"He wasn't blessed with natural hockey ability, but his pugnacious, disciplined approach made him stand out enough that he earned a tryout with the Detroit Red Wings. . . . The discipline stayed with him, whether he was coaching teenagers or deciding to get into the best shape of his life at 60."

The Romans used to say that if you can't say nothing good about the dead, say nothing at all. Bert Templeton didn't know or care about the Romans.

Some obituaries played Piestany high up in the copy. Some made mention of it a little further down. All of them played Piestany bigger than the job he did of coaching the Hamilton Fincups to a Memorial Cup victory in 1976. Bigger than his Ontario Hockey League championship teams. The juniors he coached who went on to NHL careers were briefly mentioned. His former players who went on to successes away from the rink weren't mentioned at all.

None of the obituaries mentioned his nickname, Dirty Bert. It's there every time during his coaching career—in dozens of columns, in dozens of news stories, written by the reporters when Templeton was bringing his team to town or when he was staking his team home after a win. "Dirty Bert."

Dave Branch, the commissioner of the Ontario and Canadian junior leagues, knew Bert Templeton. He knew about Templeton's rep before the coach made it to the OHL. He knew the coach from having called him on the carpet for what his teams did on the ice. Branch knew him from working beside him on the league committees. He said that Templeton's rep came from circumstances "beyond his control." Branch could have said "beyond all control." No matter. Inference: Templeton got a raw deal from history.

———

Templeton got a late start in hockey. He was born in Irvine, Scotland, and was eight or nine years old when his parents came over. He boxed. That suited his temperament. The kids he went to school with were already skating, already playing hockey. Many, maybe most, were bigger than him. That didn't matter; he started to play. He missed some things because of his late start. He made up for it with an intensity that bordered on desperation. It might have crossed the line sometimes. Many were better players, but nobody got more out of his talent than Bert Templeton. He made it all the way to that pro tryout with Detroit. He didn't make the cut—the plucky underdog story stopped there.

Templeton decided against playing minor-league hockey. He decided to throw his lot in with coaching, with getting as much out of other guys' talents as he got out of his own. With driving others as hard as he drove himself. It wasn't professional stuff. It wasn't even stuff that looked after your expenses. He wanted to coach so bad he paid to do it. He told people years later that it ended up costing him a couple of grand a season in gas, extra ice time, and equipment for the players when he started out.

The "Dirty Bert" handle goes back to a game that was much discussed and written about. The game was made for legend—almost nobody saw it. Templeton was coaching a Junior B team in Hamilton in the early '70s. His players were specialists in mayhem. Templeton's team was scheduled to meet Bramalea in a playoff series. The Bramalea players gave up—not figuratively, like so many teams in a no-win, don't-want-to-pay-the-price game or series. Not figuratively in the sense that they went through the motions. No, the Bramalea players decided to forfeit the series after a single fight-filled game. That's where it started: rumours of Templeton's players carrying foreign objects like pro wrestlers or wrapping their fists like the Hanson Brothers in *Slap Shot*. It gave the newspaper columnists grist for their soapboxes, though secondhand grist, hearsay. It opened the door for the provincial government to launch a white paper on violence in the game.

The nicknames multiplied. Dirty Bert. Crazy Bert. Bramalea Bert. Those are the ones that can be reprinted.

Not all of Templeton's teams scared opponents off the ice, but that's not to say many didn't aspire to it. Toughness became a trademark of Templeton's teams, in

Junior B first, then in Junior A. Templeton's teams became the league's toughest, the bad guys. The Ontario league made a show of being displeased by Templeton and his teams, but no more than that. It was good business, after all. It sold tickets.

In four seasons with the Fincups, Templeton was suspended seven times. He was barred from the bench for twenty-two games. No numbers on sellouts, though. No numbers on stories, real or apocryphal, about Bert inciting his players to riot, inciting opponents to riot. This much is certain: Templeton was charged with assaulting the coach of the Soo Greyhounds. (The charges were eventually dropped.) This much is shrouded in myth: opponents chasing Templeton down hallways to the dressing room, trying to exact revenge for gooning. (Former players vouch for it as fact.) It was all theatre. Or at least a lot of it was theatre, so long as you weren't on the ice against his teams or behind the bench.

"There's no denying that he had tough teams," says Sherry Bassin. "I remember I had one team that was just a bunch of kids, a rebuilding year with seventeen-year-olds. Bert had a bunch of older guys, really tough, like Al Secord, who would be a very tough NHLer but was a beast in the Ontario league. Anyway, that season, first game we play them, one second into the game, right off the opening face-off, there's five fights on the ice. Secord is just hammering this kid who was probably our toughest player. It wasn't just something that happened spontaneously; it was Bert's style. He got teams to play tough, but he did it for a reason. I was sitting there watching this beating that his team put on our kids, and it only started with winning the game that night. What it really did was plant the seed with our kids. They thought, 'God, we gotta play these guys six more times?' Those games were already lost, one second into the first game. Bert didn't give opponents any hope if they didn't deserve it."

Templeton was always compared with Brian Kilrea, the coach of the Ottawa 67's. It was a stark contrast. Templeton went about his job with a scowl, Kilrea a smile. Templeton was burning up, Kilrea lighting a cigar. Templeton felt like his job was on the line every season, Kilrea enjoyed civil-service sinecure in Ottawa. "They were both old-time hockey men, real drivers and characters," Bassin says. "Killer had much better talent to work with than Bert did. Killer had a great territory to work in Ottawa, especially back when teams drew from their own regions. You look at the teams he had, with Bobby Smith and Doug Wilson and others. All local Ottawa guys. Bert didn't have that type of talent to work with. Later on, when it just went to a draft for the league, Killer had this great support system—a bunch of scouts, part-timers, a network of friends, all kinds of guys who'd pass on information. Bert, though, had his thumbprint on everything in his organization. He did it all himself, and really he had to do it all himself. I'm sure at the start it was a matter of him having to do it that way because he didn't have any choice. In time, though, he probably got used to doing it that way. It became his comfort level."

For all of Kilrea's advantages and goodwill, Templeton was the first to win a Memorial Cup. Templeton's Hamilton Fincups won the national junior championship in 1976 and, in three rounds of playoffs, lost a single game.

That Hamilton team defied the pigeon-holing of Templeton. The Fincups had tough guys—Al Secord was one of the toughest players in any league he ever played in. But the Fincups were deep in skilled players, including Dale McCourt, who would later be drafted first overall by the Detroit Red Wings.

The Fincups couldn't have made it to the Memorial Cup final on toughness alone. The Western champs, the New Westminster Bruins, came in with their own reputation as bullies. The Fincups soundly beat them and didn't even try to scrap with them. The Fincups' toughness had a lot more to do with will than fists. They didn't up New Westminster in the final so much as chase the Bruins into every corner and try to forecheck them out of the rink. They wore out the top defenceman in junior hockey, Barry Beck, on the dump and chase, sending in three little forwards to swarm him. Templeton didn't try to turn McCourt into a goon, he just let him play his game, which was good enough to win the tournament's MVP award. Templeton didn't brag about his players' fighting after the final. He took pride in the work ethic he instilled. "We're small in size but I don't think there's a team in Canada that practises harder. I firmly believe we're the best-conditioned team [in junior]."

Just one line of Templeton's obituary mentioned the Fincups' Memorial Cup performance. The Fincups' next season wasn't mentioned at all. Templeton took his Fincups and a couple of ringers from the Ontario league to the world juniors the next year and brought home a silver medal. It was Canada's best-ever showing. The Fincups made a run at the Soviets, which never had happened at the under-20s. The Soviets ran out to a 6–0 lead and the Fincups stormed back with four straight goals. It was a 6–4 final. Templeton was sure that with more time his team would have beaten the Soviets.

———

Templeton's best coaching job may not have been that championship season. It might have come a couple of seasons later. Some would call it the best; others would say typical—others being those hung up on the Dirty Bert thing. The Niagara Falls Flyers were a brutal team, winners of just 17 of 68 games the year before they hired Bert Templeton. Templeton took over and the Flyers won 43 games, more than doubling their points (from 44 to 90). You'd have bet it was all Xs and Os until you looked at the stats.

You had to look past the names of those players who were going to wind up in the NHL—Steve Ludzik, Steve Larmer, and Mark Osborne, among others. And you had to look past the goals and assists and goals against, to the right-hand column: PIM. Penalties in minutes. Ten players with more than 100. One guy managed to rack up 218 in just 47 games. They fought and won. It was a year when the rest of the Ontario league was getting cleaned up. Penalty minutes were down across the league. The optics were better—relatively speaking, anyway. An example: the Toronto Marlies were involved in six bench-clearing brawls the year before; just one in '77–78. One exception: the Niagara Falls Flyers. They more than doubled their points, and they almost doubled their penalty minutes: 984 to 1,897.

You might have expected the people of Niagara Falls to be outraged. But if they had complaints, they weren't engraved on the plaques the city council gave Templeton and his players during the season. You couldn't have found much protest in the capacity crowds that came out to watch the Flyers at home. Nor from the Montreal Canadiens, the fabled Habs, who hired Templeton to run their farm club in Halifax after his one season in Niagara Falls.

"Bert didn't want the job because he didn't speak French—it being the Canadiens' affiliate. But they told him it wouldn't be a factor," said Templeton's friend John McLellan. Halifax was a bad fit, and maybe Templeton should have seen it coming. Bert Templeton's approach with the Fincups and the Flyers had been to demand. He had to adjust with pros. No *demanding*. No, he had to *convince*. He had to *coax*. Halifax wasn't an outright failure. Can't call it that. He had a winning record both seasons. But that wasn't enough. Two first-round losses in the playoffs. That's not failure, but it's not good enough, either. That's what the Canadiens, thought and it's what Bert Templeton realized. Templeton also realized that he was a junior coach.

"They had a coaching shake-up in Montreal and Bert thought he had a shot," McLellan says. "Then they told him he couldn't work in Montreal—no French." He landed back in Niagara Falls for a season, and then the franchise moved to North Bay. He went with the team. He had seemed like he was a season or two away from a NHL job when he signed to coach Halifax. Now he was going to North Bay instead. Some might have thought it a come-down. It wasn't. He had to do everything himself. He liked to do everything himself. He changed. He changed because he realized what he was and what he liked. And he changed his game. He changed because whatever drove him to hope for the pros, to hope for a NHL job, faded or disappeared in those two seasons in Halifax.

His players say the Dirty Bert thing was overdone by the time he landed in North Bay. They say it was never a question of winning at all costs. Never "win at any cost."

Nick Kypreos played for Templeton with the North Bay Centennials. "It was blown out of proportion," Kypreos says. "They made him out to be the worst guy in the world. If it was true, you couldn't have got players to go to North Bay. Bert made sure parents knew that their sons were going to be looked after if they played for him. He told them that their sons were going to school, were going to learn the game and were going to get some real-life training. And Bert backed it up. He cared more about the players than he did the game. He was demanding, but he was fair. My first season, Bert suspended our top three scorers for something—he never came out and said what it was exactly, probably a curfew violation. That told every-body on the team that there were rules and no exceptions."

The hockey men claim that the Dirty Bert tag wasn't a fair one. They say he was no thug and that he didn't look for thugs.

Frank Bonello, the éminence grise of the NHL Central Scouting Bureau, coached and managed teams that played against Templeton's for years. "His teams played hard. What really stood out for me was the fact that Bert made decisions about players early on and stuck to [them]. The decision came back to one question: Is he Bert's type of player or isn't he? That decision wasn't based on fighting. It was based on effort and courage. You look at one of the players Bert brought with him from North Bay, Dave McLlwain. Dave would tell you himself that he was never a tough guy, that he was a skilled guy. Fact is, Dave was a skilled player who played without fear."

During the '80s, executives with the NHL's Central Scouting Bureau served as advisors with the national junior program, particularly on player decisions. Jim Gregory, the former general manager of the Toronto Maple Leafs and a Memorial Cup–winning Marlies team, was one of the point men in the CSB offices. "Back in those days, the junior program didn't have one scout who saw all players from all the leagues, so we were brought in for input on who should get invited to them," Gregory says. "The image of Bert as a disciplinarian was fair, but only as fair as the game went. I always found him completely in control in my dealings with him. He was intense but also soft-spoken— almost shy. With Central Scouting, I used to talk to coaches after games or maybe phone them up to find out about one of their players or another team's. Bert's team's were tough but he was always polite, real thoughtful."

The reporters say he changed, that he evolved after coming back from his stint in the pros.

"In the '80s, Bert had moved on," says *London Free Press* reporter Jim Cressman, the only member of the print media to make the trip to the 1987 world junior tournament and a veteran of the junior hockey beat. "Bert was changing with the times. He knew that what had worked before wasn't going to work in the future. And he was really determined to put that Dirty Bert or Bramalea Bert reputation behind him."

The Canadian Amateur Hockey Association knew his history. The CAHA remembered the job he had done with the Fincups in the Memorial Cup in '76, the job he had done at the world juniors the next season. They kept track while he racked up eight winning seasons out of the ten that he coached in the major junior ranks. The CAHA knew his rep, but also knew better when its brass named Templeton as the coach of the Canadian junior team that was heading to the world under-20s in 1987. The CAHA had its pick of coaches in major junior—and even the collegiate ranks— and they picked Bert Templeton. Two junior coaches were selected to be Templeton's assistants: Pat Burns of the Hull Olympiques in the Quebec league and Tom Webster of the Windsor Spitfires. The staff first worked together at the evaluation camp in Calgary before the junior season started. "I knew Bert from the Ontario league but didn't know Pat," says Webster, a former NHLer. "It was pretty clear that I was going to be the 'players' coach' . . . the guy on the coaching staff who the players can talk to."

The players on the 1987 world junior team didn't remember the Fincups' Memorial Cup win or their appearance at the world juniors. They weren't old enough. They only knew what they had heard: the reputation earned long before, the baggage. Even those who didn't play in the Ontario league knew about Templeton. You might say, *especially* those who didn't play in the Ontario league.

"When we came to camp we'd heard all about this guy, that he was a tough coach with tough teams—maybe the toughest," Stephane Roy says.

Roy says Templeton's rep was in his thoughts, in his head. Roy was tough; he thought he had to play tougher. "I think that everybody tries to play tough [in their own way]. For some guys that was being ready to fight. For other guys that was not playing scared, taking hits. But yeah, playing at world juniors we knew that we had to be better than we were in our [Canadian] leagues. The level of play was just better, the game faster. But we also thought that playing at this higher level and playing for Bert Templeton, we had to be tougher than we were before. I don't think that it was something he had to tell us."

Roy and his teammates weren't able to see things as clearly as a career coach or manager did. They weren't able to look at the opportunity the way Templeton did. Sherry Bassin said Templeton had been around too long, learned too many things, saw things too clearly, not to recognize what the world junior assignment meant.

"Bert understood that coaching the world juniors was a different thing than coaching his team in the Ontario league," Sherry Bassin says. "A short series needed a different approach than a season of sixty or seventy games plus playoffs. And the fact is, Bert was never working in the 'O' with the type of talent he'd see in the world junior program. He knew it wasn't a matter of beating up the other teams. The one thing that he knew, though, is that he needed guys out there who would get his skilled players the room to use their skill. And he knew that this was going to be the best bunch of players he would ever coach."

———

When the name "Vasiliev" is mentioned to hockey men, they immediately think of Valeri Vasiliev, the fiercest, most physical of Soviet defencemen. They will think of this Vasiliev who played almost twenty years in the Soviet elite league. They will think of this Vasiliev, who was a fixture on the Soviet national team for more than a decade. This Vasiliev who was on the ice in the dying moments of the final game of the Summit Series, whose great misfortune was a mistake that led to Paul Henderson's goal for the ages.

When the name "Vladimir Vasiliev" is mentioned to former players—even *his* former players—it doesn't register right away. "You mean Vasiliev a coach, not the player?" Sergei Fedorov asks. He has to struggle to place a face to the name twenty years later.

Vasiliev—not Valeri, but Vladimir. There will be a pause. Vladimir was a player, too. Several notches below Valeri as a player. Vladimir was a forward for Red Army for two years back in the '60s. He played beside some better-known forwards: Konstantin Loktev, Venyamin Alexandrov and Alexander Almetov. He wasn't at the level of the legends. He wasn't quite at the level of those who went to world championships every spring or to the Olympics. That was the conclusion of Anatoli Tarasov, years later regarded as the father of Soviet hockey, regarded by his players as something like the Godfather of Soviet hockey. Those in his favour lived a semi-charmed life, at least temporarily. Tarasov gave Vladimir Vasiliev a look. Tarasov gave him a chance. But Vladimir didn't quite measure up.

Tarasov dispatched him to the Soviet Wings, which meant he was at the very front of the second rank. He was a journeyman player in the Soviet elite league. He just missed the dawn of Soviet-versus-NHL hockey. Missed it by dint of talent, as well as timing. He retired before the Soviet Wings joined Red Army for a tour of the NHL in 1975. The Red Army players, the national team players, were looking west in the mid-'70s. They were getting exposed to hockey in Canada and the U.S. A time of expanded horizons. Not for Vladimir Vasiliev. He had been left home. By the mid-'70s he saw a coaching job in the elite league as a chance to give back to the game. He saw coaching as a way to get to a place as a game that he didn't get as a player.

Vladimir Vasiliev was one of a significant category of coaches: those who demand from their players what they couldn't do themselves on the ice. A bunch are listed on the Stanley Cup. Fact is, few legends cut it behind the bench. There was Toe Blake, Hall of Fame player. Larry Robinson, Hall of Fame player. And a few had been players in that rank just below the legends, like Jacques Lemaire, an important player on great teams. Many more proved better coaches than players: Al Arbour, journeyman; Glen Sather, journeyman; Mark Crawford, journeyman. Scotty Bowman never made it out of junior as a player. In the junior ranks, Brian Kilrea, winner of 1,000 junior games, had cups of coffee in the NHL. And, yes, Bert Templeton didn't even make it that far. The same goes for all of sports: the guy maxing out his ability just to stick as a player becomes a coach who gets the most out of his players. That was Vladimir Vasiliev.

Vladimir Vasiliev started out as an assistant coach with Krylya Sovetov. He worked under Boris Kulagin.

Kulagin had been the assistant to Tarasov for ten years with Red Army and for the Soviet team in the Summit Series. He had been head coach of the Soviet team that spanked the stars of the World Hockey Association two years later. He had the top job for Soviet national teams that took titles at world championships in the mid-'70s and gold at the 1976 Olympics. No matter. Kulagin couldn't coach his way out of Tarasov's shadow. Kulagin didn't get the seal of approval that Viktor Tikhonov got. He didn't get the head job with Red Army. He had to settle for the head job of Krylya Sovetov, the Soviet Wings. He took over a mediocre Wings team and built it into a powerhouse. His Wings even knocked off Red Army in '74, as the protégé Kulagin beat out the old master. Still, he would always be thought of as a poor man's Tarasov. All the same, he was an astute coach in his own right. Example: Tarasov hadn't thought much of Valeri Kharlamov when he first saw him play. Too small, Tarasov figured. Kulagin convinced Tarasov to give Kharlamov a chance. And, of course, Tarasov took the credit for finding that greatest of all Soviet players.

Kulagin was hard to forget if you had seen him. He sucked stogies. He had a face like one of those guys on the officials' viewing stand when the tanks and missiles rolled

through the streets of Moscow for the May Day parades.
Kulagin gave Vasiliev a job. Kulagin had been a player a lot
like Vasiliev—not even as good, with two goals in fifteen
elite league games with VVS in '48. Kulagin saw a lot of
himself in Vasiliev. Everyone knew that Kulagin could teach
players. And Vasiliev got an education in a couple of years
of working with Kulagin. Vasiliev also studied at the Sports
Academy in Moscow.

He went from Wings and the classroom to Khimik,
a.k.a. the school of hard knocks. His Khimik teams often
finished with losing records. That wasn't a mark against
him, or them. It was just a fact of life in the Soviet elite
league. Red Army had the strongest team because it could
"recruit"—maybe "draft" is the better word, or "poach" or
"pillage"—the best players produced by the other clubs.
Dynamo had stroke, too. Khimik, though, was one of the
smaller fish in a smaller pond. It was based in Voskrenesk—
only kilometres outside of Moscow, but it might as well
have been a thousand. "The entire hockey establishment
was centred in Moscow proper," Vasiliev says. "We were
like a farm club to the bigger Moscow teams." The best
thing that can be said about Khimik was that the team was
competitive under Vasiliev. The best thing that can be said
about Vladimir Vasiliev was that he squeezed the most out
of his players, that he made them better players. Even
though that meant that he was ultimately making them better players for Red Army or Dynamo. "The Khimik job was
a difficult one," Vasiliev says. "Under the . . . communist
system everyone had to go and serve in the army. It was supposed to be an honourable deed." That didn't make it any
tougher for a coach, even a true believer, to swallow.

———

The Soviet hockey brass named Vasiliev as its national junior coach in the fall of '85. He looked at his WJC assign-

ment differently than Templeton would a year later. Templeton was comfortable with his lot in junior. He wasn't looking to get out of North Bay. He knew his limits. Vasiliev wanted out of Khimik—*up from* Khimik. He wanted to get to Moscow. He had bigger ambitions. He wanted to work behind the bench of the team where he hadn't been able to hang on as a player: Red Army. He wanted to play a role on a team that never had selected him, the national team. He wanted those things in a way that one of the legendary players couldn't know. He wanted Valeri not to be the Vasiliev people thought of when the name was mentioned. He saw the Soviet junior team as the natural step up. He was working with the players who were going on to Red Army, to national teams, to world championships, to Olympic Games, to the pantheon of Soviet hockey. He hadn't even been a spare part in the Big Red Machine. A victory at the world juniors would make him a cog in that machine. A bunch of titles would have elevated him to the status of mechanic. He made the leap: these players would carry him to the next level.

Any coach who has been a player will tell you that the charge one gets from working behind the bench is the nearest thing to being on the ice. It's the reason players wean themselves out of the spotlight by taking on coaching jobs instead of finding a desk job. The better the team, the greater that vicarious thrill.

Vladimir Vasiliev had one thing in common with Bert Templeton: the national junior program gave him the opportunity to work with the best talent he'd ever had. Khimik wasn't the best of anything. The team he coached at the worlds in Hamilton ranked up there with the best of the Soviet junior squads.

Some coaches try to avoid the spotlight. Vasiliev's predecessor with the Soviet junior team, a soft-spoken and almost courtly man named Igor Dimitriev, was one of those. Vasiliev was the farthest thing from him. He did everything but light himself on fire to attract attention.

Vasiliev went beyond shielding his players from the media at the tournament in Hamilton—an approach that coaches adopt occasionally in an attempt to keep their teams focused on the game. He shut down all access to the players and threatened and cursed any journalists who even strayed near the Soviet team. He kept his players in a virtual lockdown. He didn't allow them to attend tournament functions, like the official dinner. Organizers planned a shopping excursion for the Soviet juniors (and even offered them some pocket money)—Vasiliev vetoed it, though he did manage to pick up some things for himself.

Selmar Odelein a defenceman on the '86 Canadian juniors, never met Vasiliev and didn't even know his name. Didn't have to. The memory stuck for twenty years—the memory of Vasiliev behind the bench of the Soviet team that won the world juniors in Hamilton in '86. "This guy had just about the loudest voice I ever heard," Odelein says. "The guy shouted all game. He shouted at the refs. He shouted at us. And did he ever give it to his players. He never let up. Even when they were up 4–1 in the third period, he was shouting like they were down a goal. They presented the gold medals—no change of expression, just a stone face, no smiles or anything. Not that I remember anyway. Whatever he did for that team, it worked, because I think our team in '86 was better than the one that won the year before. The Soviets were a much better team [in 1986] than they were the year before."

The Soviet victory in Hamilton, the 4–1 win over the Canadians, was a bitter pill for the losing side. A couple of bounces, that was the difference some would say over the years. Players on the Canadian team, holding their silver medals, told reporters in Hamilton that the Soviets were players and actors. They maintained Vasiliev's players suckered the ref into penalty call after penalty call and that was the difference. It was either stuff that Vasiliev encouraged or stuff that Vasiliev ignored. The Canadians thought it was outside their own code. Their take: they wanted to play *by* the rules, Vasiliev's team to play *with* the rules. They wanted to win by physical sacrifice, Vasiliev's players by sacrificing their dignity.

How the Soviet teens felt about the charges was not established. Though Vasiliev had promised reporters that they would be able to interview the Soviet juniors after the tournament, he never lifted the embargo. They boarded the plane for home without speaking to the media.

Some signs suggested that Vasiliev's team would have a good chance to repeat at the 1987 WJC. They won the Four Nations tournament just weeks before the WJC. They beat the best that Europe had to offer. Vasiliev knew not to fix what wasn't broken. He took the same squad to Czeckoslavakia. They had five players back from 1986, including Konstantinov, Davydov and Zelepukin.

Coaches always take their own. They always take a couple of players from their club teams to tournaments like the world juniors or the world championships or even the Olympics. It's like they get a free pass. It sounds like favouritism. It sounds like a perq. It may be, or it may be useful to coaches. Tough enough to get to know all those players they meet for a first time. Better to have some sort of read on the room by looking at the players they know. That, plus they win the loyalty of the players from their club team. Vasiliev took Valeri Zelepukin to the world juniors in '86. It made sense at a couple of levels. Loyalty figured in it— payback for Zelepukin's past service with Khimik. Another loyalty—to thine own self be true—figured into it, too. Vasiliev figured that Zelepukin would benefit from his experience at the world juniors, and Khimik would be a better team with a better Zelepukin. No such rationalizing would be needed a year later, though. Vasiliev had reason to make the pick on Zelepukin's merit. Zelepukin was a useful player—not a star on offence, but a reliable player, one who wasn't going to hurt you on the ice. Zelepukin wasn't trouble off the ice, either. No attitude. He bought in. The other players liked him, and the younger players respected him. Vasiliev took Zelepukin because he was a player he knew, and more. "He was a kid with a strong will, a warrior, and also a very modest person," Vasiliev says.

Vasiliev had to weigh risk and reward. He wanted to take Zelepukin to the world junior in Czechoslovakia, but he knew that there was a snag—a big one. He knew that Zelepukin was going into the tournament with a banged-up shoulder. He knew he was less than 100 percent. How much less was the question. "At first I didn't want to take him on the trip," Vasiliev says. "He didn't want to have surgery until after the tournament." Zelepukin was a 1968 birthday; he'd have another shot at the world juniors. Vasiliev could have told him "better luck next year" or "put Khimik ahead of personal goals." Vasiliev decided to take Zelepukin. He claimed that there weren't any players, even older ones, even healthy ones, who could have filled in for Zelepukin.

———

Fedorov doesn't have much to say about Vasiliev. "I don't remember much about him," Fedorov says. "I think that he was like most Soviet coaches, really. He shouted. He was tough. What I remember thinking is that we had a great chance of winning the tournament. He coached the championship team the year before. He was bringing back five players from the team that won the championships the year before. The players won at the European tournament. It wasn't the best team I ever played for, and I was so young— I was a '69 birthday in a '67 tournament. But we had a good enough team to win. And we had a coach who had won before."

Checking In and Facing Off

The Canadian team checked into a hotel in beautiful downtown Nitra when it arrived in Czechoslovakia. One star would have been too generous. "A dump." Shawn Simpson says. Even if it had been plusher there was no danger of the players ever coming back on holiday. "It was a depressing place," Kerry Huffman says. "It was an industrial town. The snow that fell turned grey. The sun never came out. Everywhere we looked there were these really poor people, asking us for stuff. Nobody was about to go away on his own. We just stayed at the hotel."

Hunkering down would have been easier if the team had brought along a nutritionist. Or even a cook. Attention to diet was still a few years away, at least in junior hockey. Top junior players ate as poorly as the average teenager of the time—back then even worse, given the hours and travel that was their grind. It was hard to imagine junior players had ever eaten worse than this team. Marathoners carbo-load. The Canadian juniors did so by default. The teenagers ate french fries three meals a day. Appetizers, main course and dessert. Fries. The juniors' stomachs growled when they thought about a real dinner. The stuff down in the dining room didn't even look like real food. "Fries, that's all we could choke down," Theoren Fleury says. "Nothing else was edible. They told us that they were going to get someone back in Canada to send us food. About a week into it we got some Kraft Dinner. Kraft Dinner never looked so good."

Steve Nemeth didn't gripe. He stayed curiously upbeat. The two guys on loan from the NHL, Steve Chiasson and Yvon Corriveau, had experienced a taste of first-class treatment when they were on road trips to New York or Los Angeles or Montreal. They'd had a taste of the meal money and bright lights. Now, they wondered what they'd got themselves into. The guys from the junior clubs were used to bunking on the road at Motel 6s and Super 8s and, if they were lucky, Best Westerns. Nitra was a real step down. Not for Nemeth, though. "It was an upgrade for me," he says. "I'd been with the national team at the Izvestia tournament [in the Soviet Union]. I spent weeks on beds that were like slabs of stone. The food was even worse. You were worried about getting sick in Czechoslovakia. In the Soviet Union you were worried about getting poisoned."

The Canadian juniors had a whole floor to themselves. They rearranged the furniture to suit them. Theoren Fleury, Mike Keane, Greg Hawgood and Yvon Corriveau put their beds all in one room of a suite. They played cards and joked during the day. They stayed up all night. They stared at the ceiling in the dark, talking to one another all night.

Theoren Fleury can recall the conversations to this day. "It was unbelievable how close we got in that time," Fleury says. "You can spend time together with a junior team and get to know someone over the course of a season, but we were thrown together for a few weeks—just packed in with no break. It's a completely different thing. You end up knowing the guys in a whole other way. In a couple of weeks all of a sudden you're like friends for life. You know the other guy like your brother. "We talked all night long.

We'd ask Yvon what the places were like where the Capitals stayed. You know, it was like a kid who'd been to Disneyland coming back to school to tell everyone what he did on his vacation—that's how someone who'd played in the NHL was to us. Keaner and I talked about the Moose Jaw barn—the 'Crushed Can'—where you might as well have played outdoors in the middle of the winter, that's how cold it go. I kidded Keaner and the other guys picked up on it. I said, 'Keaner, there's never been any guy who's gone harder after a girl than you, never . . . calling her from the road, sending her gifts.' He'd say 'So what?' And I said, 'So what . . . she has a boyfriend, so what.' And the guys just laughed all night long."

———

One of the principals didn't make the trip to Nitra: Tom Webster. He could only follow it in the newspapers. "I worked with Bert and Pat at the summer training camp. But afterwards the coaching job with the New York Rangers was offered to me and I had to take it," Webster says. "I couldn't turn it down. And the fact was I understood that an assistant coach's job wasn't as crucial as a head coach's job—and with Bert in charge, an assistant's job was even less crucial. Bert liked to run his own show. It was like I would have been a spare part. But I just figured that they were going to be fine."

That put Pat Burns in a position he was unaccustomed to and uncomfortable in: the ex-cop had to be the good cop to Templeton's bad cop. Glowers had to give way to back slaps—the players had to think that those back slaps were coming from a bear pawing them. Burns's role would be hard to imagine years later—grown men, NHLers who played for Burns, figured he was ready to snap at any moment. They wouldn't just fear his wrath—many actually would fear physical harm. Scared shitless wouldn't be too strong. "Being the players' guy wasn't something I'd ever really done," Burns says. "For sure not with juniors. But that's how it had to be when Tom took the NHL job. Bert didn't do the players' guy thing at all."

DECEMBER 26
TOPOLCANY
CANADA 6 SWITZERLAND 4

It had to look daunting at the start: seven games in nine days. It seemed like the Canadians decided to pace themselves just after the first intermission, once it appeared they were heading for a rout. Pat Elynuik scored on the first shift. Elynuik and his linemate Dave McLlwain both scored on another early shift. McLlwain added a shorthanded goal midway through the first period. The Swiss looked badly outclassed, but then came back at the Canadians suddenly, and the clock couldn't tick fast enough. Their energy level flattened. Jet lag and travel may have been part of it. Overconfidence definitely was. Jimmy Waite was given the start in the Canadian goal. Templeton decided to save Simpson for what figured were going to be tougher games down the line.

Canadian goals: Elynuik (2), McLlwain (3), Nemeth
Swiss goals: Kuenzi, Walder, Mattioni, Nyffenegger

Other results
    Soviet Union 7 Poland 1
    Czechoslovakia 4 Sweden 1
    Finland 4 United States 1

DECEMBER 27
TRENCIN
CANADA 6 FINLAND 6

Through the first two games of the tournament the Finns looked like the best *team*—not the best collection of prospects, not the overwhelming favourites, just the twenty teenagers who played best together. More than the sum of their parts. Everyone filling a role with no personal agenda beyond winning. Only one of them, forward Janne Ojanen, will play in the NHL (Ojanen's career numbers in the NHL: 98 games, 21 goals and 23 assists). No Finns will be named to the 1987 tournament's all-star team, though Markus Ketterer will be named the WJC's top goaltender. (Ketterer will spend two undistinguished seasons with Buffalo's AHL affiliate, the Rochester Americans.) Yet the Finns smoked a strong U.S. team, led by Brian Leetch in their first game, and were unlucky not to beat the Canadians on the tournament's second day.

Canada's top line emerged: David Latta and Pat Elynuik centred by Dave McLlwain. McLlwain, the kid who had never given major junior a thought even eighteen months before, bumped Pierre Turgeon onto the bench. McLlwain's game was all speed. He was the fastest forward on the squad—when he took off he stretched opponents' blue lines, especially on the bigger ice surface. Turgeon wasn't benched outright. He scored a power-play goal against the Finns, but he was going to see limited ice time the rest of the way. Not a personal issue. No problem with French players. Templeton liked Turgeon as a kid, but had no time for him as a player at this level. "Turgeon at the world juniors would get killed if you got him off the bench," one teammate says. "He was still a boy. And this was hockey like he didn't see in the 'Q'." Dave Draper the chief scout said Turgeon didn't pack his game when the team travelled to Europe. "It was a far tougher road trip—going to Eastern

Europe in those days—and some kids, whether it was home-sickness or something else, just couldn't cope. That was Turgeon."

The Canadians didn't try to beat the Finns with speed—or at least speed alone. They went after the Finns like Templeton's veterans chasing Sherry Bassin's kids almost out of the rink. They tried to intimidate the Finns. Not that Templeton had to make that message explicit or even write it on a blackboard. At the time almost any collection of Canadian juniors would have approached it the same way. "That Canadian team was a bad bunch," says Goran Stubb, a Helsinki-based scout who has worked for the NHL's Central Scouting Bureau for years. "It was bad on the ice. Pushing, slashing, cross-checking after whistles. But the worst thing that I heard was off the ice. The Finnish players told me that the training staff of the Canadian team was spitting at them when they came on the ice before their game. They would have no reason to make this up. I believe them. And I think that was the attitude that the whole team took. We had many Canadian teams come to tournaments in Europe and there were many teams that played tough hockey but didn't cross a line. But this bothered me. There was a lack of respect. I don't blame the players—they were just teenagers—but the staff of the team shouldn't do things like spitting on the [opposing players]. It's not an example adults should set for youngsters."

Wally Tatomir, then a trainer with the Windsor Spitfires in the Ontario junior league, was loaned to the national program for the under-20 tournament. "Things were pretty good for our team," he says. "I don't know about 'attitude.' We were all pulling together. We saw things off the ice, kids begging, people just getting by, some real poverty. The people [in Czechoslovakia] were good to us, but being away in a tournament like that and having games reffed by guys who never saw things your way, yeah, it could feel like it was you against the world."

Tatomir denies outright the idea that he or anybody else on the Canadian team spat at Finnish players. "Nothing like that ever happened," he says.

Canadian goals: Latta (2), Corriveau, Turgeon, Chiasson, Shanahan
Finnish goals: Seppo (2), Kiuru, Ojanen, Kivela, Wahlsten

Other results
    Soviet Union 8 Switzerland 0
    Sweden 15 Poland 0
    United States 8 Czechoslovakia 2

DECEMBER 28
Day off

DECEMBER 29
NITRA
CZECHOSLOVAKIA 5 CANADA 1

The short bus ride back to the hotel was the highlight of the day.

The Canadians were outplayed. Not by a little. By a lot. Czechoslovakia scored three unanswered goals in the third period. The Czechoslovakians peppered Shawn Simpson with fifteen shots in the third period. "They gave me the player of the game award but I didn't think I deserved it at all," Simpson says. "I think I played sorta stinky." The Canadians looked like they were in trouble— they lost to the Czechs, the Czechs were routed by the U.S. and the Americans were in turn blown out by Finland. The Canadians looked like they were struggling. Pierre Turgeon was less of a factor than in the previous two games. Chances of a medal for the Canadians seemed slim.

Canadian goal: Hawgood
Czechoslovakian goals: Lubina (2), Hostak, Latal, Kron

Other results
   Sweden 8 Switzerland 0
   United States 15 Poland 2
   Finland 5 Soviet Union 4

Everybody took notice when Finland played the Soviets. Form went out the window. The Soviets, defending champions, swept the Four Nations but the Finns beat them. Or maybe their own goaltender beat them. Ivannikov was named the top netminder of the Four Nations, but he had a horrible game in the Soviet Union's first real test at the world juniors. The Soviets outplayed the Finns, but three dubious goals cost them the game. The Soviets' vulnerability was exposed—a huge fall-off in net from the '86 championship team to the squad the next winter.

"It was like we were climbing stairs and we missed the first step," Pavel Kostichkin says. "That first important game is the toughest to lose. It's hard to recover after missing the first step and keep climbing the stairs. In a short tournament you must come together very fast. In a short tournament there isn't room for stars or for one player to carry a team. It must be many players contributing and all players being friends. After that loss early in the tournament, we lost confidence."

DECEMBER 30
NITRA
CANADA 18 POLAND 3

It wasn't the best example of mercy as a Canadian virtue. And though the score was ridiculously one-sided, a dark cloud blew in.

Shawn Simpson had been bothered by tendonitis when he reported to the Canadians' training a couple of weeks before. A hyperextension. No matter. He thought that a WJC gold medal was going to cap a turnaround for the ages. The year before Simpson had played behind the worst team in Canadian junior hockey. The Soo Greyhounds had been brutal. Simpson had handled being showered with rubber. He had shown enough for the Washington Capitals to draft him in the third round in the spring of '86. He figured he could play behind Canada's best juniors, even if he was banged up. He figured he couldn't let this pass. Simpson wanted to tough it out. Maybe he would have still started if he had been too proud. He did the tougher thing. He told the team he was hurting. Couldn't go. "It was getting worse and worse," he told Jim Cressman. His tournament ended against Poland. He tried to get a glove up over the crossbar when a Pole fired the puck head high. "I fell back on my glove and it felt like I almost pulled the shoulder right out," he says.

Now the absence of Sean Burke, the national team goaltender, the prospect heralded as the next Patrick Roy, seemed to loom larger. Simpson's injury and Burke's absence looked like death blows to Canadian medal hopes.

Canadian goals: Nemeth (2), Sanipass (2), Shanahan (2), Fleury (2), Metcalfe, Turgeon (2), Elynuik (2), Wesley, Corriveau, Latta, Chiasson, Joseph
Polish goals: Niedospial, Merta, Kasperczyk

Other results
    Sweden 5 Finland 0
    United States 12 Switzerland 6
    Czechoslovakia 5 Soviet Union 3

The unexpected good news for Canada was that the
Soviets' tournament was falling apart. They managed
only two wins, over the outmatched Poles and Swiss.
Years later the Soviet coaches would claim that their team
was living down to expectations—that the Four Nations
result wasn't a real indicator of the level of talent. "We
knew our players weren't as strong as the team that won
the year before," coach Vladimir Vasiliev says. "We
decided to take some younger players to get some experience [for the junior tournament the next year]."

Vasiliev's assistant Valentin Gureev concurs: an off year
for the Soviets. Gureev takes it one step further. "In
Hamilton, our team was much stronger and so were the
Canadians," he says. "The previous year, all the lineups
were more talented and were better overall."

Now, with the Soviets fading from the medal picture,
the remaining contenders would be in a dogfight for
gold.

DECEMBER 31
Day off

Brendan Shanahan's byline appeared in the *London Free
Press*. Jim Cressman ghosted a first-person column by
the player the reporters had covered on a daily basis for
the last two seasons.

Subject 1: The Canadians watching the Soviets' practice in Nitra. "Holy smokes, the Russians practice hard,"
Shanahan noted. "They were really flying. Maybe it's
because they lost for the second time."

Subject 2: Shanahan captured the Canadian juniors' creeping claustrophobia: "So it's New Year's. Talk about life in the fast lane. Happy New Year's in Nitra consisted of sticking your head out your hotel room door at midnight and yelling, 'Happy New Year, guys!' Real exciting. Swig back that glass of water." He mentioned that the Canadian juniors had to settle for a vicarious celebration—that they could hear the on-ice officials, the refs and linesmen, bringing in the new year on the floor above them at the hotel. Shanahan didn't begrudge the officials their relief. The officials "take their jobs seriously but it's been a great experience so far," he wrote. "They're just doing the best they can when they're on the ice."

Dreading and Mourning

For decades the scene has played out behind junior-hockey arenas across the country: fans, friends and family gathering to send off teams. No one wants to be the straggler who has to be told that the bus is leaving. All the players walk by the coach, who sits in the front seat on the right side of the bus. He gets two seats. An assistant sits behind him. The players always sit in the same seats. There's no switching. A trainer walks back and counts heads. When he determines that attendance is complete, the bus pulls out of the parking lot. Statistics Canada has never done a hard, official count on it but there's no doubt that a junior hockey player spends as much time on a bus as he does on the ice through his career. Nothing is sadder than a player who sits on a bus for six hours before a game and six hours after, but doesn't get off the bench during the game. Or doesn't even dress for the game, getting back in his civvies after skating in the warm-up.

There's less of a crowd at the arena when a team heads out for a road trip in the morning. Players are dropped off by family or by billets. Others catch rides with teammates.

No autograph seekers. No excitement after a victory or despair after a loss, just resignation at a day wasted.

That's the way it is in the Ontario Hockey League and the Quebec Major Junior Hockey League. Neither, though, has anything on the Western Hockey League. The Saskatoon Blades meet at the arena in the early morning and ride all day and all night, arriving in Seattle twenty-two hours later, weather permitting. Not that it's the longest ride, just a typical ass-buster. Players across the three leagues have tales of bus rides gone bad. The flat tires and mechanical breakdowns don't make the news. Nor do most accidents narrowly averted. Every once in a while a driver has a medical emergency or starts to nod off at the wheel. That will make the news. Everyone has a bus story. This, though, was the most tragic.

It was Swift Current, Saskatchewan, mid-morning, the penultimate day of 1986. The Broncos were boarding the bus for the 250-kilometre ride to Regina. A small crowd saw the team off, at least what would be a small crowd somewhere else. But then again, Swift Current (population 17,000) was the smallest burgh in Canadian major junior hockey. It wasn't a long road trip—or at least it wasn't supposed to be. When four of the Broncos come back, they will return to a crowd of 3,500—not to cheering fans but to mourners.

———

The Canadian juniors got the bad news getting off the bus before practice in Nitra.

Nitra was the town where the Canadian juniors were staying and playing and practising. The snow on the ground was tinged with soot and truck exhaust. Not even twelve hours were left in the calendar year of 1986.

It was the usual drill. Team officials passed out mail to the players, letters from home, cards signed by schoolkids, wishing them luck. "Some yelling," Shawn Simpson says. "Joking. Laughing. That's what you'd have expected."

The team officials' faces were stony, like they would have been after a bad loss. The players thought it was Simpson's injury or the team's fading medal hopes. It wasn't. The adults on the trip had heard something. They had been waiting to break it to the team. They had been on the phone to Canada. They had heard about the bus crash. They didn't have the details.

The players made their way to the dressing room. Jim Cressman walked around the rink, around the neighbour-hood around the rink, looking for a phone. The players were on the ice. Cressman called the *London Free Press* offices. He called the Canadian Press office. He got through. He got the name of the team. He took down the names of the dead. He made his way back to practice, back to ice level.

Templeton whistled an end to practice and headed off the ice. A few players lingered to shoot the puck on empty nets—Simpson was done, and Jimmy Waite couldn't take any chances. After they showered—cold water, moldy floors—and changed, the players boarded the bus. A low hum, no chatter. No one remembers who was the bearer of the bad news. It was as if someone hit the mute button. They knew: something bad had happened to a junior team back home. "Everyone is thinking, 'Is it my team?' 'Is it someone I know?'" Shawn Simpson says.

The odds: the Canadian team had twenty players. Subtract Steve Nemeth because he was on loan from the national team program. The remaining nineteen players were drawn from seventeen teams. There were thirty-nine teams in the Canadian major junior ranks. Odds were about even, a coin flip, that the bus that had crashed was carrying teammates of somebody on the bus.

The details trickled out. First they heard that it was four dead. Then that it was the Western League. Sighs of relief heaved by the players from Quebec and Ontario. More details: it was the Swift Current Broncos. Nobody on this Canadian team was pulled from the Broncos' lineup. The Broncos of the 1986–87 season were a young team, barely competitive. This was the Broncos' first season back in "Swift" after several seasons in Lethbridge. More sighs. Cressman came back to the bus with the list of names. He didn't read them out—that wouldn't have felt right. He just had the players pass the list around. He told a couple of players where the accident had happened. On the road from Swift to Regina, the Trans-Canada Highway. Just four kilometres out of town. Black ice.

Steve Nemeth was unnerved. Though he had come over from the national team, the news hit close to home. Swift Current had owned Nemeth's rights before trading them to Prince Albert before the season. "I thought, 'It could have been me if circumstances were a little different,'" Nemeth says. "Just the fact that four guys in their teens died . . . that's enough to shake you up."

Greg Hawgood looked stricken. He could picture exactly where the bus had gone off the road. It was more than that, though. Three of Hawgood's teammates with the Kamloops Blazers had been traded to the Broncos a few weeks before. He looked at the list of victims when it made its way back to him. Their names were not on it. He passed it to the guys sitting behind him. "You're hoping it's not them but then again you're sorry for the four players," Hawgood said. "You never think about it until something like this happens, but the miles put in by a junior team are incredible. A lot of time after games you can't see the road. The driver is just going by the lines."

Pat Elynuik couldn't even speak. He was waiting for the names. It wasn't just that Pat Elynuik and his Prince Albert Raiders had had a near miss the season before, that the Raiders' team bus literally had been blown off the road by a prairie wind. No, Elynuik's linemate and closest friend on the Raiders the previous season, Scott Kruger, had been traded to Swift Current in the fall. "We would hang out and play cards," Elynuik says. "We just got along better than most guys. I missed him in PA for sure." Elynuik wants to hear those four names. Odds are that Scott Kruger's name won't be on that list. Nor Kruger's little brother, Trevor, a sixteen-year-old backup goaltender. "It was a tough five or ten minutes before we got the names," Elynuik says.

After Hawgood read the list he passed it along. It passed through the bus. It was passed back to Elynuik. The names: Chris Mantyka, Trent Kresse, Brent Ruff. And Scott Kruger. "I swallowed hard when I knew that Scott was one of those who had been killed," Elynuik said. When the bus pulled away from the arena, Elynuik still felt sick. He knew that all four players were going to be mourned, but if one's life story was going to be told it would be Brent Ruff's. The sixteen-year-old brother of NHLer Lindy Ruff of the Buffalo Sabres, Brent also had been regarded as perhaps the best player of his age in Canada. Maybe that's what made Elynuik feel sick—the idea that his friend was going to be overshadowed in this way. Losing his life as the second star. Maybe there's another reason—the idea that Scott Kruger was playing out his last season of hockey at this level, no real prospects as a pro. Kruger was the smallest guy in the WHL, all of 135 pounds. He could have played in Theoren Fleury's shadow. "He was like a pinball out there," Greg Hawgood said. "He had to keep moving because Western league guys aren't going to do you any favours just because you're small." If only he had not hung on for one more year, if only he had walked away. One thing about the grief there were no maybes about—it was all new to Elynuik. "I had led a pretty lucky life, I guess," Elynuik says. "Scott was the first person I really knew who had died. No family, nobody in school. Everyone was always there."

Before he sat down next to the teenager, Jim Cressman didn't know about Elynuik's friendship with Scott Kruger.

Cressman wasn't pouncing on grief. He was just grabbing an empty seat. He wasn't looking to get quotes to fill up his story for the paper. It wasn't opportunism. Cressman didn't know that the teenager was overcome until he sat down next to him. That was when Cressman put it together. Tears welling up in his eyes. He told Elynuik to let it out, to do what he had to do. Elynuik did his best to get through it. He didn't react with anger, didn't bawl his eyes out. He kept in what he could. "When he started talking, he talked about going bowling with Scott Kruger, about hanging around the hotels or the dressing room," Cressman says. Not the heroic stuff, not game-winning goals, not fights. Just the mundane stuff that goes on behind the scenes, just hours, *days* on the Iron Lung, just the things that get the teenagers through long days and long seasons. Elynuik poured it out. This was a teammate who'd never make it to a reunion, to a golf tournament, to the retirement of his number or anything like that. Elynuik was thinking about what should have been.

Steve Nemeth was still thinking about what might have been: Swift Current had traded his rights for Kruger's. "[That hit] even closer to home," Nemeth said. "That could have easily been me in that seat. I just felt a shiver when we got the details and the names. These things might hit you harder in your late teens. You don't have any practice in dealing with tragedy. But maybe you have a better ability to bounce back when you're young. And maybe it was a good thing emotionally for us to have games and this tournament to worry about—that we didn't have a chance to get preoccupied with the accident."

No one was there to talk them through the grief on the bus back to the hotel. No one. That is, if you don't count the reporter with his notebook out or the hard-ass coaches at the front of the bus. "If something like that had happened with a Canadian team ten years later there would have been a lot more support for those kids—a sports psychologist with the team or maybe a grief counsellor brought in," Cressman says. "They might have had family around that they could at least talk to. But here were these kids in a pressure situation in this depressing place and they get hit with news like this. It hit some of these kids really hard. Some of the players were old beyond their years—Steve Chiasson was a good example of a nineteen-year-old who was more of a man than a boy—but others were pretty fragile."

—

On the other side of the world, prairie stoicism was already chipping away at grief. The Western league temporarily suspended its schedule. The Broncos' owners and management considered suspending operations for the season, but decided to support the players if they voted to continue playing. "It's up to the players and fans now," said team president John Rittinger, whose family had billeted Chris Mantyka. "We aren't ready to throw in the towel. If [Chris] was going to die, this would have been the way he wanted it to be. He just loved hockey so much." By the time the Canadian juniors retired to their hotel, preparations were already taking place in Swift Current. There were going to be funerals across the Prairies—Kresse's in Kimbersley, Mantyka's in Saskatoon, Ruff's in Warburg, and Kruger's in Swift Current. There was also going to be a separate memorial for all four. No church in Swift Current could have accommodated all who wanted to pay their respects, all those whose lives had been touched by the four players and the teammates who survived. So the team and the mayor and others were organizing a memorial service at the Broncos' home arena, the Swift Current Civic Centre. The mayor, Len Stein, was writing a speech for the service: "Solidarity of sorrow." Fans would not only be in the stands. Plans were made to lay plywood on the ice, and hundreds were going to take their places there, right where those four young men had skated, where the Western Hockey Leaguers on the Canadian junior team had played games only weeks before. Flowers were ordered, more than fifty bouquets. Team officials were combing the office for photos of the players—what should have been artwork for hockey cards was going to be framed by wreaths. While all of the preparations were being made in town, the players gathered at the arena, even those who had been injured in the crash, like Kurt Lackten, who had broken ribs, and Bob Wilkie, who had injured a hip. They put the season to a vote. Before the crash it had been a season that didn't hold much promise—the players would have been pressed to find any redemption in a "rebuilding year." Unanimously, they decided to play out the rest of the season.

Team officials expressed doubts about the players' readiness to get back on the ice. Rittinger said that, despite the vote, some of the players "aren't ready mentally. . . . There were kids on that bus who've seen their friends die."

When a team struggles as hard for points as the Swift Current Broncos did in the fall and early winter of 1986, its players will always have a place in the hearts of fans who watch them. Most of these kids would likely be out of hockey in a few years. The odds are long enough that any player with a winning junior team will go on to the pros, longer still that any player, even on a championship team, will emerge as a pro star. Incredibly, though, one player on that bus would go on to have a distinguished professional career. A Hall of Fame career, in fact. Twenty years later he would still be playing. He would see his name engraved on a Stanley Cup, have an Olympic gold medal draped around his neck. Joe Sakic was one of those who voted to continue the Broncos' season. Sakic would always be reluctant to discuss the bus crash and the teammates who lost their lives—then again, Sakic would always seem reluctant in front of a microphone or a notebook.

Two years later, the team's name would be engraved on the Memorial Cup: Swift Current Broncos, 1989. It would be an inspirational story for the ages. Trevor Kruger, Scott Kruger's little brother and a survivor of the crash, would be the Broncos' goaltender that year. Darren Kruger, Trevor's twin brother, who would join the team after the bus crash, would be one of the championship team's leading scorers. The 1989 final would be a celebration of Saskatchewan hockey, the Broncos edging out the host Saskatoon Blades. And the championship would cap an amazing season, the Broncos losing only two contests and tying one in thirty-six regular-season home dates.

Some of the dark clouds never lifted, though. Not for good. Years later, storm clouds blew in again. More pain. Unthinkable stuff. Graham James had been the Broncos' coach at the time of the crash, and he would coach them to the Memorial Cup. He had won coach of the year awards in minor hockey, not just in Winnipeg, but for all of Canada. He had been regarded as a coach on the rise. Coach of the St. James Canadiens. The coach who brought Theoren Fleury to Winnipeg to play midget hockey for the Canadiens. It would eventually be alleged that James kept psychologists and psychiatrists away from the Broncos' players. Hockey fans, hockey executives, families, players: nobody thought that it was odd then. Nobody questioned the coach of the year. They trusted James. They simply trusted a coach who said it was best for the team, for the players, to work through the grief of the crash on their own. Those at a distance had no way of knowing. Those inside might not have known, but some were in denial. James was sexually abusing one Swift Current player, Sheldon Kennedy, who also played for James and beside Fleury on the St. James Canadiens, and another whose name would be withheld. Players from the Western league on the Canadian team's bus in Nitra might not have been close enough to those on the Broncos to know about

James's secret life. There were rumbles though, whispers. Broncos officials talked about the deaths of four players bringing the team together, even closer than before. It might have not only brought them together but also given James the cover he might not otherwise have had.

Before the Face-off, and In the Dying Moments

JANUARY 1
PIESTANY
CANADA 6 UNITED STATES 2

Bob Corkum skated across the centre red line during the warm-up. Look at it as an innocent mistake and you're not giving a teenage hockey player enough credit. Look at it as a breach of etiquette and you're soft. Look at it as a provocation and you're Shawn Simpson or Steve Chiasson or one of the other players in the Canadian lineup. The Canadian juniors wanted to be the ones delivering a message. Especially when the U.S. had players who should have known better. Darren Turcotte should have known better, born in the States, growing up in Canada, learning to play there and learning junior hockey as one of Templeton's players in North Bay. Adam Burt and Mike Hartman should have known too—they also played for Templeton's Centennials team.

Shawn Simpson was angry about not playing, about being hurt. Corkum didn't know that Simpson wasn't playing when he did his fly-over too close to the goaltender.

Simpson gave Corkum the axe, a two-hander ankle high. Mayhem ensued.

The officials didn't even have their skates on. The referee was Hans Rønning. IIHF officials ran to the referee's and linesmen's dressing room. They told Rønning to get out on the ice. He laced them up fast. He was waiting for an arena worker to open the Zamboni gate. He was standing on the other side of the glass and watching the two teams talking trash, pushing, shoving, slashing. Ten years of refereeing, and he had never seen anything like it. Bad: nothing in the rule book seemed to apply, nothing came to mind. Worse: Rønning hadn't seen how it started, who was at fault, where the blame lay. The ref came out on the ice and picked two players: Steve Chiasson for Canada, Mike Hartman for the U.S. Random, like their numbers fell out of a bingo-ball tumbler.

Canadian players at international events count on a raw deal. It was the same thing this time. They figured the IIHF was out to hit them where it hurt worst. "Seeing [Chiasson] thrown out meant he was going to miss that game plus the next," Everett Sanipass says. "That really got to us. Like they were trying to hurt us by taking away our captain . . . taking a personal shot at us. That was all the motivation we needed. It was a big mistake for the Americans to challenge us."

With the fire lit under them, the Canadians responded with their best game of the tournament. The warm-up was more dramatic and more evenly matched than the game. Canada jumped out to a 3–0 lead. The U.S. scored twice to narrow the lead early in the second period. The Canadian first line cranked it up after that, Elynuik scoring twice, Waite stopping twelve shots in the third period.

Canadian goals: McLlwain, Sanipass, Nemeth, Elynuik (2), Wesley
American goals: Turcotte, Young

Other results
    Czechoslovakia 9 Poland 2
    Finland 12 Switzerland 1
    Sweden 3 Soviet Union 3

The tie knocked the Soviets out of the medals. Sweden was going to need a win against Canada to keep its hope for a medal alive.

JANUARY 2
TRENCIN
CANADA 4 SWEDEN 3

Two wins in their remaining two games would give the Canadians a shot at a medal. It looked better on paper than it did to the players. They weren't pessimistic, but they had their doubts after Shawn Simpson went down with his bad shoulder. Sean Burke's absence made it seem even worse. It was Jimmy Waite, a seventeen-year-old, tiny-looking kid from Chicoutimi, or nothing. Medal hopes were riding on a goaltender who didn't figure to play in the WJC.

"All of a sudden we're looking at this young kid that we know nothing about and he doesn't speak English, not one word," Theoren Fleury says. "It was the strangest thing. Our whole tournament was riding on a guy that we couldn't even speak to. Makes doing the pep talk pretty hard."

"Maybe they didn't know, but I was sure that I could play [at this level]," Jimmy Waite says.

It is highly doubtful that Waite had any idea that he was about to embark on the greatest goaltending run in the history of the Canadian junior program—maybe in the history of the WJC. One moment started it all.

The Canadians were soundly outplayed through two periods. The Swedes had twenty-four shots on Waite and gave up only nine. But Canada led 3–1 going into the third period, thanks to power-play goals by Dave Latta and Greg Hawgood. The Swedes rallied to tie the game with less than five minutes to go on a goal by Ulf Dahlen. It looked as if Brendan Shanahan had won the game for Canada with his goal with just two minutes left to play. That only set the stage. Glen Wesley tripped Tomas Sandstrom on a break-away on the very next shift. Penalty shot.

"I can see it now just as clearly as I saw it then," Fred Walker says. "Jimmy had an angle that he gave the shooter—and it looked like he was giving him the whole glove side to shoot at. That's what I thought when I was watching it . . . he's going to score on the glove side. But it was amazing. Jimmy forced him to go that way and took it right away from him. I mean, it was a remarkable save for any goaltender at this level, but with a whole tournament on the line, with an underage goaltender in a tournament for nineteen-year-olds, it took a tremendous amount of nerve."

Others were surprised by Waite's performance, but Stephane Roy says he wasn't. He had a decent eye when it came to goaltenders—his brother Patrick had won the Conn Smythe backstopping the Canadiens to the Stanley Cup the previous spring. "I can honestly say that it didn't surprise me that Jimmy made that save or that he came on and played so well for us," Roy says. "I played a lot against him in the Quebec league. I knew how good he could be. The idea that he wouldn't be the starting goaltender in this tournament—I thought that the other guy must be really good or they're just holding Jimmy back because he's sev-enteen. And I knew what Jimmy was doing on that penalty shot. He had amazing skills, for sure, but he also had this confidence. Maybe the other guys couldn't tell because of the language barrier. A game, a penalty shot, with the tour-nament on the line, was no different than shooting around the puck at practice for him at that point. He was incredi-bly cool."

The final shots on goal: Sweden 36 Canada 15.

One player was more relieved than any other. "In that game, the team realized that we weren't carrying him," Shawn Simpson says. "He was carrying us."

Canadian goals: Latta, Metcalfe, Hawgood, Shanahan
Swedish goals: Franzen, Sandstrom, Dahlen

Other results
    Czechoslovakia 8 Switzerland 1
    Finland 13 Poland 3
    United States 4 Soviet Union 2

The host Czechoslovaks were in position to clinch a gold medal with a win in their final game against the Finns in Nitra. That would give Czechoslovakia a 6–1 record. Even a tie would do the job for the hosts. The Canadians thought the Czechs were the best team they had played in the tournament. It looked like Canada was going to vie for the silver medal.

JANUARY 3

A day off gave the players time to ponder the hypotheticals, the unlikely scenarios. A Finnish win over the Czechs and a Canadian win over the Soviets would give Canada a shot at the gold. Complicating issue: that 6–6 tie earlier in the tournament. The first tiebreaker—head to head—would be out the window. The second tiebreaker wasn't favourable for Canada: goal differential. The Finns stood at 40 for, 20 against, plus 20. The Canadians stood at 41 for, 23 against, plus 18. The running up of the score against Poland looked like the Canadians being ungracious: 18–1. But they could have used two or three more, the way it turned out. Their real issue traced back to a seemingly inconsequential game. They didn't beat up on the Swiss in the tournament opener, jumping out to an early lead, then coasting for two periods.

It was hypothetical, a long shot. Still, the players had their hopes up. "We know we've had doubters, but we've snuck back in the picture," Shanahan told Jim Cressman. "Now we're right at the top of the list. We're going to be greedy. We want the gold medal."

Hope and Fear

Other results
    Finland 5 Czechoslovakia 3
    Poland 8 Switzerland 3
    Sweden 8 United States 0

These games wrapped up before the tournament's finale. Tournament officials had thought this final game between Canada and the Soviet Union would have medal significance when they drew up the schedule. They thought two of the other three games might factor into the medals as well (they wanted to avoid a team having to run up the score against the Poles or Swiss to clinch a medal).

Tournament officials figured it would be a good bet that either the Canadians or the Soviets would be contending for the gold medal. They figured it was a good bet that *both* would be looking at the gold—the case in the previous two tournaments. They figured they were going to be presenting medals to one of these teams in the postgame medal ceremonies, maybe to both teams. Good optics: players donning medals while still in uniform. Good optics: stands packed because of the feature matchup. The arena had only opened weeks before. It was brand new. "We thought, if everything went as planned, the first event at the arena had a chance to be a historic game," says Josef Kuboda, the head of the organizing committee in Piestany.

The tournament could easily have ended with a game that meant nothing in the medal standings. It could have turned out that the last game of the tournament would have had much less significance, maybe none. If Jimmy Waite hadn't been brilliant against the Swedes. If he had given up a goal on the Tomas Sandstrom penalty shot. If Canada hadn't run up eighteen goals against Poland to pad its goal differential. The biggest *if*: if Finland hadn't upset the Czechs.

The Canadian players boarded the bus in Nitra in the late afternoon to take them to Piestany. The other games that day were played in the early afternoon in other nearby cities. Poland and Switzerland strove for self-respect in Topolcany: Poland secured the booby prize, avoiding relegation to the B pool, earning the right to return next winter for another week of ass-kicking. Sweden and the U.S. rounded out their schedules: the Americans didn't even show up for a game when two points would have kept alive their chances for a bronze. The critical game was in Nitra: Finland versus Czechoslovakia. The hosts needed only a tie to clinch the gold. The late start for Canada and the Soviet Union was scheduled to allow the other teams to bus in for the closing ceremonies and the end-of-tournament banquet. The final game was scheduled for Piestany because the IIHF officials were bunking there—Piestany was dull and grey, but an improvement on the other host cities.

The Canadian players boarded the bus not knowing the results of the other games. They got word of the scores—most importantly, the Finns' upset of Czechoslovakia—when the bus pulled into the parking lot behind Zimny

Stadion in Piestany. Almost immediately they started doing the math—goals for and against, two points for a win, one for a tie. The basics: a five-goal win for Canada meant gold. A win by less meant a silver. Bronze was already clinched. Canada had nine points going into the game in Piestany and so did Sweden—Canada had the tiebreaker because of the 4–3 win over the Swedes and because of Jimmy Waite's stop on the penalty shot.

"A lot of us were trying not to get our hopes up," Everett Sanipass says. "That way we wouldn't be going into that final game too flat if it was just for a silver. Maybe a few of us were looking forward just to getting home. The energy all changed when we heard about Finland winning."

"For me, the most memorable thing that Steve Chiasson said in that tournament, he said on the bus after we got the news about Finland winning," Scott Metcalfe says. "Steve was just sitting in the back of the bus. He didn't yell or even raise his voice. He just smiled and said real calmly and quietly, 'Things are falling into place.' No excitement. Like Clint Eastwood would have said it. He made it seem like he knew that it would."

Even Clint Eastwood would have had trouble keeping a straight face if he had looked at the team that had made things "fall into place." The other team in the gold-medal chase couldn't have been more different from the Canadians. All but one player on the Canadian team would play in the NHL, and a few would log more than a thousand games. The Canadians needed help for a shot at the gold medal from a Finnish team that would send only one player to the NHL. "It was a remarkable team," scout Goran Stubb says of the Finns. "They really played as a team first. They were very hard-working, very disciplined. I think that they were the best team in the tournament. To this day I think that."

The Canadian juniors walked into the arena through the back door. They lugged hockey bags like handbags in their excitement. The chatter grew louder, more excited. The sound of teenage euphoria. Some would play for Stanley Cups, for other championships, but most would never feel so excited about a hockey game again.

The sound of adult panic—that would have been the sound of the soles of Dennis McDonald's loafers on the unfinished cement floor of the arena. He was running from one end to the other. He was going from the executive box to the VIP section. He was flashing his pass to soldiers standing by the IIHF officials. He was trying to chase down the supervisor of referees and linesmen, Rene Fasel. McDonald had been as excited as the players when he heard the news about the Finns' victory. That excitement turned to dread in the arena when he received another bit of news. The referee assigned to the Canada–USSR game: Hans Rønning of Norway.

Canadian officials—really, officials anywhere—worry about the politics and favours in situations like this, one country looking after a friend. Norway seemed to have no dog in the hunt, no agenda. A Norwegian ref might have looked like the model of neutrality. But McDonald's worry wasn't favouritism; it was a question of competence. "The first thing I thought about was the tournament in Hamilton the year before," McDonald says. "He worked a few smaller games in Hamilton and he was the lowest-rated official there. He was out of his league—just not ready or qualified to work a game like that." Nothing McDonald had seen in the tournament gave him any confidence about the ref. Rønning worked the Canada–U.S. game—it was like peering into a gas tank by the light of a match, but somehow he survived it.

McDonald made his case. McDonald pleaded. McDonald cajoled. He asked for the assignment to be changed, for a more qualified ref. Sabetzki, Fasel and the other tournament officials didn't budge. Rønning it was.

McDonald shifted into damage-control mode. He asked the officials to speak to Rønning. He wanted them to tell Rønning to try to establish control early. He wanted them to tell Rønning to speak to both coaches, to the captains of the teams. Just settle them down. Just tell them that the game was going to be called close. Just let them know that it was a hockey rink, not a battlefield.

Bert Templeton would have listened. Templeton thought his players were goals better than the Soviets, maybe even five goals better, if they played it straight and got a fair shake from the ref. It was less likely the message from Rønning would have been understood by Vladimir Vasiliev. Probably would have been tuned out by Steve Chiasson, still pissed over the match penalty against the U.S. Ditto the Soviet captain, Vladimir Malakhov. Wouldn't have even understood it. But McDonald made no headway with Fasel. The message to McDonald: worry about your own team behaving. Don't expect us to discipline your team for you.

There was a scene within a minute of the teams skating onto the ice for the warmups—strife brewing even before the television feed started. Signs of real trouble.

There were symptoms of a team nearing the summit and slipping into the chasm at the same time. Same glowers cast before the game against the Americans. The same sort of trespassing at the centre line, encroachment along the DMZ, that foot beyond the red stripe. "The trouble had already started at the very beginning," Vladimir Vasiliev says. "At the red line during the warmup, the Canadians would skate closer and try to hit our guys with their sticks on the hands or legs. I know, the Canadians had this approach to scare their opponents."

"That's just what junior hockey teams in Canada did, and they probably still do it," Everett Sanipass says.

McDonald sagged. "It should have been an exciting time," he says. "I just sensed something bad was going to happen."

It was more than a gut feeling. McDonald knew the numbers. Canada had the second-most penalty minutes in the tournament (106 PIM) going into this game. Par for the course. The Soviets had spent the most time in the box. The margin over the Canadians: four minutes. Unusual, almost unprecedented, for a program that supposedly aspired not only for victory but the moral and aesthetic high ground.

McDonald didn't know one set of the numbers, though. If he had, it would only have made him more worried. Twelve of the 110 minutes in penalties had been assessed as bench minors against Vasiliev—one minor per game on average. An inexperienced ref and an experienced ref baiter: that was a bad combination. The Soviet coach was going to try to rattle a ref.

McDonald didn't know the intentions of Pat Burns, either. If he had, it would have had him in a flop sweat. Burns had told Jim Cressman that he was planning "to stir things up." He was going to try to throw gasoline on the fiery Vasiliev. The players' coach was going to bad-cop the Soviet coach. For fun, for his own amusement, as much as for team spirit. Burns figured the language barrier wouldn't be a factor in the bench jockeying.

McDonald walked by the television cameramen to his seat. He looked at the monitors as the broadcast was ready to start and the teams about to step on the ice. He saw the graphic on the screen.

ZSSR 0 KANADA 0

A Beginning and a Middle But...

First Period

Cue the DVD. Let it run from the start. The CBC broadcast opens with a shot of the Soviet team celebrating the year before in Hamilton. Cuts to flag graphics: the Hammer and Sickle on the left, the Maple Leaf on the right. "Brought to you by Esso."

The pre-game package starts with footage of Templeton at practice the day before the U.S. game. He's standing to one side of the ice, hands in the pockets of a red Canada jacket. He yells and chews gum. Then an exterior shot of Zimny Stadion—which viewers might presume to be a stadium named after Zimny but is in fact Czech for "ice arena." Flags of the nations in the tournament wave in front of the arena.

Then a tournament recap: game footage of the U.S. win. Dave Latta hits a streaking Pat Elynuik with a pass on a two-on-one for a goal against the Americans. Game footage from the game against Sweden: Jimmy Waite's glove save on Sandstrom's penalty shot.

Assorted establishing shots: an old church off

Piestany's town square, old television antennas, a Piestany family gathered around a small black-and-white television set, fans in the rink waving Canadian flags passed out by CBC Sports, local fans wearing fur hats, packed stands.

Continue watching as the CBC broadcast cuts to the Czechoslovakian feed. Low light makes it look gloomy. Blurry. Murky. It opens with a wide-angle ice-level shot from the Canadian end of the rink that makes the rink look as big as a football field. Players almost ghostly. Through the television screen looks like through the looking glass.

Cut to the bench. Pat Burns, glowering, gum-chewing, clapping his hands: "Come on, come on." Wally Tatomir walking around in the background. Shawn Simpson standing behind the Canadian bench, bright red locks. Looks like he'd fit in as a member of Journey or some other '70s hair band. A tight close-up of Luke Richardson. And then the coach. Moustached. Lean. Stoic.

Listen to Don Wittman give the basic set-up. "Canada is assured of a medal," he says authoritatively. "The colour will be determined by the outcome of this game." Metaphysical certainty.

Listen to Sherry Bassin soapbox-sermonize. Bassin looks ready to jump out of his skin. He calls the Canadians' rebound from the loss to the Czechs "remarkable." He cheerleads. He says that all Canada has to do is "put more pucks in the net." He knocks Vasiliev. Bassin says Anatoli Tarasov called Vasiliev's work in the tournament "the worst coaching job ever."

Look at the teams set up for the opening face-off. Count the hits in the first ten seconds after the puck drops. Shesterikov doesn't play the puck on the face-off; instead he throws an elbow at the head of McLlwain. No call. McLlwain cross-checks Shesterikov. No call. Elynuik takes a slash from Popov. No call. Latta is hooked to the ice. No call. The puck hasn't left the face-off circle yet.

Watch the first shift unfold. Too many big hits, clean and otherwise, to catalogue. Elynuik ducks a flying elbow from a Soviet defenceman along the boards. Popov lines up for a knee-on-knee hit with Elynuik on the rush, Elynuik jumping out of the way. Chiasson levels a Soviet with his head down thirty feet from the puck. Every time two players cross paths sticks are up, elbows up, Irish up. Rønning is even accidentally knocked flying at one point by a Canadian d-man lining up a Soviet winger. It's as if the hit knocked the pea out of Rønning's whistle. No calls as the bad behaviour escalates.

"Some good bumping early in this game," Wittman says.

Hit pause. Bounce the understatement off the bumpers and the bumpees. "It was strange," Greg Hawgood says. "We came expecting them to do the things that Soviet teams were known to do—puck possession, building up to the rush, carrying the puck over the blue line. But right from the start they were playing like a Canadian junior team. We didn't expect the dump and chase from them, but that's what they did. They didn't play the usual European defence—positional stuff. They were running us and trying to take our heads off. Whatever game we were prepared for, we got something different. We were fine like that, though. If they wanted to play us playing our game, I figured they were making our jobs easier."

Press play. Check out the Czech graphic. Check out the tournament recap.

KANADA	SVAJCLAR	6—4
	FINSKO	6—6
	CSSR	1—5
	POLSKO	18—1
	USA	6—2
	SVEDSKO	4—3

Wait for the first scoring chance. Three minutes in, the first shift for the line of Everett Sanipass, Theoren Fleury and Mike Keane. Fleury takes the face-off against Sergei Fedorov. It's Fedorov, even though there's no name on his sweater. He's the only Soviet player who is anonymous in this way. Sanipass sets Fleury up with a nice pass around Vladimir Malakhov, who is looking and leaning the wrong way. Fedorov tries desperately to get back for a defence-man who was caught flat-footed. Fleury dekes Ivannikov and tries to drag the puck over to the goaltender's glove side. Ivannikov dives desperately to block the puck. Seconds later in the neutral zone, Fleury catches Kostichkin with his head down. It's the best shift from the Canadians. It's clear that Fleury's line will be effective in this game. They won't be intimidated. Skill and will.

"Everett had a reputation as a tough guy, but he was better with the puck than he was given credit for," Fleury says. "We got going good on the first shift. We went in confident but getting off good at the start, that was a confidence builder."

Wait for the first goal. It comes on the Fleury line's next shift. Less than five minutes in. It starts with Fleury firing a cross-corner dump-in from centre ice. Keane chases it down and fires a shot from a bad angle that Ivannikov kicks twenty feet out into the slot. Sanipass takes one swipe and misses. Mogilny is there on the backcheck, but the puck bounces past him. Fleury cashes it in with Ivannikov so far out of position he's almost standing beside the net. Ivannikov flops back into the picture only by the time that Fleury starts celebrating. Fleury throws his hands up in the air and runs around the Soviets' end. His linemates swarm him. He and Keane exchange helmeted head-butts.

ZSSR 0 KANADA 1

Hit pause during the replay on the broadcast. The cameras miss Fleury skating back to centre ice and then sliding on his knees, holding his stick like a machine gun and pretending to empty a clip at the Soviets' bench. "It was an inflammatory act, completely unnecessary, lacking any sort of respect," CAHA president Murray Costello says. "When Fleury got to the bench, Bert Templeton didn't say anything about it. It was evidence that any semblance of discipline was breaking down or just never there."

Hit play. Wait for the second goal. Next shift. Ten seconds after the Canadian elation. Glen Wesley turns the puck over to Valeri Zelepukin at the Canadian blue line and Zelepukin drives on Jimmy Waite. Hawgood's a helmet shorter. Can't fend off Zelepukin. Two, three shots in tight on Waite. Wesley's trying to hold up Sergei Shesterikov. Wesley goes down. Waite goes down. Shesterikov finishes off a rebound from the edge of the crease.

ZSSR 1 KANADA 1

Remember a golden rule of the game. Nothing hurts worse than giving up a goal on the shift right after your team has scored.

Determine whether it applies. Look for the Canadians to crash. It doesn't happen. No sticks slammed. No heads hanging. They have to stay fired up just to stay standing.

Look for slashes, high-sticks, elbows, pushing and shoving after whistles. It happens every time. Just a question of how intense.

One chain of events on one stoppage midway through the period:

Keane slashes Kostichkin just before the whistle;

Kostichkin eats a cross-check from Chiasson;

Fleury sneaks up on Kostichkin from behind and slashes him across the back of the knees;

Kostichkin falls to the ice and Sanipass, skating by, knocks Kostichkin's helmet with his shinpad.

Follow Kostichkin. Imagine a pinball machine letting loose four balls at once. Imagine eight guys square-dancing in a mosh pit. It's hard to pick up every cheap shot because each is just one of three or four simultaneous exchanges of unpleasantries around the Canadian net. They're hard to pick up because Fleury steals the show, dropping at the end of the sequence as if he has been shot. It's a tough game in the flow of play. It goes from tough to cheap after the whistle. And it hardly needs embellishment—if the ref isn't handing out minors for aggravated assault, the players are kidding themselves if they think diving will draw a penalty.

"I expected a whistle," Pavel Kostichkin says. "So many fouls and nothing came from the referee. It was not like hockey that I had played. I couldn't do it [during play], but when it stopped I looked to see if the referee had a whistle. I thought after the first shift that something bad could happen. Every shift the bad thing was getting closer."

It cuts both ways, of course. No blood on the ice, but not for lack of trying. A Canadian player takes a run at Mogilny in the Soviet end of the rink. "*Mol-igny,*" Wittman calls him. Mogilny rolls with the hit. Fair, smart. Then he gets his skate up knee high or so, sort of a spinning back kick. Can't be just chance: he tries it later in the same shift along the boards.

Cue the understatement again. "A lot of chippiness," Sherry Bassin says. Chiasson makes it personal—he fires the puck off Zelepukin's cup three seconds after one whistle, as if trying to win a stuffed doll on the midway.

Get the first-hand accounts. "It wasn't just the dump and chase and bodychecking they took from Canadian junior hockey," Greg Hawgood says. "It's like they got one of those Rock'em Sock'em fight tapes."

"It was the dirtiest game I've ever played in," Theoren Fleury says. "Everything went. Any slash below the waist, no whistle. Two-handed baseball swings, no call. Go into the corner, count on getting kicked."

And all the cheap stuff eclipses some legitimate heavy hitting. Smirnov knocks the wind out of Sanipass, who's caught trying to find the puck in his skates. Igor Monaenkov runs over Yvon Corriveau, a check as heavy as any Corriveau had to suck up with the Washington Capitals. Even Dave McLlwain, never mistaken for an enforcer, the erstwhile boy scout, has to watch out for a Soviet defenceman's skates when McLlwain knocks him upside down like a stuntman.

Realize that the other guys can play. Realize that these guys might be the best two-win team in the history of the tournament. Alexander Kerch carries the puck down the right wing into the Canadian zone. He pulls up in the corner and then carries the puck back to the blue line. Then across to the left wing. Then right in on Waite for a point-blank scoring chance. Kerch skates more than a full lap of the Canadian end. Four defenders have a shot at him and he eludes them all. Waite has to bail out his teammates or the play would result in one of the most memorable goals in tournament history.

See it the other way. The Soviets have to be convinced that they can't buy a good bounce. Not on Kerch's play. Not when Konstantinov hammers the puck off the post seconds later.

Don't buy the hype. Bassin cites Konstantinov's measurements: "six feet four, 215 pounds." Minimum exaggeration: four inches, twenty pounds.

Look for a trend. Canada's forecheck produces turnovers in the Soviet end. Puckhandling on the Soviet blue line: like playing catch with fine china, like playing badminton with live grenades. Konstantinov is no stylist but he gets the job done. Malakhov, Smirnov: brutal.

Look for it on two goals late in the period. Harmless-looking play at the start: puck rolls back to Malakhov inside the Soviet blue line. The big defenceman tries to get the puck to sit down. Latta raps Malakhov's gloves and steals the puck. In alone on Ivannikov. His wrist shot whistles by the Soviet goalie.

ZSSR 1 KANADA 2

Sanipass runs all around the Soviet end. Chaotic, but effective. First he steamrolls Ivannikov. No call, of course. Then Sanipass's pressure forces Davydov to throw it over to Mogilny just as he's crossing in front of the net. The young winger thinks he's free and clear and leaves the puck in the slot—a drop pass. Hard to tell who he had in mind for the pass. Fleury pounces, two strides and a deke to beat Ivannikov.

ZSSR 1 KANADA 3

Feel the temperature rise. Fleury's goal comes late in the period, but the best measure of escalating hostilities comes two or three seconds after the buzzer. Medvedev lets loose a slap shot ankle high at Wesley two or three steps away. Medvedev looks right at him before he does it. Might be payback for Chiasson's jock-rattler. Or maybe just a fitting way to wrap up twenty nasty minutes, something less than a showcase for junior hockey, at least in the eyes of IIHF types. Wesley looks ready to go after Medvedev but his teammates talk him out of it.

———

Intermission
Sit tight. Change of plans for Fred Walker. Walker was going to have Everett Sanipass as his guest during the first intermission. Instead, Walker asks Sanipass if he can come on after the second period so he can get Fleury on the air.

Look at Theo Fleury. It's not that he looks so small next to Fred Walker, who is a good six-four, maybe more. No, it's how young he looks. He looks like a thirteen- or fourteen-year-old. He looks like a thirteen- or fourteen-year-old version of Joe Strummer—hyperactive, hyperenergetic, hyperenthusiastic.

Listen to Fleury. He sounds like a thirteen- or fourteen-year-old, too. So excited, like a kid on his birthday. So nervous, like a kid called up to speak in front of the class. Walker asks him how he scored the second goal. "Y'see, I just knew, I knew their style, circle back, circle back, y'know, until they get the play set up," Fleury says. "And I just moved right in, right in behind them." Walker asks him about the physical play. "Oh, it's a real physical game," Fleury says, stammering. "It's probably one of the more physical games I've been involved in. Tempers are high. The boys are up for the gold medal. Everybody is so tense. Tempers are flying. It's really tough out there . . . I can't believe it. It's so tense. It's so tense." Walker asks him about the mood before the game. "No one was talking or nothing, eh," Fleury says, now just lost in thought, rambling. "Everyone was in their stall, with their head down. Thinkin' about it. Thinkin', Thinkin'. We gotta beat these guys."

The shot of Fleury dissolves to one of the Zamboni clearing the rink. Walker tries to throw it back to Wittman and Bassin. Fleury jumps in and shouts over him: "I'd like to say hi to the people in Russell, Manitoba, and all the fans out in Moose Jaw, Saskatchewan."

"You just did," Fred Walker says.

———

Hit pause. Imagine what it would be like if the Canadians were to win this game by five or six goals. Imagine if they cover themselves with glory. Everyone loves a winner. Everyone jumps on bandwagons.

Hit play. Bookmark this. Brian Williams, in the CBC studio in Toronto, starts writing postscripts after twenty minutes: "You have to be impressed with the job Bert Templeton has done."

Listen to fate being tempted. Don Cherry, also in the studio, offers up his game plan for success: "Go in, bang 'em around and they'll back down."

———

Second Period

Look for a sign that the dark clouds will lift. Look for a sign of respect for each other and respect for the game. Malakhov takes a penalty on the first shift of the second period. Linesman Peter Pomoell is about to drop the puck to start the Canadian power play, then stands up. An announcement over the public-address system in Czech: officials make it known to the benches that there will be a pause here. A moment of silence for the Swift Current Broncos. Expected: the Canadian players stand up on the ice and on the bench. Many heads hang. Unexpected: the Soviets all take off their helmets, either holding them under their arms or setting them down on the ice. No glowering. No death stares. Defenceman Dmitri Tsygurov stands at attention opposite Dave Latta out at the blue line, stiff, bolt upright, his skates so close together his ankles almost touch. The camera pans the stands. Not just silence, but stillness, too. No rocking back and forth, no whispering to one another, no sideways glances. Not on the ice, not on the bench, not in the stands. None of the Soviet players know where Swift Current is—some of the Canadians don't. The Soviets couldn't have known whether any of the Broncos had been teammates of players in the Canadian lineup.

Five minutes pass. The Canadians are on the power play for four of those minutes. The Soviets are reeling.

Rønning is making an attempt to assert some sort of control over the game. Quick penalty calls. Quick whistles along the boards. His learning curve is a minute-to-minute thing. Maybe McDonald worried too much.

The game goes from furious boil to simmer: less pushing and shoving, less stickplay. Maybe it's the power plays. Maybe it's nervous energy burning off. Maybe the Canadians see their chance at the gold. Maybe the Soviets just want to get home. Maybe fatigue sets in. It looked uglier in the first period than it does in these first five minutes of the second. Turgeon—yes, Sneaky Pete, as Templeton called him—stares down Popov after a whistle. Stares *up* is more accurate: Popov is half a helmet taller and built like a freight train. Turgeon even feints as if he's going to throw a punch. Popov doesn't even blink. No chance of Turgeon suckering Popov, and it seems no chance the game will get ugly again. Too much at stake.

Round up the usual suspects. Some don't need inciting. Some being Fleury, Sanipass and Keane. They were effective in the first, playing "with an edge," Fleury says. Now they can't gear down. They don't gear down. An innocent-looking check against the boards: Igor Monaenkov carries his stick a little high, rubbing Fleury on the boards—but then again, it wouldn't have been high on anyone except the five-foot-six Fleury. Fleury shoves back. That lights a fire under Sanipass: a high stick up around Popov's throat. And there: the first punch, a left hook thrown with real authority. Popov misses Sanipass by inches. Meanwhile, Monaenkov goes for the classic Greco-Roman stuff, pushing down on Fleury's neck till he's at 90 degrees, can't see anything but Monaenkov's skates. The linesmen, Poemoell and Gorski, try to break things up, skating into the middle of things, while Rønning blows his whistle on the perimeter—not that anybody notices.

Remember a moment when you've failed to act quickly enough. Remember a moment when you needed to

make a quick decision and dragged your feet instead.
Rønning skates over to the off-ice officials. He speaks to
them, his back to the benches, not even glancing over. A
minute passes. Almost two. He has yet to make a call. The
captains come over, Konstantinov and Chiasson, and
stand off to either side. Eventually Fleury and Sanipass
come over to the box. Popov and Monaenkov, too.
Double minors.

Hit pause. A shot from the Soviet penalty box with the
Canadian penalty box in the background. Fleury is standing up. He points to Monaenkov. He's going a mile a
minute shouting at him. Wired. Just as he'd been revving
during his interview with Fred Walker. Almost incoherent.
Lost in the moment.

Press play. The three-on-three figures to be a dicey situation for Canada, considering that the Soviets can take
advantage of their speed, that they won't even let the
Canadians see the puck. Those fears seem warranted when
Templeton sends out Wesley, the seventeen-year-old, and
Hawgood, the undersized tenth-round pick of the Boston
Bruins. Not an issue. Wesley manages the puck coolly,
like a veteran NHLer dropping in on a shinny game.
Hawgood, too. And then Davydov slashes Steve Nemeth
behind the Soviet net. A petulant, needless penalty for
a tough guy, but Davydov is supposed to be a pure-skill
type. It seems out of character for the team and for the
player.

———

Move up to the edge of your seat. No chances for several
shifts, then shoulda-been-goals come seconds apart. First
Monaenkov turns the puck over at centre ice and Shanahan
has a clear breakaway, Fedorov the closest one to him.
Ivannikov has his best moment of the game, a glove save on
a snapshot just inside the post.

Sigh. The Canadian players know that they're giving life to a Soviet team. They know that they're not halfway to the five-goal margin necessary for sole ownership of the gold.

Then Kerch wires a shot from the face-off dot off the crossbar, Waite just waving at it when it's already by him. Then Kostichkin deflects a Tsygurov shot from the point and the Soviets are back in the game.

ZSSR 2 KANADA 3

Look again for the Canadians to fade. Look again for the gas to run out at the end of a tournament. Look for the Canadian player who has travelled the most, who has been away from home longest, who has felt like an outsider—or at least never quite one of the guys. Steve Nemeth is out on a penalty kill. Popov is handling the puck inside his own blue line, the last man back, looking for forwards streaking up the ice. Nemeth looks like he's giving just token pressure. Popov is lulled to sleep. The puck takes a funny hop and Nemeth steals it from him. A turnover. Like Latta's goal. Like Fleury's second goal. Nemeth lets loose an almost-full-windup slapshot on the breakaway. Same place as Shanahan was looking: waist high, glove side. This one is just too close, too fast, for Ivannikov. Shorthanded. Unassisted.

ZSSR 2 KANADA 4

The puck is dropped at centre ice. Hawgood drops a big hit on Konstantinov, shoulder on sternum. Canada kills the penalty effectively and at the next whistle the broadcast breaks for a commercial. "We'll return to our live coverage in Piestany right after we pause for this message," Wittman says. We're given no notice, but it's the last game action we'll see. The commercial appears on Canadian television while, half a world away, things are set in motion. Things that will deny the Canadian teens any shot at glory, or even near-glory. Things that will follow coaches and players and officials for the rest of their lives.

Blood Spilling and Night Falling

Hit pause before the broadcast comes out of the commercial. Ask if anyone saw it coming. Ask if anyone saw anything like it coming.

The Soviets' assistant coach says he saw the signs in the warmup. "We were standing at the red line with our backs facing them, some of our guys got hit," Valentin Gureev says.

Some say they saw signs long before that. "We just had a big, tough, inexperienced and young team," Shawn Simpson says. "We didn't have anyone who had been through this before."

Press play. A slow-motion replay against a soundtrack of piercing whistling in the crowd. The replay advances slowly. Sanipass hooks Shesterikov up around the shoulder as he carries the puck in front of the net. Shesterikov is spun around and falls to the ice.

Wittman describes it in the voice-over: "Well, we had a real skirmish just moments ago following a face-off." Wittman makes it sound as if it's done and over. Clearly not so. Clearly not so when the feed switches to live action.

"It all started when Sanipass and Shestirikov collided . . ." Wittman says while Sanipass and Shestirikov trade punches and the skinny Gorski tries to separate them. Gorski has trouble even holding Sanipass's arm. Gorski ducks low so he doesn't eat a stray shot, a real danger when the two are trading and connecting with flush right hands.

Wittman has it half right: it started and ended when Sanipass and Shestirikov collided. He can't describe all the action in front of him. It's happening on too many fronts. It would be like trying to give a blow-by-blow of a battle scene in one of Peter Jackson's *Lord of the Rings* movies.

Rewind and focus on each fight. Number them. Put them in escalating order.

No. 1: Chiasson and Smirnov pair up. At the start, nothing much.

No. 2: Tsygurov, the Soviet defenceman who had stood at attention during the moment of silence, gets into it with Chris Joseph. They're rolling around on the ice within seconds, Joseph doing his best to pin him and punch him at the same time. Joseph gets Tsygurov's helmet off after a right hand. A couple more punches and Joseph gets the glove off his right hand.

No. 3: Kostichkin pairs up with Fleury. Fleury doesn't turtle—he *is* turtled. He's pinned, tied up so that he can't move his arms, more threatened by suffocation than getting nailed with a knockout punch. "The guy had me in some sort of death grip," Fleury says. "I played more than 1,000 NHL games and I never felt anything like it. He was the strongest guy that I ever played against. I wondered what the hell I got into."

"I know that [the Canadians] didn't think we could fight, and it was true that we did not fight in international tournaments or in our elite league at home," Kostichkin says. "But in hockey there is fighting. We would train or practice, we would get angry at each other, and we would fight—maybe not all of us and maybe not the way

Canadians would fight in games. But we were young men and we all wanted one thing—to play. When we fought it was usually when there were no referees or coaches. It was more like fighting outside the arena than inside."

No. 3A: Chiasson tries to separate Kostichkin and Fleury. Smirnov headlocks and bulldogs the Canadian captain. They scrap full bore. Down to their knees. Then down to the ice.

No. 4: Sanipass and Shestirikov are chucking them. A vicious tilt. More than a dozen punches. Gorski seems to have separated them—they're six feet apart. But then Sanipass does something you don't see in a season of games. You hardly see it in boxing. A clean one-punch. No wrestling. No locking up. No grabbing the other guy's arm to get leverage. Sanipass just whistles a right hand over Gorski's shoulder and right into the mush of Shestirikov. Shestirikov is knocked flat on his ass. What Sanipass does is like push-starting a car while you're on roller skates. The physics are all wrong, but that doesn't matter when the spirit is willing.

No. 5: An epic encounter between Mike Keane and Valeri Zelepukin. Pomoell seems to have quelled the pushing and shoving. Zelepukin goes behind the net. Pomoell and Ivannikov stand between Keane and the Russian forward. Keane pulls away from the linesman and starts skating full speed around the net, pulling up his sleeves. Keane finally catches up to Zelepukin. He's giving away at least fifteen pounds but he's landing punches like a piston churning. Zelepukin stands in and trades. He doesn't back down. Stiffer. Slower. But never bailing, never clinching, never even wrestling. Just throwing right hands of his own.

Hit pause. Lock in on the image of Keane reaching back to throw a right hand. See him not as a hockey fighter but as a boxer, one of the old-school brawlers, nothing scientific about him. "Keaner was the best fighter in the

Western league back then," Fleury says. "He was fighting that guy [Zelepukin] like it was for the world title. I don't know if anyone ever landed so many punches as Keaner did in his fight. He was one of these great middleweights who just didn't fight that often in the NHL—like Steve Thomas or Todd Gill or guys like that."

Hit pause. It would be an unforgettable moment, a scary moment, an appalling moment, a thrilling moment and many other things. It would be different things to different people. And it would be all those things to all those people if this had been the end of the fight. It's not. It's not climax. It's prelude.

Press play. The camera stays tight on Keane's pounding of Zelepukin. Blurs across the screen. First a red Soviet sweater. Then a couple of white Canadian sweaters. The camera pulls out. A shot of the ice surface from centre to the Soviet goal. Now there are a dozen fights. Some numbers you can make out. Some you can't. The *Lord of the Rings* principle applies. The fights in the movies were choreographed—they had to be listed and blocked out somewhere. The scene in Piestany is much messier, spontaneous, improvised. Many players—maybe most—will leave the ice surface without knowing the names of the guys throwing punches at their heads. They didn't even get the numbers.

Pause. Review. Replay. Replay again and again. Determine how the benches cleared. No telling from the tape.

Ask the players. Ask the Soviet players who sent them. Several Soviets say they don't know who—they don't even know if anyone sent them.

"[Most of us] didn't have any idea how to fight," Fedorov says. "I had never been in a fight. The idea that we were sent out there to fight, that wouldn't make any sense. This thing just happened, and we went out just trying to do what we thought we had to do. Davydov was the first guy off the bench. I don't know who the second was, but I might have been the third guy off the bench. I don't know why I had thought I had to do that—Alex and I were the youngest guys on the team and we were trying to prove that we belonged on the team. They were all '67 [born in 1967], and Alex and I were just kids [born in 1969]. Maybe I thought that I didn't want them to think that I was a scared kid. I grabbed one guy—I have no idea who it was. We started fighting or wrestling around at the blue line and ended up in the corner. I have no idea what happened, but I know how it all happened. It all started with Zelepukin. He was just getting pounded by some guy—same thing, no idea who it was—and he couldn't protect himself. Afterwards his shoulder was out of [the joint]. I don't know if he was hurt before the game but he was in a lot of pain afterward."

Ask the Canadian players who sent them. The Canadians say they know Templeton and Burns didn't send them. They say nobody sent them and Templeton and Burns were powerless to stop them.

The first one to leave the Canadian bench was Luke Richardson—at least that's the way most remember it. He saw Davydov and another Soviet jump and he gave chase. He didn't jump over the boards reflexively. He waited to make sure that they were heading for the scrum. That's not a story he has been perfecting and cleaning up over the years; that was his statement right after the fight. "[Davydov] was past our bench and past the blue line before I went," he said. "When you see them go right to the pile, you go. I didn't grab anybody right away. Then I was fighting some guy, and it was probably the first time it had ever happened to him."

Mike Keane says any coach would have been powerless to stop players from coming off the bench. It wouldn't have made any difference if it had been national team coach Dave King or any other sportsmanship-preaching CAHA golden boy behind the Canadian junior's bench. So says

Keane. "It's not something that Bert had to think about. If the players didn't get off the bench and defend our teammates, Bert would have been criticized just as much and someone could have been badly hurt. The first thing you have to do is defend your teammates. There's just no way around it."

Hit play again. Look closely. There's no making out the numbers in half the fights.

A few scraps stand out.

No. 1: Pat Elynuik tries to break up a fight in front of the Soviet net—two unidentifiable players rolling around on the ice, too pooped to punch. He reaches down just to separate them at arm's length. He does this with all the violence and urgency of a guy picking up a dropped penny. The Soviet goaltender Ivannikov grabs him from the back and starts swinging. Elynuik is no fighter, and he tries not to look eager or even interested in fighting Ivannikov. Another Soviet player presumes Elynuik jumped the goalie. Bad luck for Elynuik: it's Vladimir Konstantinov. The way Ivannikov has played in the tournament, the Canadians would have directed him to a safe house rather than have him knocked out of the game.

No. 2: Keane vs. Kostichkin. Kostichkin lets Fleury out of the straitjacket when the benches clear and finds Fleury's Moose Jaw teammate waiting for him. Keane's first opponent, Zelepukin, has gone to the Soviet bench, to the team doctor. Kostichkin loads up on the first punch, a home-run swing, a right hand that goes whistling over Keane's head, a perfectly timed bob and weave. The counterpunches, two flush left hands before the camera pulls away.

No. 3: Greg Hawgood draws Vladimir Konstantinov, who had moved on to his next bout. No good for Hawgood. "I didn't know who he was, but as soon as I grabbed him I realized that this guy was really strong," Hawgood says. "I got in a couple of good shots. I could tell that he had never fought before, but that didn't matter. He was strong and he was a fast learner. In Canada you knew that you were supposed to fight a certain way—head-butts weren't supposed to be part of it. Didn't matter to him. Just whatever worked. Next thing I know is that I'm in a lot of trouble."

Next thing he knows, his nose is broken. "The greatest head-butt I've ever seen. The best of all time," Brendan Shanahan says.

"I don't know what happened to the guy [Konstantinov] was fighting," Sergei Fedorov says. "I just know that Vladi didn't look good when he got back to the dressing room. They must have had a real fight because he was real beat up if he won."

No. 4: The battle of the backup goaltenders: Shawn Simpson vs. Vadim Privalov. It plays out as farce rather than drama. Simpson manages to keep his mask and helmet on—he had to put them on before going onto the ice, since he wasn't wearing them on the bench. He manages to rip Privalov's mask off early in their "fight." That reveals a head of blonde hair only slightly less massive than Simpson's MTV-worthy mullet. It's impossible for either to hurt each other, given the padding. Absurd but irresistible: a pillow fight to the death.

"I was 150 pounds soaking wet," Simpson says. "I wasn't stupid. I went looking for a fight that I had a chance to win, or at least not get killed. It was a tough tournament for me. I didn't think that I'd have any chance to contribute. So maybe I was getting out my frustrations in the fight. And maybe I hadn't fought a lot, but I saw lots of them. I knew what to do."

No. 5: Two Soviet players, one of them Smirnov, the other unidentifiable from the video, double-team Stephane Roy. Wittman sees it right away. Roy kneels on the ice, Smirnov knees him in the face while the other Soviet player holds Roy down. It goes on for a minute until Roy is just a heap on the ice.

"Nobody took it worse than Stephane Roy," Theoren Fleury says. "I sat next to him afterward. It was like science fiction—the guy with two heads. He had something coming out of his head, all swollen, about the size of a volleyball." Says Brendan Shanahan: "You could see the bootmark on his forehead. He could have been killed."

Don't adjust your set. The screen goes half grey. The lights are dimmed in the Soviet end. Then the picture goes to black. All that can be seen on the screen is the white lights of the scoreboard in the arena:

4 2

13:53

USSR—CANADA

Hit pause. It's going to be known as many things. "The Punch-Out in Piestany" will be an alliterative favourite. The mention of it will sometimes draw a blank from a casual fan. Even those with a faint interest in hockey will clue in with a mention of "The Night the Lights Went Out."

Shawn Simpson: "It was black on the screen, but down at ice level you could still see what was going on. Not really clearly, but it wasn't pitch black. There were still fights going on. But even before the lights were turned off guys were getting arm weary. It was already starting to die down."

Fred Walker: "You really wonder about turning out the lights—it probably meant less as far as stopping the fights than for face-saving for the officials."

Press play. 5:00 flashes in the column for Canadian penalties. As if one major is all that's going to come out of it. Then the clock begins to run. 13:54 . . . 13:55 . . . 13:56 . . . and then, for some reason, 13:5. The lights come up.

Richardson and Kerch are still wrestling, Richardson with a bear hug, Kerch stuck with his head down around Richardson's knees. Davydov and Konstantinov jump in. So does McLlwain. Two or three players and suddenly it's a rugby scrum, a tangle of bodies moving from one end of the ice to the other.

Zelepukin skates off the ice to get repairs, Hawgood to get his nose put in joint.

Nemeth skates off the ice and tries to find tournament officials and the referee to make the case that Canada wasn't the first off the bench. He takes it upon himself. It probably should be the captain's responsibility, but Chiasson might not be the best one to represent the team's interests at this point. Nemeth figures he should skate into the leadership breach. He is, after all, the one player on the Canadian team who had been playing with and against men, the one who has a comfort level in foreign arenas. Nemeth looks for someone in the hallways outside the officials' dressing room to explain to him what the Canadians should do next. Should they go to the dressing room while penalties are assessed? Or should they wait at the bench? He doesn't get any word directly, just second-hand and third-hand. Go to the room, time will be added to the start of the third period, wait for word about penalties. Nemeth skates back to the bench. Delivers the message to Templeton. No change of expression. Stony.

Pause again. Pomoell and Gorski are talking to arena workers at the Zamboni gate. Rønning is nowhere to be seen.

Listen to Wittman. "I wouldn't be surprised if the game is over. I won't be surprised if the game is called . . . I don't know which team left the bench first, but I think Canada might have been the first off the bench."

Listen to Bassin. "I don't want to sound like a homer, but I think when the fight was on, the one Russian player jumped over. . . . There's gonna be a complete reorganization. There's gonna be some committee work."

Cue Everett Sanipass once more. Look for it. Look for the remorse. Look for the fear. Look for the sinking feeling. Look for the realization that trying to do the right thing has made everything wrong.

"Obviously a bit too aggressive . . . we took a bit too much . . . I—I was gonna settle it down . . . I wasn't expecting for the other guys to do it . . ."

It dawns on Sanipass, while he's talking, in the first few short sentences while he catches his breath. Better that he take the fall than everyone else. Better that it fall on him than be spread around.

"They were stickin' us and everyt'ing . . ."

He claims, the Canadians claim, provocation, even self-defence. He opens his eyes wide. The sweat is pouring into them, stinging. He struggles to stay composed. Bites his lip. Drops his head. Almost hyperventilates. *My fault. He's saying it's my fault. Is it my fault? All this. For all my teammates. In front of all these people. All those people back home.*

Fred Walker tells Sanipass that they're looking for him in the dressing room. It's all Sanipass can do not to break down on the spot.

Hit pause again. Look at the equipment strewn all over the ice: the gloves, helmets, sweaters—equipment no one will don again this day, or ever again.

Not Prevailing and Not Existing

Hit play. *Pause it when the camera catches Bert Templeton on the bench as his players head to the dressing room.* Dread all over his face. More like a mourner than a coach. Even before the lights went off. His shot at something close to the big time, his shot at shaking the Dirty Bert label, is up in smoke. He knows what will happen. "Bert kept saying, 'They're going to kick us out,'" Dennis McDonald remembers. "He kept saying, 'We're going to get screwed.'"

Hit stop. It's too painful to watch.

———

The crowd of four thousand had nothing to watch other than arena workers gathering up equipment. It looked like a freeze frame. It looked like a still life.

Dennis McDonald was trying to keep the Canadian team's medal hopes alive. He was trying to save the game.

Gunther Sabetzki convened and presided over an emergency meeting in an office at the arena. In attendance were the managers of all the tournament teams and Sabetzki. McDonald suspected it would take some serious lobbying just to get it to a vote—to convince any of the officials that the game could be completed, or at least that the teams shouldn't be disqualified. Wittman said that he had "never seen anything like this" and called the brawl "unprecedented" in international competition, but that wasn't entirely true.

Slava Fetisov had provoked a bench-clearing brawl with a U.S. team at the world championships in May '85. The outcome: two ejections, four majors and a game played to a conclusion (and the Soviets came away from the tournament with a bronze medal). The rule book seemed to cover bench-clearing: ten-minute majors and ejections for the players who left the bench first. And that certainly seemed to be the spirit of the law when you weighed the penalties that came out of the pre-game scrap between the Canadians and Americans: level the penalty against a couple of players, one from each team, spreading the justice around. That approach seemed to recognize that the instigators should be punished and protection should be afforded those who were just caught up in events not of their design.

Those other two bench-clearings differed from the one in the final game of the 1987 WJC. The scrap between the USSR and the U.S. at the 1985 worlds differed because of the presence of mind of the combatants. "I came off the bench and ended up with Fetisov," says Neil Sheehy, a former NHLer and now a player agent. "I saw Fetisov stick one of our guys right in the face, and the Soviets had ten guys on the ice at the time that the fighting started—they were in the middle of a line change. I didn't get thrown out of the game because I wasn't the first off the bench and I didn't drop my gloves. And most of the other guys did the same thing. It wasn't how you'd fight in North America, but we all knew the rules in Europe—if you drop your gloves, you're out. The international rules are a lot harder on dropping your gloves rather than coming off the bench." The Canadian juniors' pregame brawl with the Americans earlier in the 1987 tournament differed from the melée with the Soviets simply because of scale and situation. Fact is, the scrap with the Americans wasn't as violent and no one left the bench—everyone was already on the ice.

Medals for the Canadian juniors—remember Don Wittman's pre-game comment about those "guaranteed medals"—were only one of McDonald's concerns. An immediate concern, yes, but maybe not the most serious one. He knew that Sabetzki's dislike of the Canadians bordered on hatred. *The man wouldn't put maple syrup on his pancakes.* This was an opportunity for the last word in *schadenfreude.* Here was the chance of a lifetime to humiliate the Canadians. Suspensions were out there, for players, even for national programs. And relegation to the B pool would have been the crowning insult.

McDonald was going to war without an ally he could really count on. The American team's manager, Art Bergland, told McDonald in the stands during the fight on the ice that he could count on his support—except if no one else took the Canadian side, which is exactly what happened.

"I can't say that I was really surprised that the vote was eight to one," says McDonald. "All the teams and Sabetzki voting to throw us out. I was alone and I knew it going in. There's something fundamentally wrong with the idea that a team that stood to back into the gold medal, Finland, voted us out of the tournament. Same thing with the Czechs, who moved up from bronze to silver. Sweden votes to throw us out—they get a medal that they'd already been eliminated from. Sweden wouldn't have won a medal any other way. It was just wrong. It was a railroading."

McDonald was hot under the collar. Sabetzki and the other officials said that the Canadian team was still welcome to attend the tournament banquet after the medal ceremony. McDonald seethed. They were taunting him with their fake smiles. McDonald told them to drop dead. Sabetzki and the tournament organizers dropped the mock sportsmanship and told McDonald to get his team out of Piestany. Then they told the military officers that they wanted the Canadians out of there. The word got to McDonald: have your team on the bus in half an hour and get out of the country.

The hearing was a tough moment. A tougher one awaited: breaking the news to the coaches and the players.

Ignorance was short-lived bliss. In the dressing room the Canadian players were still hoping to take home the gold medal. They were still concentrating on what they thought was a game at hand but was in fact a game at an end. The innocence of youth wasn't tempered by adult doubt.

"We were trying not to get distracted," Mike Keane says. "We were just trying to get prepared to go back out there to finish the second period and play the third. As far as we knew, the game wasn't over. As far as we knew, we were going back out there. We took off our skates, but no one was taking off his equipment."

"My nose was broken but I was getting it looked after because I wanted to get back out there and play," Greg Hawgood says. "I didn't think for a second that I wasn't going to be able to play—never mind that there'd be no game."

"I was trying to get it together," says Everett Sanipass. "Fred [Walker] came in and tried to calm me down and let me know that he wasn't blaming me. It was tough. I was shaking. I don't know if I ever felt quite like that before."

"Maybe we got caught thinking about the game the way that we thought about hockey in our own [Canadian junior] leagues," Scott Metcalfe says. "Back then there were a lot of bench-clearings, but I doubt very many of us had been in a game that was cancelled or forfeited outright.

We'd been in games where a bunch of players on both sides had been thrown out—first guys off the bench, third men in, the ones who provoked it. But playing a game with a shorter bench, that was always a possibility in our leagues, and any real trouble after that was pretty rare because you didn't want to shorten your bench even more. That and everyone got [the fighting] out of his system."

Dennis McDonald didn't have any fight left in his system. He felt defeated on every count: no game, no medal, no justice. He walked into the dressing room feeling defeated not once but over and over. He struggled to come up with a way to break the news to the players. He didn't know how to describe the ultimate screw job.

"I remember Dennis walking into the room, more disgusted than disappointed," Kerry Huffman says.

Everett Sanipass remembers McDonald walking into the room madder at the team than he was disgusted with the IIHF officials.

"I said, 'We're out. It's like we don't exist. It's like we were never here,'" McDonald says.

That much everyone agrees on. "It's like we were never here": a perfect epitaph. It was all a great illusion. It was like a magic show. The lights came on and it was like the international officials had made the Canadians disappear.

One snag: some players remember McDonald adding a footnote that gnawed at them then and gnaws at them still.

"He said, 'They voted us out and I can't say I disagree with them,'" Brendan Shanahan says.

Others will remember it as: " . . . and I agree with them." Others don't remember anything at all like that.

Still, McDonald didn't bother to conceal his disappointment with the coach and the staff. The Soviets jumping first didn't mitigate Canada's case with the international officials, and it didn't get the Canadian players and coaches off the hook with McDonald. McDonald doesn't talk about it now, but Murray Costello will. "It was the failure of the coaches more than the players," Costello says. "Bert Templeton wanted to run the whole show—that's what he was used to doing, and that's what he did with this team. He refused anybody's help. Before the tournament and during it he ordered CAHA staff out of the dressing room. He wanted control and it ended up with a complete loss of discipline. That's what we thought at the time, and when we brought [Templeton and Burns] in to debrief them, they didn't say much . . . they didn't volunteer any information. They were generally unco-operative."

McDonald took this as a tacit admission of guilt, but Burns says that wasn't the case. He and Templeton were frustrated and angry that they were going to be scapegoated. "Anyone in hockey knows that in that situation there was nothing—nothing—a coach could do. At the start we were trying to hold players back. As soon as our guys started to go over the boards I tried to hold some guys back. I was thinking, 'I gotta have some guys we can finish the game with.' We didn't send players, but eventually we were powerless to stop them. Anybody in hockey knows that, but there was no convincing those guys [the CAHA] of that."

Some players acknowledge that team discipline was an issue before the Soviet game. They will talk about it guardedly and ask that their names not be used. They will ask to leave out the names of their teammates.

———

Listen to one player tell it.

"We were a dysfunctional team. It was a real gong show. We were a bunch of the best players in the country and we turned real negative. Not about each other—but we joked that the only thing we all agreed on was that we hated the coach and we were down about the program.

"Bert Templeton was more than a hard-ass. He was angry. He would get under your skin. When they were selecting the team, they brought every player in individually to talk to them and let us know if we made the team or got cut. And even for the guys who made the cut, really good players on the team, Templeton couldn't find one good thing to say about them. It was that way all the time with him. I remember I had one screw-up, nothing major, against Poland—a game we won easy. I saw him the next day at the hotel, just walking by, and he was trashing me. Maybe he was one way with North Bay and another way with us, but we still felt like black sheep. It was hard to respect him when he didn't respect us. It's a hard thing to say—it's like ganging up on a guy who can't defend himself—but that's just the way we felt.

"It wasn't just the coach we hated. We felt like we were treated like shit by the CAHA. We went through the try-outs in Ottawa and right up to the end of the tournament, when Dennis McDonald said that he didn't disagree with the decision. They treated us like meat.

"We became sort of a rebel team. We broke curfew when we were in Switzerland and a bunch of us got trashed. Two guys were eyeballing these two Swiss girls who wanted nothing to do with us. When the two local guys took them up on the dance floor, [a couple of players] pissed in their beer pitchers. When we hung out at our hotel in Nitra, the Swedes were going around like Boy Scouts in corduroy jackets, all clean-cut. We were the Bad News Bears, all scruffy, not giving a shit. And really, that's how we played and acted the whole tournament. Ugly.

"If Dennis McDonald was sour at us before the brawl—and I'm sure he was—it was because we didn't get with the program. It didn't feel like there was a program there. We made up our own program. And I guess Dennis McDonald, whether he'd say so or not, made a connection between our lack of discipline off the ice and what happened against the Soviets."

McDonald coming into the dressing room was like an adult arriving on the island in *Lord of the Flies*. Or at least it would have been if it didn't look so familiar to CAHA officials. It wasn't the first time that the players had taken over the program. Canada had taken a solid team to the 1984 WJC in Sweden but had crashed and burned. Afterwards, it came out that several players had snuck out of their hotel and gone bar-hopping before important games.

The CAHA officials were certain that some of the juniors had shown up for games hungover. They resented that the players had looked at the WJC as some sort of frat party. Even some players on that '84 team had complained. "We didn't have discipline," said Sylvain Cote, who had been a seventeen-year-old defenceman on that team. "A few guys were more worried about going out and having a few drinks. That was my first [world juniors] experience. I was just like a rookie there. I had to keep my mouth shut and sit in the room and get some rest for the game. I was looking at the other guys and thinking, 'Something wrong is happening here.' That was the only thing that hurt the team's chances."

There was no indication that the Canadian juniors broke curfew in Nitra. Coaches always presumed that a resourceful hockey player with bad intentions can find trouble anywhere. But Nitra, as grey as the smoke from its factories, as joyless as its breadlines, would have tested that theory. The odds of finding good-looking puck bunnies and a friendly bartender in Nitra were no better than of finding a four-star restaurant. It was one thing to party in Sweden like the 1984 team did, but another thing to do so on the other side of the Iron Curtain. Worse still to be in a luckless little industrial town. But the way the Canadian officials saw it, the real damage had been done by the time the team arrived in Nitra. The team's partying in Switzerland during the exhibitions had hurt Canada's medal chances, though they couldn't have seen it coming. A more decisive victory over the Swiss in the WJC opener would have left the Canadians needing just a simple victory the Soviets, not a five-goal rout. But goal-differential numbers were not the real problem. The CAHA officials saw the beer party as a symptom. If they were going to scapegoat, they would see it as a symptom of teenagers who were trouble, teenagers who were inclined to act out.

But if the Canadian team's officials were going to step back and see the big picture, they'd have understood that it was not only the juniors' failure but also their own. They presumed that the teenagers would be transformed into model Canadian youth the moment they pulled on the red and white sweaters, and that they would remain chaste, sober and God-fearing right through to the medal cere-mony. The officials should have anticipated that, left alone, the players would stray.

———

The messages came not just from the coaches but also from the adults on the trip.

The message came from Templeton, who showed up back at the hotel with Sandy after a few too many drinks. The message came from Templeton, who would still be blasting the players on the way to his room. Maybe his team in North Bay would be used to it over the course of months, and to them it would have sounded different and mattered less. To the Canadian juniors—who'd had a few weeks to get to know not only each other but also their coach—the scene and his sniping played differently. These were the best players on their teams—*in Canada*— so they weren't used to someone laying into them, sober or not.

The message came from right down on the bench.

Cue the DVD again. Look for a scene at the bench—on the bench—that may or may not have provoked the Soviets before or after the bench-clearing. Nothing. Nothing to back it up other than a confession made without coercion after the incident.

Look for the trainer. Press pause. He's easy to spot. He was there in footage earlier in the game. The camera down on the bench picked him up. Think of a young Craig Stadler—walrus-like moustache, hair that looks more wind-blown than blow-dried.

McDonald had reason to be as sour about Wally Tatomir as anybody. He doesn't air old grievances—personal ones, anyway—twenty years later, but the players knew that McDonald had Tatomir on his shit list—in there with the players, the coach and others—even if Goran Stubb's story about a Canadian staffer spitting at the Finnish players wasn't true.

The incident wasn't reported on the broadcast. With fights breaking out on so many fronts, with the camera focused on Simpson and Privalov for a long stretch, and with the arena eventually going dark, it would have been easy to miss. With soldiers running up to the rinkside, with everything drowned out by the whistling, it was understandable that Fred Walker could have missed it. Jim Cressman had no way of seeing it from where he sat in the stands.

So the incident wasn't reported until a couple of days after the game. Wally Tatomir told a reporter back home—not Cressman—that he gave the Soviets' assistant coach "a right-hand shot" while the fight raged on the ice. Tatomir said that he "was holding three guys back from jumping over the boards and at the same time hollering to the [Soviets'] assistant coach to hold their guys back." Tatomir said the assistant coach laughed at him. Tatomir said that he gave the assistant coach "one shot, right in the face, and he went down."

That was Tatomir's account then. He's not quite so forthcoming these days. "A lot of things were happening," he says.

Tatomir didn't name "the assistant coach," so he didn't likely know his name and certainly couldn't have put a name to his face. Vasiliev only had one assistant coach, though: Valentin Gureev. Gureev says he has no memory of being hit.

Gureev recalls "some kind of masseur . . . running around and threatening everyone . . . don't remember his name." But he doesn't mention anything about being hit or about anyone else on the staff being hit by a Canadian trainer. No memory of something that you'd think would have stuck in his memory.

Vasiliev doesn't mention a trainer popping his assistant coach or anyone else on his staff. It seems like a detail that wouldn't get erased from the memory bank, not for a coach who can remember his line combinations from that game.

Maybe it happened the way that Tatomir originally described. Maybe it was an apocryphal story. Maybe he was cranking up the details of minor incident. Maybe Tatomir punched someone else, and in a case of mistaken identity, thought it was the assistant coach. Whatever the case, Tatomir's admission in the newspaper makes it easier to believe Goran Stubb's account of the spitting incident with the Finns. It's easy to believe a guy was spitting on players from other teams if he was taking shots at an assistant coach—or someone he *thought* was an assistant coach—of the team on the other bench. It's even easy to believe the spitting story if he didn't punch anybody in the heat of a fight but told apocryphal stories afterwards—bragging about it as if he'd done the honourable thing.

As the trainer, Tatomir was the one adult on the team the teenagers had the most contact with. The players listened to Templeton and Burns and McDonald and others, but in any dressing room, no adult feels a part of the team more than the trainer.

———

It was a poetic postscript, an almost philosophical one. "It's like we don't exist. It's like we were never here," McDonald said, words that Albert Camus could have scripted for an address to outsiders.

Soon they *weren't* there. About half an hour after the last player had skated off the ice. That was all the time it took. They weren't just thrown out of the tournament—they were being kicked out of the country. Soldiers surrounded the Canadians when they emerged from the dressing room and pointed them toward the bus. With their rifles. With dogs snapping at the Canadian kids' heels. They boarded, still bruised, bleeding. The bus pulled away, a three-hour military escort to the border. The Russians, in even worse shape than the Canadians, went to the dinner.

———

McDonald still sounds regretful and hurt today. "There's not a day goes by that I don't think about it," he says. "It's always there. And I keep thinking, 'Is there something that I could have done that would have stopped this from happening?'"

It only sounds like he's talking about any executive move he could have made in his dealings with Sabetzki and the IIHF. It only sounds like he's talking about any bargain he might have been able to strike so that Canada could have come away with a medal. It encompasses a lot more than that. It includes what he coud have done before the tournament, decisions that were made with personnel and, yes, the coaching staff. It's just a polite way—

self-accusatory—of saying that the wrong people were in the wrong place at the wrong time.

McDonald was not alone in second-guessing himself. After McDonald told the team it was over and the itinerary was changed, Templeton was pacing outside the dressing room and telling anyone else who would listen, "I tried to prepare them for anything that could have happened out there, but this is the one thing I didn't talk about."

Accusation and Plausible Denial

Press play. *Go forward a tenth of a second at a time. Slow it down. Zoom in.* The seconds before the teams have poured over the boards. Blurs. One red; two—three—white. Coming into the frame from left to right, skating from centre ice, where the benches are, to the corner in the Soviet end where Keane is pounding Zelepukin.

Listen to the commentary. There are no answers there. Not for the questions that linger, questions that weigh on the minds of those watching the game in the arena and on television in Canada and, you'd suppose, the officials charged with meting out punishment:

Which team jumped the bench first?

Who was the first player off the bench? And who was the second?

The nearest thing to eyewitness evidence is inconclusive, contradictory. Wittman: "I don't know which team left the bench first, but I think Canada might have been the first off the bench." Bassin: "I don't want to sound like a homer, but I think when the fight was on, the one Russian player jumped over."

Hit pause.

—

All these years later, you'd expect denials. You'd expect no one to plead guilty; fingers pointing at each other. Blaming the other guy. Spinning.

The outcome isn't what you'd expect.

First, Vladimir Vasiliev admits that the Soviet players were the first to leave the bench. He qualifies that, however. He maintains that he didn't send his players off the bench. Or at least he didn't mean to, he says. The players' leaving the bench was an incident that was lost in translation—not from Russian to English, but from coach to players.

"Valeri Zelepukin was playing with a separated shoulder—the left one, I think," Vasiliev says. "I knew about his injury and at first I didn't want to take him on the trip. He didn't want to have surgery until after the championships. It had already popped out once during the game. His teammates knew it was very painful for him. He was a kid with such a strong will, a warrior, and also a very modest person.

"The Canadian [Keane] started punching him. Valerka couldn't fight full strength and he was protecting himself with only one hand. And the Canadian maybe didn't know what was going on with Valerka. And I was thinking, goddamn it, this guy will pummel him. And I yelled to our guys on the ice, 'Guys, help Valerka.' But unfortunately, my players who were next to me watching the incident from the bench thought that I told them to help Valerka. And yes, Zhenia Davydov was the first one to go. Our hockey players were a close-knit unit and took care of each other. And they jumped out and so did the Canadians and the brawl began."

The bullshit detector might be flashing. Or not. Vasiliev's version is self-serving, but not as far-fetched as it sounds.

A message misheard. It seems plausible. He could have been drowned out by the fans' whistling before the benches cleared. Vasiliev had been the loudest coach that the Canadian players on the 1986 team had ever heard, but then again, Wittman and Bassin had to shout into the microphones just to be heard above the whistling during the fight.

If you accept that it was a message misheard, the question then becomes: Why was it misheard? Why would the players think he was telling them to leave the bench? How did it fit with the other messages he had been sending to them?

Vasiliev's job had been to make the Soviets more like the Canadians. He had been drilling that concept into his players' heads. The first player off the bench was Evgeni Davydov, the least likely enforcer. A coach who wanted to send a message would have tapped the shoulder and shouted in the ear of Malakhov or one of his other monster-sized players. Davydov didn't fit the profile. The book on him: soft as chiffon. But Davydov would have heard his coach knock him for not being tough enough. And it was his best friend on the club, Zelepukin, who was being punished, first by Sanipass, then by Keane. Davydov's was just an emotional reaction. That's Vasiliev's claim. It takes a bigger leap.

"Maybe it did happen that way," Sergei Fedorov says. "Vasiliev could have been yelling at guys on the ice and someone else heard it . . . got confused. I didn't hear it. By the time I went over the boards, Davydov and someone else had already left the bench.

"I don't know about the coach trying to make us play tougher or like the Canadians. I don't think that was it at all. For us, playing tough was skating through checks, going into the corners. The usual things in our game. Did we try to be tough against the Canadians, though? Just in the usual way, not by looking for fights or playing dirty. That just wasn't our game—not at all."

———

Rewind the video to the start of the brawl. Press play. Look for any weaknesses. Holes start to show in Vasiliev's story about Davydov and the other unidentified Soviet player racing to the defence of the supposedly defenceless Valeri Zelepukin. Zelepukin is knocked down, yes, but he gets up. He gets up, so the notion he was pinned down helplessly doesn't wash. He could have skated away. He gets up and Keane circles away from the linesman. Keane uses the net and Ivannikov to pick off the linesman and grabs Zelepukin. Keane starts throwing them. Zelepukin has never fought like this, and he has certainly never fought anyone like Mike Keane. Zelepukin should have been an immediate casualty. He should have been taken out on a stretcher this time—if his shoulder is separated. But Zelepukin is throwing punches. He's fending off Keane, locking Keane up with his left hand and throwing with his right. Hard to imagine he could do either with a separated shoulder. Keane should consider himself lucky that this guy didn't have any experience fighting—he looks like a natural.

Fast-forward to a point after the lights are turned on again. Zelepukin is sitting on the bench alone. No helmet. Fights have died down. Vasiliev waves his hand at Zelepukin. He points him toward the dressing room. Zelepukin doesn't seem in a lot of distress. The trainer isn't looking at his shoulder. Zelepukin steps out of the gate. But he doesn't go directly to the dressing room: he skates down to the Soviet net. He picks up his helmet, gloves and stick. His right arm is hanging down, but he's not holding it at the elbow with his left hand, as you'd expect of a player with a separated shoulder. He's not racing off the ice to the tournament doctor without getting his equipment.

Press pause.

—

Many hypotheticals are left. Few things are certain.

Maybe Zelepukin had a bad shoulder going into the tournament. Lots of players were banged up by that final game—including Keane, as it turned out. But nothing in the game before the shift that led to the fight indicated that Zelepukin was playing with a separated shoulder.

He was hooked to the ice right before the whistle. Maybe he landed awkwardly and hurt it in the process—but then there'd be no explaining how he hung on with Keane for so long. Keane had beaten up a lot of Western league enforcers, most of them healthy and ready to go, and he was scoring an emphatic decision in this fight with Zelepukin. Keane did get a fight from Zelepukin, though. Zelepukin showed up.

It seems just as likely that Zelepukin had a shoulder injury that was aggravated during the fight. That would be a less convenient story line for Vasiliev. Harder to justify scaling the boards under those circumstances.

Evgeni Davydov drills the biggest holes in Vasiliev's story. "I wasn't confused by anything Vasiliev said on the bench," Davydov says. "He told me to go over the boards. Zelepukin was hurt. I didn't mistake what Vasiliev said. He told me to leave the bench, and afterwards he said nothing to me. If I did something he didn't want, he would have said something.

"I was surprised that he picked me to go out on the ice. Fighting is not part of my game. It never was. Maybe [Vasiliev will say] he wanted me just to go to the referee, but that's not true. He wanted me to go into the fight."

Templeton also claimed that there was nothing to be lost in translation, no message that could have been misunderstood. "I saw him open the gate and send players on the ice," Templeton told reporters days later in Toronto. Templeton was hardly an unbiased witness—but he didn't know what had appeared on the CBC broadcast, what Wittman and Bassin had said during the broadcast, what Cressman had reported, what newspapers had published and what his own players had said. Unless he was telling the truth, he would have been risking embarrassing contradiction.

———

Don Cherry was the first one to float the conspiracy theory. He did it right on the broadcast. The whole thing was a conspiracy to deny Canada a gold medal. A dirty trick. A well-hatched plot: the Soviets, having dropped out of the medals, had provoked the Canadians in order to take their arch-rivals down with them.

The theory gained a lot of momentum in the press. If it wasn't unanimous, it did become the conventional wisdom.

In fairness to those who supported the conspiracy theory, they wouldn't have been the first in international sport to make the case against the Soviets. "It had happened with Soviet teams in different sports over the years, certainly in soccer," Professor Robert Edelman says.

The Soviets had invited suspicion about not competing on the up-and-up because of one of the most dubious performances in modern hockey history, the Czechoslovakia–USSR game at the world championships in 1981. The Soviets had clinched the gold going into the last game of the round-robin tournament and run up scores against most opponents. Canada needed a Soviet win over the Czechoslovakians to capture the silver medal. "It finished 0–0," hockey historian Denis Gibbons says. "The game wasn't taped or broadcast, but supposedly the Soviets passed the puck back on a breakaway."

"Any time you see the 0–0 score it raises questions about the legitimacy of the result," Edelman says.

But the Piestany game wasn't a case of a superior team lying down. Nor was it a case of a "gentleman's agreement," something prearranged, both teams entering into it. It was something much more complicated.

And in fairness to the conspiracy theorists, another Canadian team had been ambushed by the Soviets and drawn into a fight. Back in the '60s, Anatoli Tarasov was espousing sportsmanship. He was elevating the willingness to walk away from a fight to a virtue of the highest rank. He was deriding the Canadian game as a lesser form of hockey, and the Canadians' fighting on the ice as a stain on the game. Or at least that's what Tarasov was preaching publicly and writing about in his memoirs. Yet Tarasov sent a different message to his players.

"In the early '60s, Tarasov thought his team wasn't playing hard enough, so he came up with a plan," says journalist Seva Kukushkin. "He wanted his team to fight the Canadians, to send a message to the Canadians and to his own team. He wanted his players to drop their gloves and fight the Canadian team, which was on tour in Eastern Europe. Tarasov's problem [was] fighting wasn't approved of by the politicians—if the politicians from the Kremlin saw a game with Soviet players fighting a team from another nation, it would have been a scandal . . . especially if the Soviets provoked it. So Tarasov scheduled a game with the Canadians in Kalinin, 120 kilometres outside of Moscow—just far enough so that the politicians would not go to watch it. Just to be sure, Tarasov scheduled the game for an outdoor rink in the dead of winter. No politician was going to drive to a game to stand in the cold."

As Kukushkin tells it, the scene in Kalinin was the closest thing to a precedent for Piestany.

"There were fights all over the ice," Kukushkin says. "Tarasov's players didn't wait for the Canadians to drop their gloves—they [the Soviets] dropped theirs first. After two periods the Canadian officials talked to Tarasov and he agreed just to play hockey in the third period. When old-timers get together, they talk about that game. It was just a score in the newspaper so the politicians had no idea what had happened, but those who were there knew what happened—they knew there had never been anything like it."

Kukushkin says Tarasov wasn't happy with the result in Kalinin—the Soviets held their own in the brawling, but it did little to adjust the attitude of his players. "Nothing good came of Kalinin," Kukushkin says. "It was an experiment for Tarasov . . . an experiment that failed. There was no reason to repeat it."

———

The idea that Piestany was the product of a conspiracy didn't hold water. Not then. Not now.

Not then: if the authorities had a plan that Vasiliev had gone along with, he would have been spared criticism in the media. Had there been a conspiracy, the press would have heaped blame on the Canadians. That didn't happen, though. TASS, the USSR's news agency, hung the Soviet coaches out to dry. TASS declared Vasiliev and Gureev culpable. The players got off only slightly better.

"Our press did not write that the Canadians left the bench first," Gureev says. "Yes, they wrote that the Canadians were aggressive, but they did not really blame them, they blamed us—Vasiliev and me—because we could not control our players and prevent them from fighting. All the leading newspapers wrote about this incident. Everyone was craving for Vasiliev and I to be kicked out of our jobs and for us to lose our careers."

If Vasiliev and Gureev had followed the official plan, they would have been rewarded for their full co-operation. The sports ministry would have had no choice but to observe the IIHF suspension, but it wouldn't have taken long to call in the coaches from the wilderness. The ban would have been no more than a hiatus if Vasiliev and

Gureev had been going along with a plan. It would have amounted to a sabbatical, and then they would have been restored to their previous national team positions—or promoted. That wasn't the case, however.

"The hockey officials brought the coaches and all the players to a meeting," Pavel Kostichkin says. "It was very serious for the coaches, not so much for the players. The officials wanted explanations of what happened in Piestany. It was about the fight but it was also about our team performing so poorly. We [the players] were there, but we were not expected to speak unless asked to. Vasiliev was the one who had to speak. I think that we might have been asked [by the officials] to speak if they did not believe what Vasiliev said. But his explanation was simple: our bad tournament was like the fight, just hockey. It was just hockey and not everything can be controlled. The officials understood that, I think, and they did not really hold it against us."

"But back home in Moscow, everyone was against our players and me and my coaching staff," Vasiliev says. "For a whole week I was waiting to see if I was going to get banned from both club and country. And at the time, I was the second coach behind [Viktor] Tikhonov for the national team. I had to wait and see what would be the decision of the Central Committee of the Communist Party. I had a couple of friends who were up there at this level—one was responsible for soccer and the other one for hockey—and they called me one morning and told me that for sure, I was going to be banned. I started thinking, 'What was I going to do now?' But my boss, who was the director of the chemical factory which backed the Khimik club, told me not to worry, that things will eventually get back to normal. Then, at the end of the week, one of my friends at the Central Committee called me and said that the news wasn't all that bad. The decision was not to ban me from Khimik, but only from the national team."

Years later, Gureev's and Vasiliev's accounts conflict. Gureev remembers being shut out for eighteen months, but Vasiliev says he was named to the 1988 Olympic team's staff. Put it down to the passage of time.

Players back the coaches' claim that there wasn't a nefarious master plan. Just because things went all wrong for Canada doesn't mean that the Soviets had a plot. "I can honestly say that we went on the ice just trying to win that game," Fedorov says. "There was no way that the coaches told us to start a fight to get the Canadians thrown out of the tournament. If Canada doesn't get a medal, it doesn't help us. It helps the other teams—the Finns and the others. If we beat Canada or tie them, then at least we can say that we played well in one game of the tournament. [The idea of a plan] doesn't make any sense."

Though this sounds disingenuous—it overlooks years of bitter rivalry, even the mutual hatred the teams put on display for all the world to see during the game—Fedorov's version of events and motives is backed up by Professor Edelman. If the Piestany game was the product of a conspiracy, the Soviet hockey officials would have to have acted with incredible speed. They would have had to be practically clairvoyant.

Not now: the conspiracy theory isn't consistent with the culture of Soviet sports, secrets that spilled out after the collapse of the USSR. Robert Edelman leaves no room for doubt. "It never happened," the historian says. "It never would have happened. They wouldn't have ordered a coach to do this. They would have been enraged that it was allowed to happen."

Professor Edelman has no rooting interest. He isn't in the defensive posture that a former Soviet official might assume. He is not influenced by any patriotic sentiment that a Canadian hockey commentator might promote or succumb to. Edelman has dedicated more time and research and thought to the history of sports in the Soviet

Union than any other academic in the West. It seems like a small niche to carve out, but it's an effective way to gauge the bureaucracy and the people, social policy and society's attitudes. He has opened long-sealed files. He has interviewed the principals: the athletes, the bureaucrats. He has a clear read of not only the decisions that were made but also the goals that guided decision-makers.

"What mattered most to Soviet officials was how other countries and the major international sports federations looked at them," Edelman says. "To them it was important to be respected. They couldn't have influence at the international level without that respect. They couldn't have important jobs in the federations without first getting that respect. You have to understand what was of value to them. It wasn't just victory—or in this case Canadians' defeat. Some of it was material. They wanted those jobs—the travel to the Olympics or to other international events. They wanted to have all the perqs that went with the prominent jobs with the federation. But some of it was just their character, maybe an inferiority complex. [The officials] had heard snickers when they first became involved in international sport and the Olympic movement. They knew that the officials representing other nations had significant wealth. Some of them were nobility. And they looked down on the Soviets when they attended meetings in their cheap suits."

Professor Edelman has never opened a long-sealed file of orders to Vladimir Vasiliev to start a brawl with the Canadian team at the junior tournament in Czechoslovakia. He has never interviewed anybody who would admit knowledge of any such orders. Out of hundreds of interviews, not one that would back it up. Not one that would even indicate that it was a possibility.

Professor Edelman suggests that Piestany as a conspiracy falls short on the three standard counts: means, opportunity, motive.

Means: the bureaucrats couldn't have known that the bench-clearing would have brought about the disqualification of both teams. That wasn't the outcome when the Soviets were involved in a bench-clearing instigated by Slava Fetisov in an international game a few years earlier. "They couldn't know what the outcome of that fight would have been," Professor Edelman says. "The decision was out of [the Soviets'] hands. It was in the hands of the [on-ice] officials and the national and federation executives." And that was exactly the case in Piestany.

Opportunity: the bureaucrats and the coaches could not have known that, as Steve Chiasson said on the Canadian bus, things were "falling into place" for Canada's gold-medal hopes. It took the result of another game only an hour or so before the start of the game in Piestany for the Canada–Soviet Union match to have such significance in the medals.

Motive: the juniors were an important tournament, just not *that* important. The audience back in the Soviet Union wouldn't have been up there in numbers with those dialled into major international games. The audience was small anywhere outside of Canada. It wasn't the Summit Series. It wasn't the Olympics. It wasn't the world championships. A Canadian victory wouldn't have sent the wrong message to the Soviet people. The Soviets had lost other world junior tournaments without incident. A loss again wouldn't have sown the seeds of doubt about their own sports or social system, at least no more than the Finns getting the gold. This was one hockey game, no matter how important in Canada. It was not viewed as a contest with hearts and minds at stake. The bureaucrats, more than anyone, knew that. Motive? It just doesn't fit.

Edelman takes it one step further. The Soviets had motive *not* to cause an incident. Events didn't advance their cause. They were not in the Soviet officials' interests. They even hurt them on what mattered most.

At home: "In a culture where discipline and self-control were considered important virtues, an incident [like Piestany] would be embarrassing. Yes, officials wanted their athletes to be victorious, but if defeated—fairly or unfairly—they were expected to act like sportsmen. They were expected to be models for the Soviet people."

With international officials: "They wouldn't be trying to curry favour with other nations by ordering the coaches to start a brawl with the Canadians. They would have thought that an incident like that would have been a stain on their reputations and a stain on the nation's reputation."

During the CBC broadcast, Sherry Bassin took a couple of shots at Vasiliev, claiming that his job prospects would be dismal if he returned to Moscow with a team that lost five games. Edelman says this wasn't necessarily the case. Jobs weren't quite guaranteed for life, but neither were they on the line with every game or every tournament. Coaches being punished for defeat was far more likely in the pro ranks than in the Soviet sports system. The U.S. victory over the Soviets at Lake Placid was Viktor Tikhonov's first Olympics. The most embarrassing loss, the definition of a firing offence. But Lake Placid didn't end up costing Tikhonov his job. "The security of cadre": that's the phenomenon Edelman refers to when asked about Tikhonov keeping his job. The old way— Lenin, Stalin and Khruschev—sent the foreman of the tractor factory or the manager of the collective farm to the salt mines if they didn't hit their quotas. The approach in the '70s and '80s and through to *perestroika* offered the security of cadre, the confidence born of a push for continuity and collegiality. To the outside world, continuity looked like stagnation, collegiality like an old boy's network. Nonetheless, dishonour—like Piestany—was a lot more dangerous than defeat.

Conscientious Objectors or Shirkers

ress play. Look for Jimmy Waite in the brawl. It's not hard to find the goaltender. Waite's on the ice when Keane and Sanipass first drop the gloves with the Soviets. Waite's on the ice when the benches clear. He's on the ice when the lights go out. He isn't fighting, though there are fights all around him. He rests on his stick, as if imitating the classic pose of Ken Dryden in repose. Waite's decision not to fight is purely pragmatic. It is the cool response you'd expect of a goaltender in a pressure situation. "I didn't want to get thrown out of the game," Waite says. "I thought that we were going to finish the game and that we were going to win the gold. We had been all over the Soviets. I was sure that we were going to win by five goals—no doubt in my mind. I didn't want to get thrown out because I knew that Shawn [Simpson] was injured and he wasn't ready to go. He hadn't played in a few days."

Pause. Go back to the benches clearing. Press play. Look for Steve Nemeth. It's hard to find him. He's in and out of the frame. You can spot Nemeth on the periphery of fights. He skates along the boards, trying to step in between guys who trade punches or wrestle. "I was the one guy who had international experience," Nemeth says. "I knew how the officials called things—that there was zero tolerance on fighting." Nemeth's looking for order in the chaos. He seems to be one who stays focused on the gold medal. Bert Templeton doesn't seem impressed. Nemeth's teammates don't seem impressed. Nemeth skates back to the bench and tells the coach that the officials want the teams to go to the dressing rooms. Templeton doesn't react. He doesn't move. He doesn't say a word. A bunch of Nemeth's teammates are within earshot. A few look at him but don't say a word. Others are exhausted—they're leaning against the boards just to stand up. They don't even look at Nemeth.

Pause. Go back to the benches clearing. Press play. Look for Pierre Turgeon in the brawl. There's no finding him. Hard to find him during the game. Impossible when the benches clear. That one feint that he threw at Popov earlier in the second period was an empty threat. Turgeon isn't skating around looking for Popov. Or anybody else. It's hard to tell if he even leaves the bench. "It was crazy, but fighting was never my game," Turgeon says.

Press pause. Take a copy of the roster and put check marks beside their names. These are the three Canadian players who didn't fight in Piestany.

———

Many stories in the press roasted the Canadian players who seemed to glory in the brawl. One exception was a column by Al Strachan in the *Globe and Mail*: "Whether the attitude is right or wrong, the fact remains that any youngster who stayed on the bench in Czechoslovakia would have never been allowed to forget it and would have seriously jeopardized his NHL future." It seemed overblown. It wasn't. It was, in fact, uncannily prescient on one count at least—the part about "never being allowed to forget it."

Strachan and everybody else in the press failed to notice—or could not see— that one player, Nemeth, stayed on the periphery of the brawl, and another, Turgeon, remained on the bench when all others jumped over the boards. It didn't escape the notice of the eighteen other Canadian juniors, however. It sent a chill over the team. By the time the Canadians boarded the bus behind Zimny Stadion, the total freeze-out of Nemeth and Turgeon was half an hour old.

A lot of their teammates will never let go of their hard feelings toward Nemeth and Turgeon, and they were deeply felt before the players took their skates off. Nemeth and Turgeon didn't do what their teammates thought they had to do. They didn't stand up for the other guys. That's what most believe.

———

Go back to the benches clearing. Press play. Look for Stephane Roy. Look for a fight out at the blue line. Look for three *players, not two.* Roy is helpless. One Soviet is swinging wildly. Another has Roy's arms pinned from behind. Roy drops to the ice. The Soviet behind Roy lifts him up so that his teammate, Andrei Smirnov, can knee him right in the face.

Press pause. It's no longer a hockey fight, not even a third-man-in situation that usually happens when a player tries to bail out a beaten teammate. No, this is aggravated assault, something you'd expect to find on a security camera and or in evidence at a criminal trial. Don Wittman's voice breaks as he describes it. It's too hard to look at more than once.

Press stop.

Everett Sanipass was skating from one fight to the next when the benches cleared. He tried to make his way over to Roy. "I couldn't believe it," Sanipass says. "Roy was out. I thought maybe he was going to get killed. So I'm skating over but I'm tied up by one of the Russians. I'm looking for someone to help Roy out and I look over at the bench. There's this dog Turgeon, just sitting there, with his head down. He wouldn't get his ass off the bench . . . just sitting there when everyone's off the Soviet bench and at least one of our guys is in real trouble getting double-teamed. I think Bert had to tell him finally to get off the bench. They said that Bert sent guys off the bench, but I don't think it's true that he sent the team. Turgeon was the only guy that he sent—and he had to send him because of how bad it was for a couple of guys on the ice.

"When we came in the dressing room, everyone knew who fought and who didn't. Stephane Roy was crazy mad. 'Where were you when I was getting kicked in the head? How the fuck could you just watch?' he said. He said it to either Nemeth or Turgeon, maybe both. He was just saying what all of us who fought out there were thinking. Nemeth, he was supposed to be our leader, coming from the national team . . . being the CHA's guy, one of [its] favourites. He wasn't doing any leading when the fight was going on and guys were getting hurt. And Turgeon—the whole tournament, Bert couldn't play him because he was scared shitless.

"There was some yelling about it, but I can tell you that nobody would talk to those guys the whole way home after the tournament. They had a lonely trip. They didn't fight. They weren't part of the team from then on."

Another player who asked to remain unnamed called Nemeth "a knob" and Turgeon "a coward."

"It's all about the code," he says. "If the other team goes, you have to go. No questions asked. There's a way that you're supposed to handle yourself. These guys didn't have a clue. When you get in that situation, if you don't step up, you better step out."

Other players prefer not to get into the specifics about those who didn't fight, other than to say that some kept their distance.

Nemeth disputes his teammates' version of events. He doesn't claim to have been an enthusiastic scrapper, but he denies being a conscientious objector—that he stayed completely on the sidelines looking in when the fighting started. "Stephane Roy was getting double-teamed and kicked," he says. "I was over there trying to get them off him. Fighting wasn't my game. I was more of a skill guy. But I was doing what I could to help."

Press play. Search for Roy and the two Soviets. There's a glimpse of Roy and the two Soviets, but there's nothing on the broadcast either to back up or disprove Nemeth's claim. The Czech cameramen spend so much time on the pillow fight between Simpson and Privalov; as if they're avoiding the worst images. As if they're self-censoring. As if they're following orders. Or can't bear to look at assaults, either. *Hit stop.*

Nemeth won't second-guess himself, not even with any prompting. If he could do it all over again, he says that he would do no different. He defends his decision not to fight, claiming it was just as pragmatic as Jimmy Waite's. In fact, he believes that the disappointing outcome for Canada proved him right. "I knew that there was only one way that we were going to be able to win the gold medal," Nemeth says. "We had to end the fight. The European refs were different than the Canadian refs. You fight, you're gone."

But Everett Sanipass spoke for most of the Canadian juniors. Their rule of thumb: you don't fight, you don't belong.

———

The fight and the disqualification were the headline items. Another story received some play over the next few days. According to the press reports, the players on the Canadian and Soviet teams, the entire rosters, were suspended by the IIHF. They wouldn't be eligible for international play for the rest of the season and all of the 1987–88 season. The way people read it, the IIHF was just heaping another injustice on the Canadian players. And the IIHF had been sticking it to Canadian players and teams for years. Just more of the same. It wasn't a big story in Canada because most of these Canadian players weren't going to be eligible for the under-20 tournament the next season. But some would. A few who had big roles on the Canadian team in '87 had been projected as key parts of the WJC squad the next winter: Brendan Shanahan, Theo Fleury, Greg Hawgood, Jimmy Waite and defenceman Chris Joseph. It also figured to be a showcase for Pierre Turgeon, who had been invisible in the Piestany game and pretty well all the other games in the tournament.

Jimmy Waite never read any of the stories about the suspensions. "They must have been in the English[-language] newspapers," he says. "There was nothing in the French press."

Asked if he was intially disappointed about his suspension, about being denied a chance to avenge the injustice of Piestany, Waite is confused. "I wasn't disappointed because I wasn't suspended," he says. "I wasn't suspended and neither was Pierre Turgeon. We didn't fight. And I guess someone went back and looked at the tapes or talked to the officials—they didn't have to figure out who fought, just who didn't fight. That was probably easier."

It should have at least been a footnote, the fact that the IIHF didn't suspend two of the Canadians. It should have been hard to miss—two key Canadian players *not* suspended while the eighteen others were banished. Somehow this fairly significant detail got lost in the outrage.

"I can honestly say that after Piestany, nobody ever asked me about being suspended or not being suspended." Waite says. "And I didn't read the stories so I didn't know that [the suspensions were] such a big deal or that nobody knew that [Turgeon and I] were the only ones not suspended. I didn't think about it at the time."

The oversight was a small favour to Waite and a huge break for Turgeon. If Turgeon had been named as one of the unsuspended, he'd have become raw meat for Cherry and other media attack dogs. If Turgeon's free pass from the IIHF had been reported, Al Strachan would have held him up for ridicule—Turgeon would have become the player "who would never have been allowed to forget" turning his back on an outnumbered teammate. Turgeon would have been skating out of the shadow of Piestany for a long time—not just in his teammates' eyes but everywhere he played.

———

Steve Nemeth didn't understand the optics. If he had, then he probably wouldn't have stuck a "Kick Me" sign on his own back. That's what he did. There were hard feelings behind the scenes, but they could have remained an internal matter—strictly inside-the-room stuff. The individual who aired—and legitimized—the players' grievances was Nemeth himself. Unintentionally.

A couple of weeks after the suspensions were handed down, Nemeth applied to the IIHF for reinstatement. He wanted his suspension either lifted or shortened. His case was simple: he claimed he shouldn't have been suspended because he didn't fight. "I wanted to be reinstated so I could play for Canada at the Olympics in Calgary, my hometown, the next winter," he says today. "I didn't think what I did merited suspension. I didn't think that the IIHF was out to punish me so much as give the Canadian team and the national team program a hard time. There wasn't any sort of hearing or due process when the suspensions were made. I just wanted a chance to make my case."

A guy without friends doesn't need to make enemies, but Nemeth did anyway. A lot of Nemeth's teammates were pissed about his decision not to fight. They thought it had more to do with fear than self-control. One player says that Nemeth's teammates might have been more forgiving if he hadn't applied for reinstatement. "He didn't fight and maybe he couldn't," a player said on condition of anonymity. "That was bad enough. But when all of us were taking our lumps together [from the IIHF], this guy asks for a special deal. He didn't help us out on the ice and then he was ready to leave us behind because he had other things to do. It just made a bunch of us a lot madder."

Mike Keane won't give up much about those who didn't fight. There are many codes in hockey. Keane respects all of them, but none more than the one about keeping some things confidential: What happens in the room stays in the room. For the warden's son it's the Blue Wall—strictly don't ask, don't tell. Keane hates doing interviews, Theoren Fleury says. Telling him that other players have been forthcoming about their grievances with Nemeth and Turgeon doesn't warm him up. Keane says that the hard feelings might be overblown: "There were some guys who weren't involved in the fighting on both sides. At least not as far as trading punches. There were a lot of guys just standing around or pairing up but not trading punches." Keane's words on the page don't hint at, never mind capture, the disdain he plainly feels for the non-combatants (aside from Jimmy Waite).

Keane says that Nemeth applying for reinstatement didn't change things. "Maybe [Nemeth] was doing what he had to [in applying for reinstatement] just so he could play and make a living," Keane says. "I wouldn't have any hard feelings about that, and I don't think anyone should have."

Keane says all this in a tone that is completely flat. Like it's a rote answer. Like he can barely be bothered to convince a listener. Yet when Keane talks about others on that team—his linemate Theoren Fleury is the best example—his tone is entirely different. It's emotional. It takes him back. It's stuff he never wants to let go of. Keane has the game on tape somewhere. He pulls it out to watch every now and then. But he doesn't pull out the tape to watch Steve Nemeth or Pierre Turgeon.

———

Jimmy Waite believes Nemeth deserves better. He says no one should attach a stigma to his name. He suggests that players on that team who bad-mouth Nemeth are rationalizing—their criticism of Nemeth is their way to avoid second-guessing themselves. "I disagree with the other guys," Waite says. "Maybe Steve Nemeth was right to do what he did . . . trying to break up fights. He knew about international hockey. He went to the officials. If there were more guys like him, maybe we wouldn't have been thrown out of the tournament. I don't think that we had to goon the Soviets to win that game. We were winning that game with skill, not because we were physically beating them. If we had just played them straight, hard but fair, we win that game easy."

———

Turgeon stayed on the bench until Templeton told him to get on the ice—that much his teammates, and even the IIHF, agree on. But just try to get one account that everyone will sign off on. So many things happening all at once, so many stories that overlap and yet so many details that just don't fit. Everyone agrees on Pierre Turgeon—attendance was taken and he didn't raise his hand—but Nemeth's story is a little more complicated.

Waite, the one player who didn't fight but remained above reproach, defends Nemeth. Stephane Roy takes it one step further. Yes, the player who took the worst beating. "You could see where he'd been kicked right in the forehead," Shanahan says. "He was lucky he didn't lose his eye. Or his nose."

After the brawl in Piestany, Stephane Roy came into the dressing room bruised, bloodied and venting. "Where the fuck were you?" he said to no one in particular. "Two guys are on me and I get no help." Some of the Canadians are sure that he was saying it to Steve Nemeth. Roy says he wasn't going after Nemeth.

"When I jumped over the boards, I skated out to centre ice and grabbed what I thought was a decent-sized Soviet guy and started throwing," Roy says. "Then I got suckered from behind. That's when the trouble really started. The guy who came in and helped me was Steve Nemeth. He pulled one of the guys off me. Maybe he wasn't throwing punches like the other guys, but I don't think it's fair to say that he bailed out or chickened out. He didn't leave me hanging.

"I don't remember Everett trying to get to me. I'd believe it. No doubt. What I do remember is the one guy I saw who could have helped me and didn't—that was Kerry Huffman. I saw him standing there when I got knocked down. Afterwards, I was mad in the dressing room, but I wasn't mad at Steve.

"I won't doubt anything that Everett said. He has the right to say what he wants about the fight—whether it's Turgeon or Steve Nemeth. Everett was a tough guy . . . a real warrior. He would stick up for any of us. He was a good teammate. On any team you're going to have a couple of guys who aren't good teammates. And the guy who really let me down—who was standing right there and watched me trying to fight two guys—was Kerry Huffman."

Another player who asked not to be named said that he believed Roy's account. "I can see that. If someone said that Kerry was a bit of a pussy, I can see that. The tough stuff—the fighting, anyway—wasn't Kerry's game."

———

Press play. Presume that there are some who fight and some who don't. Presume that some who don't drop their gloves aren't wrapping themselves in the faux glory of fighting, and presume that others who don't fight aren't simply standing by. Presume that a couple are remembered and named. Presume that others are protected by teammates' reluctance to name names. Presume that there are still others who stand by, out of view of the camera and out of the line of sight of their teammates. Presume that there's no way of sorting out noble warriors and mere spectators. Presume that a lot of what happened and what didn't is just lost in the fog of war. Conclude that the idea of a team bonding through fighting together is folly. Conclude that nothing divides this team more than the fight itself. Conclude that this team came together quickly and stayed together for a few weeks, right up to 13:53 of the second period of the last game—or non-game—of that tournament. Conclude that there are rifts that would make for uncomfortable moments if anyone were to organize a reunion. Presume that those who wouldn't show up to a reunion have a reason not to.

Press stop.

Retreat and Exile

Press play. Wait for the graphic to come up. Hit pause.

ROZHODCOVIA
ROENNING
(NOR)
GORSKI
(POL)
POMOELL
(FIN)

Press play again and wait for the officials to come into the frame. Linesman Gorski: tall, thin, dark-haired, moustached, so unthreatening that he'd make Roberto Benigni look like a member of Tony Soprano's mob. Linesman Pomoell: not so slight, not so tall, compact, meticulous in his movement. Referee Rønning: easily the biggest of the three, wide-shouldered—hard to tell, though, because of an occasional slouch.

Press pause.

Gunther Sabetzki is playing host to officals from the

International Olympic Committee and the committee from Lillehammer, Norway, at the 1987 WJC. They're sitting beside him at the tournament finale. Just a few weeks before, Lillehammer was the IOC members' choice to host the 1994 Olympics. Sabetzki has seen to it to that the Norwegian Rønning is assigned to this final game of the tournament. Other on-ice officials at the tournament are surprised that Sabetzki is kissing up to Olympic brass with the gold medal hanging in the balance and the two most penalized teams in the tournament on the ice. So is Josef Kuboda, head of the local organizing committee and a former linesman with experience in the Olympics and world championships. "I knew it was a dangerous situation," he says. "I went down to the officials' dressing room before the game. Rønning was so nervous. He was smoking a cigarette but shaking too hard to put it in his mouth. Big trouble."

Fast forward. Speed through to the sequence right before the brawl. Pause. Rønning is standing in the corner to Ivannikov's left. Shesterikov is heading right toward the ref when Sanipass hooks him. Rønning's right arm goes up while his left brings the whistle to his mouth. End of the play, sure. End of the game. End of much more for Hans Rønning.

Press play. Advance to Sanipass throwing a big right hand at Shestirikov. Shestirikov tries to get out of the way, but doesn't. Rønning tries to get out of the way and does, gliding slowly backwards until he's twenty feet away. Skinny Gorski gamely grabs Sanipass, but the big winger can't even feel him. Pomoell jumps in between them. Pomoell can't stop the punches from raining down. Not when Gorski skates away to keep Keane from going after Zelepukin. Not with Rønning standing so far off to the side.

Rønning looks down at his skates seconds later. Chris Joseph and Tsygurov are down on the ice grappling. Rønning skates backwards slowly, withdrawing.

Hit pause. Look at Rønning talking to the penalty timekeeper.

Everyone in the arena knows Rønning has lost control of the game. Linesman Pomoell knows the ref hasn't had control since the opening face-off. Pomoell knew this had disaster written all over it, even before the game.

"If Rønning had spoken to the captains and coaches before the game or during the game . . . maybe it could have been avoided," says Pomoell. "I asked Rønning before the game, 'Do you want my help on calls—majors, misconducts?' He said no. I asked all referees this. I worked six world championships, lots of world junior and international games. Canada vs. the Soviets . . . those two teams produced the best hockey, but they were also the toughest games to work. I knew this, maybe Rønning didn't. He refused my help. Maybe it was pride . . . he might have thought that I was telling him that he wasn't good enough or that he wasn't ready. Maybe it was the fact that he was working in front of the IIHF executives and the supervisor of the [on-ice] officials. They'd think that Rønning said, 'No, I'll call my own game.'

"I had a bad feeling even before the game. I thought something bad could happen—just the situation of one team having nothing to play for and a big rivalry . . . the way that this Canadian team was playing, very rough, big hits, intimidating hockey. But I had a worse feeling once the game started. Right away on the first face-off, you can see a big cross-check. The puck hit the ice and the Canadian player cross-checks a Soviet. Rønning didn't make a call. He didn't miss it—he saw it, it happened right in front of him, he was looking at it. He just never made a move for his whistle. And that's how it was that whole first period. I don't know that he called many in the first twenty minutes. [It was, in fact, three minors, two of them coincidental.]

"Rønning could have called three penalties on the first shift," he says. "I'm not just saying that now, looking back at what eventually happened. That's what I thought at the

time . . . 'What's this guy doing? Why isn't he calling anything?' North American officials would say that they
wanted players to play . . . [to have them] decide the game
for themselves. European officials call a more technical
game, maybe. But this wasn't a European referee trying to
call a game like a Canadian or American ref. This was like
a singer forgetting the words to a song and the music keeps
playing."

———

*Go back to the start of the broadcast. Press play. Look
only at the officials.* The body language shouts out: TROU-
BLE. Maybe it is pride. Maybe it's an aloof attitude. Maybe
it's independence, even defensiveness. There's no real way
of knowing why Rønning doesn't talk to Pomoell and the
other linesman, Gorksi. It is clear, however, that he
prefers to work alone. Four thousand sets of eyes in the
arena are trained on him, that his every move is followed
by television cameras and transmitted back to the Soviet
Union and Canada. Only one set of eyes really matters here,
Rønning's, and he's watching the game like a spectator. As
if he's watching it from the stands. As if it's on the television screen. It seems like he thinks it's enough just to stay
out of the way.

Press pause.

"The game was going the way that I was afraid it
would," Pomoell says. "Rønning couldn't have handled it
worse than he did. Still, when we went into our room
after the first period, I thought that there was still a way
to save this game. Maybe he'd ask for help . . . [maybe
he'd] accept what Gorski and I could do out there. But he
didn't say a word, really. Didn't even look at us. I knew
then that bad things were going to happen. I knew that
there would be fights—I even think that I was worried
about a fight with players coming off the benches. I think

ABOVE, LEFT: Brendan Shanahan wearing the C of the London Knights and no scar tissue. The Knights retired his number even though he played only two seasons in London and made the NHL at eighteen. © HOCKEY HALL OF FAME

ABOVE, RIGHT: Theoren Fleury in a Moose Jaw Warriors sweater and fashionable Cooperalls. He went unselected in the 1986 NHL draft. Not long after this photo Fleury became a father. Within a year of leaving the junior ranks Fleury played on the Stanley Cup champion Calgary Flames. © HOCKEY HALL OF FAME

LEFT: Everett Sanipass in the colours of the Verdun Junior Canadiens. The first major junior game he ever saw he played in—in borrowed skates.
© PHOTO LE JOURNAL DE MONTRÉAL

Sergei Shesterikov's right hand whizzing by the head of linesman Julian Gorksi and just missing Everett Sanipass. Moments after this Sanipass would score a one-punch knockdown of Shesterikov. © JIRI KOLIS/SPECTRUM PICTURES

The usually easy-going Evgeni Davydov following orders—that's his version, anyway. The officials tried to break up fights when Davydov first left the bench. Soon the referee, and later the linesmen, would skate off the ice. © JIRI KOLIS/SPECTRUM PICTURES

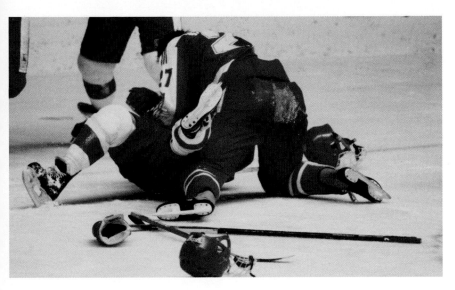

Pavel Kostichkin pinning Theoren Fleury. Kostichkin says the Soviets weren't novices when it came to fighting—they fought during practices, when referees and linesmen weren't around to break up scraps. Fleury says he doesn't know the name of the player who locked him up when the fight started but that he never played against anyone stronger in more than 1,000 NHL games. © JIRI KOLIS/SPECTRUM PICTURES

Before the lights went out. Shawn Simpson and Vadim Privalov are in the fore-ground and the television cameras in the arena focused on them for much of the brawl. Jimmy Waite stands at the left point on the Soviet blueline. At the right point, Andrei Smirnov and another unidentified Soviet player double-team Stephan Roy. © JIRI KOLIS/SPECTRUM PICTURES

Pat Burns as the Canadiens' coach, seeking a clarification from a referee. Burns says Piestany didn't hurt his chances of a NHL job because executives knew the Canadian coaches couldn't have stopped the bench from clearing. Mike Keane, who played for Burns in the AHL and with Montreal, skates in the foreground. © PHOTO LE JOURNAL DE MONTRÉAL

Bert Templeton with a Remembrance Day poppy on the lapel of his North Bay Centennials blazer. Piestany was remembered and a lot of his greatest coaching achievements forgotten by the end of his career. © NORTH BAY NUGGET

ABOVE: Shawn Simpson in goal for the Soo Greyhounds. Simpson's world junior tournament was ended by injury and his professional career by the numbers game. © HOCKEY HALL OF FAME

LEFT: Jimmy Waite as a young pro with Chicago, flashing the glove hand that kept Canada's gold-medal hopes alive in the dying seconds of the game against Sweden. Waite, who led Canada to the gold medal in 1988, was supposed to be the next Patrick Roy, but couldn't beat out future Hall-of-Famers Ed Belfour and Dominik Hasek for the starting position with the Hawks.
© PAUL BERESWILL/HOCKEY HALL OF FAME

ABOVE: Evgeni Davydov in the neutral zone, abstractedly watching teammates back-check. "Gene" didn't take the game too seriously, though he was regarded as one of the most talented Soviet players of the late 80s. © PAUL BERESWILL/ HOCKEY HALL OF FAME

LEFT: Alexander Mogilny, in sunglasses and low profile, outside an INS building in Buffalo on the day he applied for asylum in the U.S. At this point Mogilny had a team but not a country. He was granted temporary "parole" by INS officials when his flight from Stockholm touched down in New York. His defection initially threatened to sour relations between the NHL and Soviet hockey authorities. © THE BUFFALO NEWS

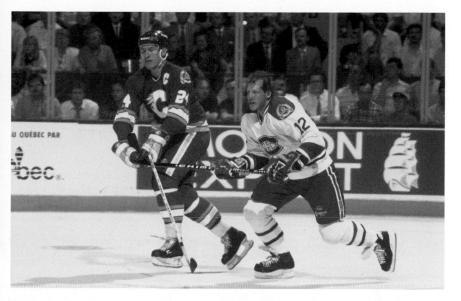

Mike Keane, sans helmet, holding up Calgary's Jim Peplinski in the 1989 Stanley Cup final. Keane was the only player on the 1987 Canadian junior team who wasn't drafted by a NHL team. He became one of eight players in NHL history to win Stanley Cups with three different franchises. © PAUL BERESWILL/ HOCKEY HALL OF FAME

Pierre Turgeon at the press conference announcing his signing with the Buffalo Sabres. Commentators suggested a player who did not skate in to defend his team-mates would tarnish his reputation, yet just months after Piestany the Sabres selected Turgeon with the first overall pick in the 1987 draft. © THE BUFFALO NEWS

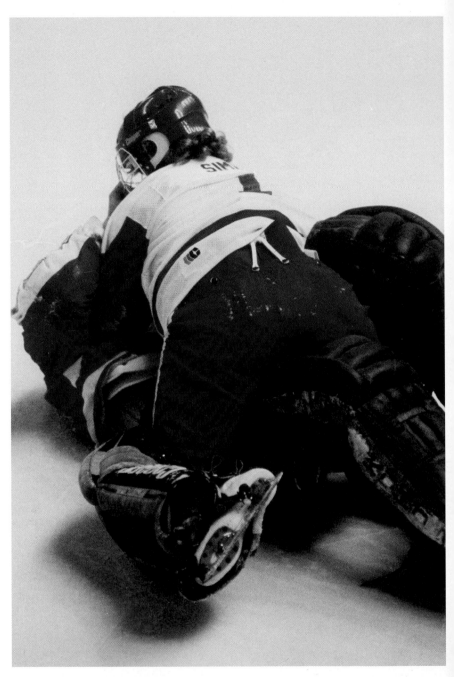

Shawn Simpson, 155 pounds, pinning Soviet back-up goaltender Vadim Privalov. Simpson says he's asked about Piestany every day, yet for many years he didn't even know the name of the goalie he wrestled. Privalov's own hockey career didn't last as long as Simpson's. © JIRI KOLIS/SPECTRUM PICTURES that he knew that, too, and felt like there was nothing he could do about it."

Hit play. View the fight once more. View Rønning's slow retreat, his placid surrender. Pomoell and Gorski have as much reason as Stephane Roy to feel abandoned. The odds aren't great to start with: five fights, three officials. Not good, but still enough to break up the fights one by one, to skate the players off to the penalty box. Five fights, two officials. Or fifteen fights, two officials. A lot harder. Pomoell or Gorski could be knocked out or cut or severely injured and unable to get off the ice—and the other linesman might not see him, might not be able to find him.

"Rønning froze," Pomoell says. "He realized his mistake and skated away from it. He quit. There were things that he could have done, even when the fights started."

Rønning doesn't do the responsible, expected thing. The light bulb doesn't go off, either—he doesn't skate to the benches before they cleared, doesn't tell the coaches to keep his players on the bench, doesn't tell them to get their players to the dressing room or risk more penalties. Just pure passivity. That's like a brain surgeon suffering attention-deficit disorder, like adjustable morals in a policeman, like pessimism in a pope. Passivity in a hockey ref is unforgiveable. Rønning should consider himself lucky that no one suffers life-affecting injuries, paralysis or death.

Let the broadcast play. Hit pause when the lights go out. It doesn't show up on the screen. It's lost in the whirl of cuts from camera to camera: Rønning skating off the ice. It happens before the arena plunges into darkness. That leads fans in the arena and in front of their television screens to believe that Rønning left the ice to order the lights turned out. The lights come back on, but Rønning doesn't return. He passes up what turns out to be a last chance to skate in the spotlight.

Pomoell and Gorski are standing at the Zamboni gate when the lights come back on. They skated there when the arena went dark. An arena worker asks Pomoell what's going on. A shrug, the universal sign for "I have no idea." Maybe they could go out to break up the few minor fights that steam on. Maybe they could go to the teams' benches and speak to the coaches. Maybe they could do something else for the referee who didn't want help, who considered the offer of help an insult, a question of his competence.

Hit stop.

———

"Gorski and I went back to the dressing room," Pomoell says. "Rønning was taking his skates off. He was unable to speak. He was devastated. He wasn't crying . . . more in shock. Then Rene Fasel came in . . ."

Fasel was the director of officiating for the 1987 world juniors. Years later, he took over as the president of the IIHF.

" . . . and Fasel was shouting. He's outraged at Rønning. He demanded the game report from him. Rønning had to know his career [in international hockey] was over. He had embarrassed the most powerful people in hockey. He had failed."

Pomoell says he has always had questions he wanted to ask Rønning about the game. He wanted to know why the ref left the game in the middle of the brawl. He wanted to know what Rønning had written in his report and whether he had any regrets. Pomoell wanted to ask him these and other things, but never had a chance to talk with him. "Rønning never refereed another game," Pomoell says. "He was broken by it. To referee, you have to have confidence, and he just couldn't have confidence ever again. I never saw him at a rink."

Pomoell presumes Rønning is too ashamed to return to hockey arenas. Pomoell presumes the Norwegian has tried to drop out of sight and succeeded. "I've worked in hockey for more than three decades," Pomoell says. "My career on the ice didn't last much long after 1987. My plan was only to work on the ice for two more seasons. I was older. I've worked in the game—no time away—since Piestany. I have never spoke to him. I've never heard from him. I've asked, but nobody knows where he is."

———

A phone call to the Norwegian hockey federation's office gets no results. The executives in Oslo either know nothing or are protecting Rønning. No, no one has been in contact with him. No, there's no Hans Rønning listed in its directory of on-ice and off-ice officials. No, no one in the federation has a phone number or email address for him. "Hans Rønning . . . I'm not familiar with this name," Norwegian hockey federation president Bjorn Ruud says.

Calls to teams in Norway, international on-ice officials' associations and the IIHF produce no leads. Nothing. Hans Rønning skated off the ice in Piestany and seemingly off the earth as well.

Calls are made to all the H. Rønnings in the Norwegian phone directory. He's not listed. Not under *his* name, anyway. The other Hans Rønnings aren't related to him. One Hans Rønning knows the location of a Hans Rønning with an unlisted number. Turns out that he gets the other's mail sometimes. He has an email address for him. He's surprised by the story of Piestany infamy—this Hans Rønning doesn't know the story of the elusive, reclusive Hans Rønning, not even that he was a referee.

The first hopeful sign: an email message sent to this address doesn't bounce back. The bad news: no reply. For days. There's no way of knowing whether Hans Rønning is still with us or whether he didn't just walk out on a chunk of ice and float out to sea.

Then, a week later, a reply. Hans Rønning agrees to talk about Piestany.

———

"The linesman doesn't have it quite right. I didn't referee another game internationally," Hans Rønning says. "I did referee another two seasons in Norway. In Piestany I was thirty-eight years old. I only had a couple of years left. I thought that [the 1987 WJC tournament] was probably going to be my last, or one of my last, international [assignments]."

The voice on the other end of the line sounds almost sunny, as if he is reflecting on good times, better times. Rønning might have been devastated by the denouement of the biggest game he ever worked, just as Pomoell says, but there's no knowing it now. Twenty years to heal. Twenty years to rationalize. "When it is just the players on the ice, then it should be in my hands," Rønning says. "But when the benches clear, it's in God's hands. There is nothing that three officials can really do. We stayed on the ice for several minutes. We tried to do what we could with the fights that were going on. But really there was nothing that could be done by us when the benches cleared."

Maybe Rønning is right. Maybe all efforts to re-establish order were going to be in vain. Maybe Pomoell and Gorski only realized their efforts were futile—even dangerous—when the lights went out. Every time they quelled a fight, another one broke out. It was like trying to push a dozen bars of Ivory soap underwater—there's just no keeping them submerged.

Still, there was a job Rønning could have, and should have, done. If he couldn't have been a soldier or a peacekeeper, he should have attended to the wounded. Roy and Hawgood's injuries were the worst on the Canadian side, but some Soviets were beaten up, too—and at risk of serious injury. Helping them to get off the ice should have been the officials' obligation, even if all other hope was lost. When action was most needed, Rønning went AWOL.

Rønning rejects the idea that his refereeing led to the fight. He squarely blames the coaches and, to a lesser extent, the players. "It is the coaches' responsibility to have team discipline in place," Rønning says. "The coaches should have kept their players on the bench. And they should have told the players on the ice not to fight . . . or to stop fighting. I think that maybe this could only happen with teenagers. Professionals have discipline and they know what is their job—some things they will not risk. What the players did was not a mature decision but a reaction—impulse is the word. They were innocents under a lot of pressure. They can be blamed, but not too much."

And what of Pomoell's question: What did Rønning write in the report that he passed on to Fasel immediately after the game? No equivocation, no hesitation, no change in his story over twenty years. If Dennis McDonald can't let go of Piestany because of his self-doubts, then Hans Rønning has put Piestany behind him because of his certainty.

"I wrote what I saw," Rønning says. "It was the Canadians who left the bench first. It was their fault that the fight happened. They started it. And I have no idea why when they still had a chance at the gold medal."

———

Press play. Search for the fight at the five-on-five stage. Roll back to the moments before the benches clear. Press play. Rønning is talking through a hole in the Plexiglas to the penalty timekeeper. He's looking at the fights raging. He has his back to the benches.

Press stop.

Fight, Then Flight

The coaches expected the bus ride from the arena to the Vienna airport to be a funeral procession. The players, though, were curiously resilient. No gloom. They were unexpectantly buoyant. Chatter and laughter rather than mournful silence. Youthful insouciance? No, it was more like teenage rebellion, defiance. Eff the IIHF, eff the Russians, eff this whole effin' country, eff what other people think.

Somebody slipped a bottle—bottles, that is—onto the bus. "They took us on a wine-tasting thing when they brought us over there," Theoren Fleury says. "One of the guys—I don't remember who—smuggled a bunch of bottles out of there. So we started passing them back and forth." Fleury. Chiasson. Simpson. Others. They tried to keep it quiet. They tried to keep it out of sight of the coaches. The players couldn't quite pull it off. They laughed. They shouted. They cared about the game, couldn't get it out of their minds. Until they left the arena. Until they boarded the bus. First minutes of the rest of their lives. They didn't act like they had any regrets, never mind any shame. That was the way they saw it.

"We were just a bunch of kids," Shawn Simpson remembers. "I don't think that we reacted any different than we would have if we had just lost a game in our leagues back in Canada. The only difference is that we had a bottle or two and we passed it around, so we were getting hammered. That wouldn't have happened back in Canada, but really we just needed to get past the tension and all the pressure. It had been a pretty intense few weeks and we felt we were so close to where we wanted to go. It wasn't just that we didn't get there, but that we weren't going to get another shot at it. Not this bunch of players as one group. We knew we were all together this one time and one time only. There probably wasn't one guy on that bus who didn't think he was going to play pro or even get a shot at the Stanley Cup. But what you see over a season or two seasons or in the pros over five seasons or more—a team coming together and eventually playing up to its potential—well, we had that happen all over a few weeks. Were we wrong to be getting drunk? I don't think that anybody who was fair and understanding would hold it against us."

"We had all been through something together," Scott Metcalfe says. "I hadn't ever thought about it like this, but I'm sure that we knew that we'd never be together again. It was something we sensed, all of us, without ever saying it. We didn't get sad about that or the game. We had a great time together with some great guys. It was something to celebrate."

While they knocked back the stolen wine, they had no idea about the immediate future. No idea that there was a gathering firestorm back in Canada, that they were going to get roasted, that this game was going to stick to their coach as if it had been stapled. They've spent so long playing—*living*—in the moment that thoughts of home are about a place they're going, not a place where they'll be received. They'd spent so long living in squalor and in gnawing hunger at the hotel that it had seemed like they were living in a vacuum. It hadn't dawned on them that it was ending. Or that something else was about to start.

The players saw that Bert Templeton was up in the front seat. Pat Burns was at his left. The coaches knew how this was going to play out. They knew that their reputations had preceded them when they were selected to coach this team, and they knew that these reputations were going to be trotted out when they got off the plane. Templeton told the players that some of the flights were going to be changing, that they were going to find out at the airport. Change of plans: the players missed that sign that maybe, just maybe, was beginning. The CAHA was abandoning them, punishing them. That's what some were going to think years later. The players missed it. Their little party continued at the back of the bus. They were so young, so unaware, so unworldly. They believed they were immune. They just sensed it. They didn't just think they were going to get second chances; they presumed it. They presumed it was their right. Athletes' privilege.

The players didn't worry about not getting a second chance, about being denied a career mulligan. The coaches did worry about those things.

Burns couldn't have been sure that this brawl wasn't going to hurt his career. By the time he boarded the bus, Templeton was resigned to the fact that he was never going to have another chance to coach so many talented players, never going to coach for his country against other countries, never going to have so bright a spotlight shone upon him.

A portent of difficult times ahead came at the border. The trip to the airport should have taken a couple of hours, nothing more—even with the military escort of soldiers on motorcycles. It should have taken only twenty minutes to clear Czechoslovakian customs. The border guard held up the bus for hours. "It was at least a couple of hours, but it might have been close to four," Jim Cressman says. "You just knew that these guards were out to make the team's life miserable. They were smiling when they were going through the bus inch by inch."

"I was going through the border and I saw the Canadian team's bus," NHL scout Marshall Johnston says. "The guards had pulled it off to the side and I could see them going under the bus and looking through bags. When I showed the customs guy my papers, he said, 'Canadian?' and I told him, 'Yeah, Canadian.' He stepped back from the car and put up his fists like he was boxing and started throwing punches. These guys heard all about what happened and they were told to do what they were doing."

A few hours later, Canada's best eighteen- and nineteen-year-old players were asleep on the floor of the Vienna airport. Some were beaten up. Some were exhausted. Some were nursing hangovers. And if they hoped that those hangovers were something that they'd be able to sleep off once they boarded the planes, then they had it all wrong. The real hangovers were going to start once they got off the planes.

"I thought about it a little later when they were laying there using their hockey bags as pillows," Cressman says. "The CAHA didn't do anything for these kids—just like it didn't after they were told about Swift Current. [The CAHA] could have looked after them. These kids were good enough to make this team. They gave up their holidays, did their best, risked getting hurt and ended up on the wrong end of a bad decision—and the CAHA basically handed them their tickets. [The CAHA officials] acted like they didn't want anything to do with the team."

They didn't have to wait to arrive home to get a taste of the criticism awaiting them. They started to take it right in the airport. Mike Smith, who was then in the Winnipeg Jets' front office, fancied himself as the NHL's most intelligent man, an intellectual who dabbled in hockey management. A guy who filed scouting reports when he wasn't writing one of his books. He also fancied himself the most enlightened hockey man when it came to outreach to Europe. He looked at executives who didn't cultivate European rosters as wine connoisseurs who wanted nothing to do with France. He didn't just hold what was the minority view for a long time—that Europeans could compete in the NHL. No, he believed in European superiority in hockey, and he would later exasperate fans in Toronto and Chicago by stocking their teams with overpriced Russians.

Smith was at the airport at the same time as the Canadian team. He laid into them—the coaches and the players. That's how Jim Cressman remembers it. That's how a couple of players remember it. Smith didn't just beat them up about their play. He beat them up about the brawl. It didn't make an impact on the players. All they wanted to do was to sleep—and sleep it off. They had fought and fought and had nothing left for arguments with the sun coming up. "Till you mentioned it, I had no idea who he was," one player says.

Most players missed Smith's tirade. Most missed another guy waiting for his flight, keeping his distance from them, walking around them to a payphone to call home: Hans Rønning. No one recalls Smith heaping any vitriol on the ref.

Tumult and Shouting

Jim Cressman sat beside Scott Metcalfe on the flight home. About an hour before they landed in Toronto, Cressman noticed Metcalfe's expression—a wince, lips tightening. "He had gone really quiet and looked like he was ready to cry," Cressman remembers. "I asked him what was wrong and he said that he was worried about what people would say about the team. I told him, 'Don't worry about it. You're always going to be remembered because of what happened. You made history.' But really, Scott was pretty close to the mark on that."

———

Even before the team boarded the bus with the Czech soldiers watching their every move, they were under the media magnifying glass back home.

Don Cherry and Brian Williams were in a CBC studio. They were doing commentary pre-game and between periods, Cherry preening, as usual, and, as usual, Williams turning drama into melodrama. But when the lights went out and the broadcast was thrown back to the studio, it took a single exchange, mere seconds, for Cherry to reach the boiling point. Williams suggested that the game, and the Canadian team's response, was "a disgrace" and even "possibly the darkest moment for Canada in international hockey." (Williams had apparently abandoned the idea that Templeton had done "a great job" sometime between the first intermission and the 13:53 mark of the second period.) Cherry bit into his lip. He looked puzzled at first, then enraged. Cherry told Williams that the Canadians were able to "hold their head [sic] up and be proud." Cherry told Williams that the bench-clearing was "just hockey" and the Soviets "planned to do this all along."

It looked like a great theatre—except, Williams insists, it wasn't. "There was nothing calculated about it," Williams says. "There couldn't have been. Everything was happening too fast. I said what I honestly thought and Don did the same. He always does that—agree or disagree with him, he doesn't plan what he's going to say. He goes with his head and his gut."

The broadcast broke for a commercial. The director on the floor clapped his hands—he knew this was broadcast gold, but not that emotions, real emotions, were running dangerously high.

"Hey Don," the director said, "when we come out of the commercial, why don't you have your hands around Brian's neck?"

"No," Cherry told him, "I might never let go of the little bastard."

Other broadcasts seemed tame by comparison. TSN's John Wells offered a rationale that, while accurate, was insufficient. "From the opening face-off this game was chippy. Almost every whistle produced pushing and shoving that threatened to get out of hand." Later, another TSN anchorman, Vic Rauter, opened a line of questions about the nations' eligibility for future tournaments or the fate of the NHL's Rendez-Vous tournament, in which the league's all-stars were to face the Soviets in Quebec City in February.

It was too soon for answers. Barely time enough to frame the questions. Speculation, though, was fair game. TSN brought in Alan Eagleson, the head of the NHL's players' association, who had engineered the Canada–Soviet Summit Series in 1972, as well as later showdowns between the Maple Leaf and the Hammer and Sickle. Eagleson claimed that the decision to forfeit the game and the tournament was simply a political power play. The result, Eagleson suggested, was preordained. That wouldn't have been the case if the positions had been reversed—if the USSR had been going for the gold and Canada had been out of the medals. "They would have found a way to have the game count or for Russia to win the gold medal," he said.

Piestany was more than a sports story. The Canadian juniors' disqualification was a lead item on CBC's *The National*, the evening newscast. Peter Mansbridge was the anchor. Footage from the CBC *Sportsweekend* broadcast was used. A viewer might expect that the script would have taken a just-the-facts-ma'am approach, the standard-issue evening newscast objectivity. This report offered anything but. The voice-overs were fully loaded with judgments: "ended in disgrace" and "disgraced and sent from the tournament" and "going home with a lot of disappointment." The anchor noted that the Canadians didn't attend the tournament banquet. He invested this footnote with a gravity on par with Gorbachev blowing off a state dinner with Brian Mulroney.

CTV commentator Pat Marsden compared the game to the invasion of Afghanistan, saying that both events proved the Soviets' "complete disregard for anybody else."

CBLT, the CBC's Toronto affiliate, had dispatched a crew to the Shanahan household in Mimico on the day of the game. The hope was for some happy-news footage of family members celebrating. Instead, the Shanahans were

captured in a downward spiral of disappointment and
anger and engaged in an open dialogue with the television
screen. The three older Shanahan brothers yelled over each
other: "The ref can't do that." "That would never have happened in the NHL." "They turn the lights out. It's so stupid." Then viewers were introduced to Rosaleen Shanahan,
mother, who said she was "sorry that it happened" but
didn't "see any alternative." She said, "We're all proud of
him." The youngest Shanahan was half a world away and
ten months from his first NHL game.

The real judgments came in the morning papers.
They weren't just there in the sports sections, but on the
front pages. Never had so many commentators had so
much to say with so few of them (none other than Jim
Cressman) in attendance at a major sports event. Though
they hadn't been there, they advanced theories quickly
and emphatically.

The New York Times rarely paid much attention to
hockey and had never before expressed interest in the WJC.
No matter. Journalism's beacon shone on events in
Piestany—the newspaper of record's was less a sports story
than a window into Canadian culture and international
politics. The report detailed how a hockey game between
teenagers threatened to chill relations between two nations.
The *Times* purpled up the prose. Diplomats were seemingly
following the lead of the teams, staring each other down as
if they were ready to drop their gloves. The story suggested
that Canadians were "reacting as if the Kremlin had
annexed Newfoundland."

The *Toronto Star's* John Robertson had taken on the
"evil empire" just a couple of days before. He had gone
xenophobic. Surprise: he didn't scapegoat the Soviets after
the brawl. He chose not to blame many when he was able to
blame a few. Canada, he wrote, "blew it yesterday—
because of an inexcusable lack of discipline on the part of its
coaching staff and an incredible lack of foresight by their

director of operations, Dennis McDonald." Robertson piled on Templeton, said he had a "long checkered history . . . as an agitator" and that history repeated itself when he "let the brawl rage." He piled on Burns, whom he described as "another notorious hothead" and a "big-mouth yo-yo."

In hockey's heartland, some opted for a middle ground, shrugging off the Canadians' disqualification. The Regina *Leader-Post* had dedicated pages of coverage to the Swift Current Broncos' tragic bus crash. It was a bad time to dump on Canadian junior hockey. It was bad form to blame it on the Canadian coaches and officials. Columnist Bob Hughes wrote that the Canadian team had been duped. The teenagers had succumbed to virtues of the national character and observed the etiquette of the Canadian junior game—no matter what the international rules were. Hughes wrote: "They indulged the Canadian hockey spirit. . . [which] carries within its bosom the rigid discipline that one does not stand idly by while a teammate is getting pummelled." Hughes ranged from opinion to rationalization: "Who, among the millions of hockey fans in this country, has not watched a bench-clearing brawl?"

The *Peterborough Examiner* tacked to the middle. Columnist Bob Feaver wrote: "Who cares about the gold medal? [The fight] is just the Canadian way . . . [Blaming Templeton, Burns and McDonald is] like blaming the bar owner for a brawl that happens outside the bar." Safe bet that he caught the bench-clearing brawl between the Peterborough Petes and Oshawa Generals a couple of months before.

Cherry wrapped himself in the flag. He continued to pillory the Soviets. He criticized anyone who was at all critical of the Canadian coaches or the Canadian team. Cherry sent shots in every direction. He poured it out to the media the way the Canadian juniors had poured over the boards. He told reporters that the brawl was "a deliberate strategy" drawn up by the Soviets. He filled their notebooks and laid into others who drew a cheque from the CBC. "Everybody here seems to think [the Soviets are] such gentlemen. They're the sneakiest dirty players in the world. And then we get Brian Williams and Don Wittman dumping on us."

Others picked up Cherry's drumbeat. Earl McRae in the *Ottawa Citizen* called out "the smug, self-righteous bleeding hearts" who trashed Templeton and the Canadian juniors. "It's you who should be ashamed to call yourself Canadians; you with your misguided pacifism at all costs; you blind and gullible appeasers who display that wonderful Canadian characteristic—eating our own."

The pundits wrote about Piestany but missed the game that the Canadian juniors played. The pundits wrote about Piestany but didn't catch the games that other Canadian juniors were playing.

The papers didn't have one word about a game— another bench-clearing brawl—played while the Canadian juniors were on their flight back home. The Verdun Junior Canadiens, Everett Sanipass's team in the Quebec junior league, didn't wait for him to rejoin the team. Or else the Granby Bisons figured the Junior Canadiens were exposed with Sanipass absent. Or maybe one or both were either inspired or incited by events in Piestany. Or maybe they just figured it was an appropriate tribute. But not one clip, not one photo, not one word appeared.

Nor was there one word in the national media about another game the next day. The Oshawa Generals and the Peterborough Petes didn't send any players to the world juniors in Czechoslovakia. There was a less obvious connection to Piestany. The Generals and the Petes poured over the boards and onto the ice of the Peterborough arena where Steve Chiasson and Kerry Huffman had played hundreds of times growing up. The Petes were the team that Chiasson and Huffman had come out to watch dozens, maybe hundreds of times, and no Petes game generated excitement like a tilt against Oshawa. Yes, the brawl made the *Peterborough Examiner,* but other than a passing mention of Piestany, the brawl didn't make it into the top half of the story. "While most of the hockey world was shocked at Sunday's international brawl between Canada and Russia [sic], OHL fans in these parts have come to expect fighting between Peterborough and Oshawa," reporter Mike Brophy wrote. Not until the eighteenth paragraph of a twenty-one-paragraph story did Brophy note that the Petes' trainer leaned over the boards and grabbed an Oshawa player. Not until that point did Brophy mention that Oshawa's coaching staff charged their way over to the Petes' bench and that arena ushers stepped in to break up a scrap between the adults in street clothes who passed for the players' father figures.

These bench-clearings weren't exceptional stories. They weren't quite commonplace, but they weren't like solar eclipses, either—not in the mid–'80s. Bob Hughes's rhetorical question seemed to apply. "Who, among the millions of hockey fans in this country, has not watched a bench-clearing brawl?" The answer: Not those delivering the news. Presumably not those reading the news, either.

———

Bert Templeton knew the media and the public would be looking for scapegoats. He volunteered for the position. Years later, many, Brendan Shanahan among them, would say that the media and the CAHA "threw Bert under the bus," but the fact is that Templeton took it upon himself to knock others out of the way and threw himself in front of the bus to spare them. He had expressed ambivalence about the players in practice and at the hotel—that he did in private. And he had to be aware that the players didn't like him—they were playing for love of country, not love of their coach. No matter. He only started to assume the role

of fall guy in the arena after the game. He had perfected it
by the time the reporters descended on him at Pearson
Airport in Toronto after he'd spent almost a full day in
transit. Tired. Feeling beaten up. And ready to step into the
path of any dart thrown at the players. "I don't know how
we're going to be portrayed at home, but we certainly didn't
go out with [fighting] in mind," Templeton said. "We've
tried to keep the team away from trouble and I think the
team has represented Canada exceptionally well. No one
honestly believed we were a threat for the gold medal.
Anybody who isn't proud of the way these kids performed
doesn't deserve to be involved in hockey in Canada. My
biggest disappointment would be if they don't receive the
support of the people who would have been jumping up
and down if we'd won a medal. Any negative comments
about these players would be totally unfounded. If there's
any blame, put it on me and I'll accept it." Templeton knew
it was an argument he wasn't going to win. He darkly predicted that Piestany was going to overshadow all his victories and all his championships. "The only bad news some
of these guys are ever going to write about me is my obituary and some of them would probably goof that up, too,"
he said. Morbid, but as it turned out, prescient.

"That's what they would call justice. That's what I
would call the shaft," Templeton said.

Templeton defended the players, but not the CAHA.
"The CAHA should have spoken up for this team,"
Templeton said. "Not one person from the CAHA has said
a word to any of the players—[not one said] that they
played well. That really hurts me because I'm proud of
those players. They tried as hard as they could. This was
the youngest and least experienced team to represent
Canada in this tournament, yet it wound up with a shot at
a gold medal. I'll live and die with those twenty kids."

Nobody from the CAHA came to the defence of the players. Not then, not in the years after. Not when the CAHA

changed its name. When it became the CHA, then Canadian Hockey, then Hockey Canada, which it remains today.

It would have been easy for the CAHA to defend the players. It would been easy for the executives to reach out to the players. It wouldn't have cost the CAHA anything but time to say something on behalf of the players. Or to say a few words *to* the players. The players figured it out early on—the CAHA was prepared to leave them out there unprotected. "On the bus to the airport and on the plane, Dave Draper [the Canadian team's manager] stayed up front," Shawn Simpson says. "He never came back and said anything to us. It was like [the CAHA officials] blamed us. That was the feeling that the players had. We knew we had Bert's support, and Bert did what he could to protect us."

It would have been just as easy to defend the coaches. The CAHA could have pointed out that Bert Templeton took his Fincups team to the world juniors ten years before and won a silver—he couldn't have become a bad coach in the interim. The CAHA could have played up the fact that Pat Burns had served as a police officer—hard to impugn him as a "goon coach" with his history in law enforcement.

Instead, the CAHA took thinly veiled shots at the players and coaches. "We have to decide on what type of discipline that we want to have on these teams and the type of personnel we want to be associated with the players to ensure that the message gets through to the players," Dennis McDonald told reporters. "Right now one would have to think that the coaching staff did lose control of the situation."

McDonald admitted that he had to "take some of the blame" himself. But he made it sound like his share of the blame was limited to the selection of "the type of personnel we want to be associated with the players." He pointed the finger at Templeton and Burns. That much everyone put together. He pointed the finger at Wally Tatomir. Only people in the game might have figured that out. And he pointed the finger at the players themselves. That's what it came down to: bad character spread all around. They lost control behind the bench; they lost control on the ice. He took the country-club route. He made it sound like the men and boys who represented Canada in this tournament weren't *our type of people*. He made it sound like next time the CAHA would send a team and diplomatic mission rolled into one.

Some players tuned out the CAHA's sniping. Some were stung but got over it. And some resent it still. "I don't mind the idea of a reunion, so long as the players organized it, not Hockey Canada," one player said.

———

One photo appeared on the front pages of several major Canadian papers: Mike Keane, with sunglasses perched on top of his head, playfighting with Greg Hawgood, tweaking Hawgood's broken nose. They posed for the photographers who were waiting for them at Pearson Airport in Toronto. The photograph captured the teenagers' resilience. Eighteen and nineteen years old and they understood optics better than the CAHA executives. Keane and Hawgood didn't run and didn't hide. They offered explanations, but didn't second-guess themselves. They were the very images of unrepentance. Defiantly unbowed, unembarrassed, proud to have played together.

They didn't look like diplomats. And if it had been a school trip, maybe a teacher would have slapped them down a bit. Maybe they'd have been expected to walk in single file.

There was no tortured introspection to be found in the accounts of the homecoming and the video clips of the players' arrival home.

"We're not ashamed of what we did," Shanahan said when he walked through customs and was greeted by 200 flag-draped supporters and family and friends. "I'd be more ashamed of coming back with some players that were badly injured. We just reacted to protect our teammates."

"I don't think a gold medal is worth our teammates being hurt," Hawgood explained. "There's no way we could have sat on the bench and watched our teammates taking a beating. We're a closely knit family and it was like someone beating up your brother."

"I'm relieved," Kerry Huffman said when he surveyed the crowd. "I didn't know how people would take it. We'd heard people were ashamed of us and that it was the black-est moment in Canadian hockey but I'm relieved people see it the way we do. We're proud we did so well and the only disappointment is that we were, in a way, cheated out of a gold medal by the officials' decision [to banish the team]."

"We tried to be as disciplined as we could, but they kept running us and using their sticks," Luke Richardson said. "They did everything they could to goad us."

Players' parents joined the chorus. Betty Chiasson had a lot more to say than her laconic son. "They got shafted," she said when she picked up her son the captain at the air-port. "My son played all the way through junior hockey and he's been in the odd fight. What junior hockey player hasn't?"

Glen Richardson sympathized with his son Luke and his teammates, but wondered if they could have come home with medals. "We should have been a little smarter than we were," Luke's father said. "You have to be pre-pared to bleed sometimes." That criticism didn't hold up. The players who were on the ice before the benches cleared were "prepared to bleed." It wasn't that Luke Richardson wasn't "prepared to bleed." He saw Davydov and the Soviets clear the bench. He wasn't "prepared" to watch his teammates "bleed."

Everett Sanipass went home to the reserve before reporting back to his junior club. Joe Sanipass had organized a party for his son, getting a hall at the local community centre and inviting a couple of hundred people to welcome Everett back. "I thought that Everett and the boys did what they had to do, and that we had to show our support," Joe Sanipass says. "Whatever happened, Everett wasn't out there to embarrass himself or disgrace the country. He and the other players gave all they had and played really hard— that was something that should be celebrated, never mind them getting disqualified."

Friends came out. Neighbours. Local politicians. Elders on the reserve. Kids. Two hundred, by Joe Sanipass's estimate.

"I didn't know anything about it until I got home," Everett Sanipass says. "I didn't know what people were going to be thinking other places, and I probably didn't care that much. I was worried about what the people on the reserve were going to be thinking of me. I hoped they thought what I did was right. I thought that they would . . . but you never know."

Everett was caught off guard. Loud music. A banner: Congratulations Everett. Speeches. Applause.

And then they started to call for Everett to say a few words. They gathered around him. They waited. And the applause grew louder. And they called out his name.

Everett Sanipass said "thank you" but nothing else. Not normal speechlessness. Not the usual I-haven't-prepared-anything-to-say. Words just didn't come out. Just saying "thank you" was a tougher fight than anything on the ice. He had just been talking into a camera in Piestany. Now he had an idea of how many people had seen the game. He could start putting faces to that audience.

"I played for my country and I had been on television but I was never as nervous as that," he says. "I was shaking, and it was just a lot of people I knew. I didn't know what to say. I couldn't really say anything. What was in my head back in Piestany—that I was getting blamed for the fight and for Canada not getting a medal—you know, I know that these people came out to support me, but, yeah, there was some part of my thinking that was still stuck on that. I didn't like that everyone was looking at me . . . everyone there for me."

"We couldn't have been prouder of Everett if he had come back with a gold medal," Joe Sanipass says. "He represented our people and our community as well as he could. He didn't make a speech. I just figured he was nervous. And what was left to say?"

———

McDonald and the CAHA miscalculated the public's sympathies. Critics of Templeton, Burns and the Canadian juniors weren't speaking for Canada. Not if a couple of polls were to be believed. One opinion poll showed 87 percent of Canadians supported the players despite the disqualification. Global Television's poll was even more one-sided—92 percent signed on to the idea that the teenagers did the right thing.

The polls didn't measure the intensity of the support. Dave Latta's first game back with the Kitchener Rangers was a road date against the Belleville Bulls. The fans in Belleville gave him a standing ovation in the pre-game introductions. "That was pretty classy of them," the Rangers' captain said. "I'm burnt but after a thing like that you just want to go hard on every shift and do your best." He scored a hat trick. Kitchener won, 7–2.

The Canadian juniors' most enthusiastic and loudest champion was, of course, the *vox populi*. Don Cherry was out in front in defence of the Canadian team and the coaches. Cherry led the attack on the Soviets and any critics of the Canadians. "What if it was your kid being ganged up on by ten Russians. Would you want [his teammates] to sit on the bench picking their noses?" Cherry said.

Cherry had a serious challenger for status as the juniors' most flamboyant supporter—and this famous name went beyond offering mere moral support. The eccentric owner of the Toronto Maple Leafs, Harold Ballard did Cherry one better. "The day after the fight, Mr. Ballard was walking through the office and a few of us were talking about it," says Bob Stellick, then the Leafs' public relations man. "He asked us if there was anything he could do for these kids, and I said, 'well, you could give them medals.' I didn't really expect him to do anything, but right away he told me to look into it—and of course with Mr. Ballard it had to be top-end, no-expense-spared stuff. The biggest medals, encased in glass." Ballard would claim that it was entirely an act of public-spiritedness, but it was more than that.

No. 1: Ballard was the contrarian—especially when it came to playing the media game. He loathed most of the commentators who were taking swings at the Canadian team. He couldn't have stomached the idea of agreeing with them.

No. 2: Ballard hated Communists in general and the Soviet Union in particular. No use for them at all. Didn't want them playing in his arena. Ever. If the Canadian juniors lost their medal because of a Soviet plot, he thought someone should make restitution. And if it could be him, if he could get some headlines, all the better.

Like Cherry, Ballard had a clear read of public sympathies. "Mr Ballard did a lot of outrageous things, but he also did a lot of things—some high-profile, some behind-the-scenes—that showed he was in touch with the man on the street," Bob Stellick says.

Once the medals were struck, Ballard brought in as many players as he could—almost all from the Ontario league—for a presentation prior to a Leaf game.

(Templeton was offered a limo from North Bay to the Gardens, but he insisted Ballard pick up the tab for air fare.) He wanted to make as big of a splash as he could, and would have staged it on a Saturday, a "Hockey Night in Canada" date. The juniors' schedule didn't permit it— just too many conflicts with their own teams. So Ballard set up a presentation for a weeknight game. "It was maybe the loudest roar from the crowd all season," Stellick says. "There was no putting the medals around the players' necks—they were in glass casing. But that didn't take anything away from it at all."

Not for those watching, not for those being honoured.

"A medal from the tournament would have been great, a gold medal even better," Shawn Simpson says. "But those medals from Harold Ballard signified a lot more for us. We didn't need a medal from that tournament to know what we were about. But if we had those medals, we'd never know the public's appreciation."

Greg Hawgood: "It took weeks, maybe months, for me to get my medal. They did send me a letter first. The letter said that they were sorry it was taking so long, but that it was going to take some time to get it just right. When they sent it, I thought it was just great. I've seen other medals from the junior tournaments and world championships and the rest. This medal wasn't maybe as important, but it definitely was a better-looking medal and it meant a lot to me.

"It was a special thing for me, especially going on to play for the Leafs," Luke Richardson says. "Trophies or medals aren't something you think about or look at every day. They aren't something you look at or pull out of a drawer. Sometimes you don't even know where they are. I won't lie: I'd like to have had a medal from the tournament. And I think we earned that and deserved that. But I look at that medal from Harold Ballard as being as legitimate as any we would have been given at the tournament. I know where it is exactly—in my father's safe."

Maybe that's why the Canadian hockey establishment never mended fences with the players from the 1987 junior team. It's tough to have taken twenty years to admit that you've been wrong, but especially when Harold Ballard had it instantly, almost instinctively, right. It's hard to look like you're attempting to do the right thing now, to make a gesture to this team, when it comes too late for Bert Templeton and Steve Chiasson.

———

Cherry and Ballard didn't need any encouragement, but a few Soviet hockey officials incited them anyway. The Soviet national team was travelling across Canada on an exhibition tour during the 1987 WJC. Back in the USSR, official reaction to Piestany was unequivocal. TASS drew targets on the backs of Vasiliev and Gureev. Soviet hockey officials in Canada—at least some prominent ones—sent out a different message.

Anatoli Kostriukov, head of the ice hockey department of the State Sports Committee, just happened to be in Ottawa with a national side that was routing Canada's Olympic team at different stops across the country. The Soviets had just defeated Dave King's team (the squad that Steve Nemeth had spent the season with prior to the world juniors) at the Civic Centre. Kostriukov was in Ottawa when the lights were turned out in Piestany. He watched the game on the CBC.

Kostriukov bristled when he was swarmed by reporters, when asked if the Soviets were to blame. "How do the Canadians misinterpret these things?" he said. Then combative call-outs gave way to diplomatic spin. "The incident involving the brawl at the world junior tournament saddened us deeply," he said. "It's too early to decide who to blame for the brawl as the team has not yet returned to Moscow." And then, finally, he hinted that the old way, the presumption of the moral purity of the Soviet Union and the demonization of the decadent West, might not be operative anymore. "I still believe that there can be no excuse for what has happened," he said. "The ice hockey department will soon analyze the Soviet team's performance at the championship and those guilty of the incident will be strictly punished."

Kostriukov stopped short of an apology, a contrast to Yuri Korolev, the USSR's Sports Committee's head hockey coach. Korolev seemed prepared to express regrets. "Please believe us, we feel very, very sorry about the incident," Korolev said through an interpreter. He seemed ready to fault the IIHF. "We think Mr. Sabetzki interpreted the situation improperly. In my opinion the game must be finished. The Canadian team could have won a gold medal. The referee [should] have penalized an adequate number of players. [Rønning] couldn't control the game."

But Korolev must have thought he was going to be perceived as weak, because he abruptly changed tone. He wanted to make clear that he wasn't exonerating the Canadian juniors. He wasn't about to assign blame—any blame—to the Soviet juniors. "We read in the Canadian papers that the fighting was inspired by the Soviet team," Korolev said. "I don't blame anyone. We don't feel guilty about what happened in Czechoslovakia. Soviet players never use dirty tricks. Our players cannot fight. They have no experience. They can't take the sweater over the head. We don't coach fighting."

The most caustic comments issued from the most likely source. Viktor Tikhonov coached the Soviet team that was wrapping up its tour. Tikhonov's condescension almost needed no translator.

His statement was curious. He didn't seemed to be concerned with the Soviets' performance at the WJC or the bench-clearing in Piestany. No, he cut straight to interviews Shawn Simpson and Kerry Huffman had given to the CBC. He expressed outrage that Simpson and Huffman said that they would do it all over again. No apologies, no regrets.

"If it was in my power I would withdraw them forever from hockey," Tikhonov says. "Their declaration was heard by millions. The influence was very negative on children."

Tikhonov was assuming the role of protector of Canadian youth. He went after those who were speaking too freely, too openly, too honestly. Not surprising.

He also lit into Bert Templeton. If Tikhonov had a say in it, there would have been no "security of cadre" for the Canadian juniors' coach. "The same thing was said by [Templeton]. If one of our coaches said this he would never work again as a coach."

It was an old-school, pre-*glasnost* management strategy: watch what you do, but watch more closely what you say.

———

It was easy to laugh at the Soviets' finger-pointing and Tikhonov's attempt to crush the dissent of independent-minded Canadian juniors. The IIHF was a greater concern.

It looked as though the IIHF was determined to give it to both sides worse than Stephane Roy took it: players, eighteen-month international suspensions; coaches, three years. Sabetzki could have pursued relegating Canada and the Soviets to the B pool. Implications: severe. Complicating issues: numerous.

No. 1: The 1988 world juniors were already scheduled for Leningrad. Demoting the USSR to the B pool would require another team to come forward to host the tournament.

No. 2: The IIHF would be cutting off the tournament's biggest—in fact, sole—source of media income: Canadian broadcasting. The CBC wouldn't pay to broadcast a Canada–Italy game, or other similar one-sided slaughters in the B pool.

No. 3: It would be tough to promote the world juniors as a representative tournament without the two hockey powers.

Sabetzki decided relegation would be too bitter a pill to swallow. He stuck with the suspensions alone. That was the ruling immediately after the tournament.

The CAHA was positioning itself for an appeal but was doing anything but talking tough. In fact, officials sounded like they were standing up to the bureaucratic bully—and cowering at the same time.

"We have to try whatever is available to us," CAHA president Murray Costello said. "There has to be the ability to appeal to the council. We were punished severely. If this, for example, had happened in the second game of the tournament, would they have done this with the effect on the marketing, promotion and ticket refunds?

"Disputes are supposed to go to the disciplinary committee and I'm a member," Costello said. "But Sabetzki has imposed decisions on his own before and that's what worries me. He's an old man, he's very stubborn and obstinate. I'm afraid he's going to ramrod something through without at least consulting us."

Bottom line: don't get your hopes up. "There's no appeal," Costello concluded. "He already said publicly that further action might be taken against us."

———

Public opinion gave Sabetzki an opportunity to relent. He realized that no one would come away satisfied with a tournament without the two most famous programs. It was the world's tournament more than *his* tournament. There were no worlds without Canada and the USSR. He stopped short of admitting he was wrong. He knocked the player suspensions down to six months; that way Canada could have Fleury, Waite and others back for the 1988 junior tournament. That way the Soviets could have Mogilny and Fedorov in their lineup. Sabetzki stuck with his original suspensions of the coaches. Moot point: He had reason to presume that the respective federations weren't about to bring back their coaching staffs after Piestany.

A footnote: the black cloud kept right on following Nemeth. It turned out he didn't need to apply for reinstatement—Sabetzki's decision freed him to try out for the Olympic program. But after announcing to the hockey world that he didn't fight in Piestany, he failed to make the Canadian Olympic squad the next winter.

PART II

WHEN THE LIGHTS CAME BACK ON:
An Account of Young Men Defeating Rivals, Beating Demons, Taking Refuge and Defying Human Nature

"NATURE, Mr. Alnutt, is what we were put in this world to rise above."

—Katharine Hepburn to a Canadian companion in *The African Queen*

Return and Redemption

The Soviet hockey bosses moved the 1988 WJC from Leningrad to Moscow. The decision to take the tournament to the capital might have been a matter of logistics, Leningrad lacking the resources to host the tournament. Or it might have been a purely strategic move—Moscow being the least friendly setting for other teams in the field. Moscow made it a home game for the Red Army players who filled most spots in the Soviet juniors' lineup. If it had been a strategic ploy, it failed. Canada won its third gold in seven years—its third in *six* tournaments if you throw out the DQ in '87.

Canadians made up half of the tournament all-star team: forward, Theoren Fleury; defenceman, Greg Hawgood; goaltender, Jimmy Waite. All returning players. Chris Joseph, last seen rolling around the ice at the start of the brawl against the Soviets, took up a place on the Canadian blue line again. These four had been just eighteen in Piestany. Others from the '87 squad would have been eligible, including Pierre Turgeon, Brendan Shanahan and Glen Wesley, but they were already on NHL rosters.

The returning foursome made the most of a second chance. Fleury wearing desire all over his face, instantly upping the pace and energy on every shift, furiously forechecking, causing havoc—not quite the same havoc as Piestany, but havoc nonetheless. Hawgood rushing the puck, working the point, leading all Canadian scorers, looking for the world like a shorter but no less effective Brad Park. Waite reprising—transcending—the game against Sweden the previous winter, stealing victories, giving teammates the confidence that comes only with the knowledge that goaltending will give them a chance. Joseph following Steve Nemeth's lead, coming over with the Olympic team's program, waiting for the junior squad in Moscow after the Izvestia tournament, bringing international experience into the room.

"Piestany was a huge motivation for us," Hawgood says. "It also made us smarter about the international game, more focused. I don't want to say Piestany was a good thing, but there was some good we took away from it."

Piestany wasn't a huge motivation for the CAHA, though. No, Piestany was a huge piece of baggage, one that the organization couldn't put behind it quickly enough. Piestany gave Hawgood, Fleury, Waite, and Joseph *want*. For the CAHA Piestany imposed *need*. "Looking back on it, Moscow in '88 was the most important world junior tournament for Canada, ever," CAHA President Murray Costello says. It could all have come apart very easily for the program if we didn't ice a quality team and quality players."

"There was three times the pressure on us putting this team together," says Dave Draper, back for a second time as chief scout. "Coaches, players, everything—we just felt like we couldn't afford mistakes."

By the fall of 1987, hockey executives at all levels were concerned about the image of the game. Piestany was a famous case, but just part of it. Even the 1986 Stanley Cup final between Montreal and Calgary was marred by a bench-clearing brawl. Before the 1987-88 season, the NHL instituted tough new rules—automatic ten-game suspensions for the first guys off the bench—that effectively put an end to bench-clearing.

The CAHA cleaned up the image—from one year to the next it couldn't have been more different. Dennis McDonald recruited "the right kind of people." The CAHA brought in Dave Chambers—*a career varsity coach*—to work behind the national juniors' bench. Dave Draper had known Chambers for years, going back to their days at St. Michael's, the Toronto Catholic high school and elite hockey program. Draper knew Chambers was as far away from Bert Templeton (and the Dirty Bert image) as could be. Chambers: York University, players making it from mid-terms to games, young men bound for white-collar jobs down the line, young men knowing that their competitive hockey careers were going to end on campus in the school colours. Templeton: North Bay Centennials, players catching buses to games all over Ontario, boys who dream that they'll play in bigger arenas, juniors is just a stop on the way. Dave Chambers wasn't a cleaned-up version of Bert Templeton. The difference between them was the contrast between new school and old school—even new school and *no* school. The CAHA wanted something as close to Father David Bauer as possible. Someone who offered a values-based approach. Someone who was a diplomat, an ambassador. And the fact is, both Draper and Chambers had played for Father Bauer.

Chambers was so unlike many previous coaches of the Canadian juniors that it unsettled Murray Costello. "He was so low key, I didn't know what to make of it," Costello says. "I asked Dave Draper, 'When's this guy going to snap out of it?'"

The players were just teenagers but they knew all about optics and politics. "Even at nineteen I wasn't so naïve that I didn't know what the CAHA was doing when he was named coach," Hawgood says. "It had nothing to do with the quality of coaching—I don't know if anyone would say [Chambers] was a better hockey man than Bert Templeton. The CAHA wanted to put some distance between Piestany and the program."

Dennis McDonald pushed for the changes. He drew up the blueprint. The short-term tournament setting needed a different approach—it was one thing to build a team, as most junior coaches do, over the course of a season or more; another to do it over three weeks. It seemed like every waking moment was accounted for, micromanaged. It wasn't the old-time-hockey approach, going with gut and instinct. The coach wouldn't make it up as he went along— he had to be an organization man. "Dennis McDonald doesn't get the credit he deserves for his contribution to the program," Hockey Canada president Bob Nicholson said years later. "He came up with a lot of the ideas that we've put into place and refined over the years."

The Canadian teams that dominated the WJC in the late '80s and early '90s—winning gold in seven of eight tournaments—looked a lot more like the Canadian squad in Moscow than the Bad News Bears from Piestany. "We had to go back to look at everything we did with those players," McDonald says. "Just like we couldn't have them run their own practices, we couldn't—and ethically *shouldn't*—let them manage themselves off the ice. We had to give them the right guidance and support to give Canada the best chance of winning."

Some thought it was a little touchy-feely. McDonald thought it better to err on the side of over-managing. He thought that what worked in a usual junior hockey setting wouldn't work in a short, intense tournament with players and coaches unfamiliar with each other.

None of the Canadian juniors knew Chambers, not even by reputation. Chambers left them scratching their heads at the start. They were still scratching their heads about the coach when they were being presented the gold medals at centre ice. It was their first and only brush with "the old college try." The Canadian players had hated Templeton during the '87 tournament, though they came to respect him afterward. Still, they had fed off negative energy. They had played for hard-asses—if not with their junior clubs, then somewhere else along the line. They weren't used to being *inspired,* being *mentored.* They were used to being *pushed,* being *driven.* They might bitch and moan about coaches like Bert Templeton, but it was the Bert Templetons who had the players on the pros' radar. College players coached by tenured faculty didn't go to the NHL. Guys who had been browbeaten by junior coaches either resigned to, or resentful about, their lot riding the buses—those were the players on the NHL's radar.

"He seemed like a nice guy, but he didn't swear the entire tournament," Fleury says. "He would go, 'gosh' or 'darn.' He wasn't like any other coach I ever had. He would say, 'We can't be out there doing that . . . *stuff.*' Then one of us would stand up and say, 'We're playing like shit.' I thought [Chambers] was gonna faint."

For Fleury, from one year to the next, between his eighteenth and nineteenth birthdays, life had changed. This unfamiliar coach was the least of it. Things had changed in hockey. He had been undrafted in 1986. Calgary picked him in the draft on the basis of his play in the 1987 WJC and to the continued amusement of all other NHL franchises. Things changed away from the arena. He became a father. He looked like a big brother to his son. "I had to grow up fast," Fleury says. "I had responsibilities to look after. Maybe it made me more desperate to make it. I'd always wanted to make it [to the NHL] for myself. It's another type of pressure when you're not doing it for fun but to put food on the table for your kid and your wife."

Some CAHA officials were opposed to selecting Fleury for the 1988 squad. They thought he was just too volatile, no matter what skill he possessed. Dave Draper fought hard to get him in the line-up. "I wasn't sure myself," Draper says, "but I went out and interviewed him a couple of times at least, just to get a read of him. I got a sense that he desperately wanted to redeem himself." Others were won over by Fleury's play and his commitment. Chambers named Fleury team captain—one of the few things that the CAHA ever did that didn't amount to scapegoating the players from Piestany. Fleury felt it was a message. He felt it was a way to bring him back to earth. He felt it was an emotional challenge. "I realized that I always played with an edge but that I couldn't cross a line," he says. "I couldn't be selfish and do something that would hurt my team-mates. I had to think real hard about that wearing the C. And really, it was good for me and good for the team. It was a lesson that I learned, and I think other guys learned, from Piestany."

Hawgood says that it felt different the next year, a different team dynamic. Maybe things were a little more subdued. Or focused on playing. "Piestany was something that we knew couldn't and shouldn't happen again," Hawgood says, "even if we weren't wrong in doing what we did. That was just the reality. And I think we had a different type of team."

It was like being back in grade school, when teachers told them to behave on class outings because they were "representing the school." Chambers took the team on cultural day trips. To museums. To the Moscow Circus. To historical landmarks.

There was no Animal House back at the team's hotel. No making the floor their own private clubhouse. Then again, there wasn't the same sort of claustrophobia. "We couldn't even think of doing it," Hawgood says. "It was the biggest hotel I've ever seen. Thousands of rooms. Hundreds of rooms on our floor. The hotel was so big that all the other teams in the tournament were staying there and we never saw them the whole time, not in the lobbies or the lunch room."

The roster of the team that went to Moscow was deep in talent: Joe Sakic, Mark Recchi, Adam Graves and Eric Desjardins. All went on to significant NHL careers. It was their first turn in the spotlight—guys who would play in Stanley Cup finals. That Theoren Fleury played a bigger role than them is no surprise. That Greg Hawgood and Jimmy Waite were leaders would years later have come as a surprise to hockey fans. And Greg Hawgood and Jimmy Waite were arguably more valuable members of that team than was Fleury.

"I felt like I was playing for something that I should have already had," Hawgood says.

"I didn't think like that because at eighteen or nineteen you think you're going to play forever and play for Stanley Cups," Jimmy Waite says. "I tried to have a good time as well as a good tournament. I remember our hotel was right next to Red Square and we went on a tour there."

Hawgood didn't go, though. Not to Red Square. Not on a couple of other tours that the program arranged— probably less for educational purposes, probably more as a way of breaking up the pressure and monotony. Monotony suited Hawgood. He stayed in his room a lot. He played solitaire. He looked out the window. He looked at his food long and hard before he ate it.

"I just went to Moscow for one reason, and maybe having done it once before, it took something out of it," Hawgood says. "Not the goal or the pressure. Not the satisfaction. But this wasn't the first time. I think the other guys going through it might have been more excited about it—maybe they had more fun. It wasn't about fun for me, though."

It was about results. For Hawgood. For the other returning players. For the Canadian team's executives, too. And it was about results that were impossibly narrow, and got progressively narrower.

DECEMBER 26
CANADA 4 SWEDEN 2

Fleury scored the goal that made the score 4–1 in the third period. Waite stopped 18 of 20 shots.

DECEMBER 28
CANADA 4 CZECHOSLOVAKIA 2

Fleury scored the winning goal midway through the third period. Waite raised his game, stopping 24 of 26 shots.

DECEMBER 29
CANADA 4 FINLAND 4

Fleury and Hawgood set up Canada's fourth goal, scored by Dan Currie. Waite stopped 31 of 35 shots for an outplayed Canadian team that managed less than half that number of shots on the Finnish net.

DECEMBER 31
CANADA 5 UNITED STATES 4

Fleury scored a goal. Joseph scored the winner. Hawgood picked up two assists. Waite stopped 21 of 25 shots, turning back a late rally by the Americans.

JANUARY 1
CANADA 3 SOVIET UNION 2

Fleury scored the opening goal, which Joseph set up. Hawgood picked up an assist. Waite put in a performance that a capsule summation would do no justice to.

It was a familiar theme. Waite would have been *the* goaltender of the 1987 WJC if Canada had not been tossed out of the tournament. He was *the* goaltender of the 1988 WJC in Moscow and had no serious challengers. He was the player of the tournament, just as indisputably. Canada winning without him? Canada winning with any of the goaltenders who had come to the tournament before? Unthinkable. That's what Sherry Bassin says.

"That's no knock against the guys who played for me at world juniors—they were great—but there's no doubt Jimmy was the best goaltender that we sent to [the under-20s]," Sherry Bassin says. "In either of those tournaments you can make the case that he was the best, and there have been a lot over the years—like Roberto Luongo or Jose Theodore."

Craig Button, the veteran scout and former Calgary Flames general manager, goes beyond Bassin's estimation of Waite's performance. "That game against the Soviets in 1988 was the single greatest one-game performance by a goaltender I've ever seen. He was not going to be beaten. Even the Soviets knew that after a while. You could look over at the bench and see them sag. They poured in all over him—it's not that they stopped or gave up. They knew that they were a vastly superior club to the Canadians, one of the best teams ever. It was one guy who really beat them."

Two games remained, but they were likely the most anticlimactic in the history of WJC. They had all the suspense of a coronation.

JANUARY 3
CANADA 8 WEST GERMANY 1

Canada took 50 shots. No further explanation necessary.

JANUARY 4
CANADA 9 POLAND 1

Canada took 52 shots. Ditto.

Fleury hadn't dispelled all doubts about his ability to play in the NHL, but he was sure he'd make it. Like many scouts, though, he was even more sure that the other Canadian members of the 1988 WJC all-star team were going to have major NHL careers. "I was sure that Greg Hawgood would have been a fifteen-year NHL player," Fleury says. "He was the best nineteen-year-old defence-man in the world—you'd figure he'd be in the NHL for-ever. And Jimmy was incredible. I was amazed when I had a chance to play on a Stanley Cup winner the next season but I thought Jimmy was going to win Stanley Cups, Vezinas, whatever. Nothing would have surprised me about Jimmy, the way he played for us in the tournament. There were guys you just knew would play in the NHL—for us, Joe Sakic, for sure. The U.S. had Mike Modano. The Russians—nobody knew if they'd ever come to the NHL, but you figured Mogilny and Fedorov were going to win gold medals and be the world's best for a long time."

Escape and Exile

It's usually easy to project how history will judge atheletes. More so than, say, politicians or artists or almost anybody else. Athletes are measured by titles, by wins and losses, by statistics. In hockey, players head to the Hall of Fame if they hit benchmark numbers and compile a resume featuring trophies, All-Star berths, and championships. Show enough skill on the ice and enough nerve in pressure situations, head to the Hockey Hall of Fame. It's clear cut. Almost all the time.

It's hard to say how history will judge Alexander Mogilny. Hard to slot him. He'd show flash skill on the ice, yet he'd be perhaps his most artful off the ice. He'd never be regarded as a hard-nosed player, yet he'd do something so brave that his teammates regarded it as reckless. He'd never be thought of as a team player—not then, not later— yet he would do something that would benefit not only those who played beside him, but a whole generation of Russian players: he'd open the gates to the West that his countrymen would skate through.

Canadian hockey fans saw that thrilling, improbable

win over the Soviets in Moscow. They saw the most important Canadian hockey victory in the most hostile of settings
since Game Eight of the Summit Series, back when the juniors were toddlers.

Don Luce saw that game, but not with a rooting interest.
His rooting interest was for his employer, the Buffalo Sabres,
the team he used to play for, the one he was now scouting
for. He was looking at players, not countries. He saw an
amazing talent in Alexander Mogilny. He wasn't alone. That
was the consensus of the scouts in attendance. Mogilny was
the best junior player in the world—the next big thing.

He was the lone Soviet player to squeeze onto the 1988
WJC all-star team. "If he was free to go, he would have
been the top pick in the draft," Luce says. He made a note
to himself: *If we have an extra draft pick, we could do
worse than waste it on a guy who likely will never make it
out of the Soviet Union.* At some point the possible
rewards justified buying a lottery ticket.

Don Luce knew about Mogilny only what he saw on
the ice. He had heard little about his personal story. Not
the goods. Not that he was a curious young man, one who
looked for answers in a system that didn't brook questions.
Not that he had come so far to Moscow and was disen-
chanted with not seeing his family for eleven months at a
time. Not that he was curious about a world that he hadn't
yet seen. Again, this colours inside the lines but does not
draw the big picture. And Don Luce had no way of knowing that Mogliny would turn out to be a critical player in
shaping the NHL. He had no way of knowing that in the
near future that Mogilny's name wouldn't be found in lineups but in headlines.

Weeks later, Mogilny was the youngest player on the
Soviet team at the 1988 Olympics in Calgary. His place on
the roster looked like a sign that he was being groomed for
a lead role down the line, the next Kharlamov. At least it
did until Soviet coach Viktor Tikhonov slugged the

eighteen-year-old Mogilny on the bench in an inconsequential game against Finland. Supposedly something to do with selfish or lazy play. Not the Olympic spirit you'd expect. Not out of character for Tikhonov, either.

Mogilny is reluctant to discuss the incident with Tikhonov in Calgary. "It's a long time ago," he says. "I understand a lot more today than I did as a young man. I understand why he did what he did. That is a lifetime ago."

Maybe Mogilny and Tikhonov could have reconciled. Maybe the player could have "got with the program." Soviet coaches and officials tried to get Mogilny to buy in, but ultimately he wouldn't. He didn't want a military life, which was just part of the package for members of Red Army and the national team. He declined to take an officer's rank—open, almost casual defiance. Mogilny wasn't just bitter about Calgary, but pessimistic about the prospects of life with the program. Tikhonov was the national team coach, not going anywhere for the foreseeable future, not about to back down or blink or make exceptions for Mogilny. He had already made Mogilny's Olympic turn miserable. He had a chance to blow up the teenager's career. At that point, Mogilny wanted out. To what, he didn't really know, but out to anything else would do.

Alexander Mogilny knew about *perestroika*. He knew sport wasn't the biggest thing that was broken in Soviet society. People living in hunger, lining up for food that wasn't there—that was bigger than sport. He knew this was the case in Moscow. He knew that this was the case back in his hometown.

Sport, like so much of Soviet society, was failing. The Soviet sports system was still turning out talented athletes, Olympic gold medallists, championship teams, but resources for the sports programs were being cut to the bone. Sport by the late '80s paid out more in tax than it took in from the government.

But sport in the Soviet Union was transformed about as quickly as a coach changed lines. The closed society opened for business. Everything amateur was put up for sale. The supermarkets' shelves were empty, but Soviet sports programs were well stocked with talent and pro teams were cordially invited to load up their shopping carts. First, Soviet soccer players were being sold to European clubs. By 1988 Tikhonov was admitting that high-ranking officials were negotiating with the NHL and that veteran players such as Slava Fetisov and Igor Larionov were likely headed to North America. It seemed, however, that the Soviets were negotiating for the release of the veteran players only. The authorities set a benchmark at age twenty-eight—only at that point would the hockey bosses shop their talent. For Mogilny it wasn't simply a matter of having to wait his turn; Mogilny had a reasonable concern that he might play in some type of exile before his twenty-eighth birthday, like Helmut Balderis—that his rocky relationship with Tikhonov or his status as an outsider might come back to haunt him, even if he put in his time and paid his dues.

Mogilny saw the West as an opportunity and an escape. And he saw risks in waiting. "It's not complicated," Mogilny says. "I had to do what I thought would help me become the best player I could be. I thought that I had a better chance to do that in the NHL than in the Soviet Union."

At the 1988 NHL draft the following June, Don Luce convinced the Sabres to spend a spare fifth-round pick on Mogilny. "It seemed like a small price for a longshot that could really pay off," Luce says. "We had no idea what was happening with [Tikhonov and Mogilny]. If we had known [that he was unhappy], it probably would have changed things. More teams would have been interested."

Mogilny's discontent became clearer the next season. He had been just one player in the roiling mob in Piestany, and the unsuspecting victim of an outrageous attack in

Calgary. In the Soviet elite league, though, Mogilny was acting out. It reached a breaking point when he was suspended for ten games without a month's pay and stripped of his title of "honorary master of sport." He was suspended for what Robert Edelman described as "the most violent on-ice fight in recent memory, severely injuring a Spartak player."

Mogilny won't talk about the incident, about the fight and the suspension. He acts like he has no memory of it.

Only a few weeks later, the Sabres made their first contact with their draft gamble. Luce introduced himself to Mogilny at the 1989 WJC in Anchorage, Alaska. Luce waited for Mogilny outside the Soviet dressing room after a game. He gave the player his business card and told him to call him someday. "I didn't even let myself think about it," Luce says of the likelihood of Mogilny calling him. "Maybe as something in the long run—the *long* run. But I didn't have my hopes up. Really, I just wanted to shake his hand."

Four months later, Luce's home phone rang. "I thought it was another scout playing a prank, someone pretending to be Alex," Luce says. "I hear how he has defected at the world championships and wants to talk to the Sabres. I played along for a bit and then I realized that maybe it was him. As soon as I realized it *was* him, everything changed. In an hour, Gerry Meehan [then Buffalo's general manager] and I had our tickets to Stockholm."

Mogilny's defection was headline news, not only in the sports pages but in the political circles, too. Many had defected before him—artists, writers, dissidents of different stripes, ballet stars, soccer players—but never a hockey player. The Soviets had sent some players and coaches to the European leagues prior to that. But never had anyone walked away from the national team.

"Walked away" wasn't a figure of speech. That was literally what he did: walk away. In a *Toronto Star* interview,

Slava Fetisov had mentioned that the Soviets could "walk away from the team" anytime but wouldn't risk losing the chance to "return to the motherland." No one believed it was that easy to defect, and no one believed that the players were so attached to the USSR, either.

In the West, people presumed that flight would require planning and daring, but Mogilny didn't have to crawl under barbed wire or break a KGB agent's tackle. He was being watched, but only some or most of the time, and maybe not that closely. The most daring thing might have been his decision to drop by Sergei Fedorov's room and try to talk his linemate into walking out with him. He knew Fedorov could have called team officials and tipped them. He also knew Fedorov might even have been implicated— that the officials would at least suspect that Fedorov knew what Mogilny was up to. And maybe that was Mogilny's intent—not to urge Fedorov, but to push him out of the hotel and into the free world. Fedorov declined, but kept Mogilny's overture a secret until the Soviet Union's collapse three years later.

Mogilny wasn't fearless, but he wasn't terrified, either. He wasn't fooled by the idea that his status as a national team member offered a truly privileged position in Soviet society. His only habit was independent thinking. He knew the risk wasn't walking away. No, the real risk for Mogilny was staying. That placed his career in greater risk than going to North America. There was the risk that his family would suffer in the fallout from his decision. But his family faced no greater hardship than their day-to-day existence. They were questioned by the KGB but otherwise suffered no revenge. The lack of high intrigue leads you to wonder how it had never happened before.

Logistically, defection was easy for Mogilny; emotionally, it was hard. "I didn't do it lightly," he says. "You don't do anything lightly . . . not when they convict you of treason and refuse you the right to see your family. But many things could have happened if I had not left the team in Sweden."

At the same time, he makes it sound like his defection was impulsive. "It wasn't something that I had thought about all my life," he says. "I didn't have a clue that I'd be the first."

It's impossible to say whether it was impulsive, calculated or instinctive because Alexander Mogilny shows his cards only when it suits or amuses him. One possibility: Mogilny hadn't thought about his defection straining the Soviets' negotiations with the NHL—his former masters threatened to walk away from the talks that opened the door for Fetisov, Larionov and Sergei Makarov among others. Another possibility: Mogilny had factored the effect his defection might have and didn't care. He said at the time: "They write that I was thinking of myself, but who will think about me when I finish playing hockey in the Soviet Union?" One last possibility: Mogilny realized that the Soviets would complain loudly and seem indignant, but would continue to negotiate with the NHL. Though he is hardly reluctant to appear self-centred, the third scenario seems the most likely.

One story circulated briefly after Mogilny's flight— that he had met a girl, a twenty-three-year-old biology major, at the 1989 WJC in Anchorage, Alaska, and had fallen for her. The idea of puppy love inspiring his defection made for great copy—could have been movie-of-the-week stuff—but it was quickly shot down. Those who pursued it didn't know that such a three-hanky story line would have been laughted out of a dressing room. Don Luce believes Mogilny just saw which way the wind was blowing. According to the scout, the teenager was almost a visionary.

Mogilny moved in with Luce and his family when he arrived in Buffalo and spent his first season in the scout's household. Other teenage sensations had billeted with team officials, but they had faced nothing like Mogilny's culture shock. Then again, Mogilny had already stared down far tougher things.

"Pretty quickly, we realized that he was a very special character," Luce says. "He was extremely cautious about other people but extremely confident in himself. He was highly intelligent. He was getting the hang of the language faster than people realized—he understood almost everything you said to him after a while, but he was reluctant to talk himself. He kept his cards very close to the vest. He didn't want people to know everything that he knew. He was just twenty when he came in 1989, but he still had this sense of himself. He'd get a reputation later on as someone who isn't a team player but I never thought that was fair or accurate. If you can score 76 goals in a season like Alex did, I don't know if he's being a better team player by shooting [rather than by] passing the puck. He was great with our family and we've stayed close to him and even his parents later on. He was a young man with an old soul. He was very sensitive to people. He was very aware of things going on. And I think when it came to the changes in the Soviet Union, he was way ahead of the [hockey] scouts and executives."

The Mentor's Cruelty and the Enemies' Acceptance

Years later, the players who were on the ice when the lights went out moved on to the NHL. And years later, the stories about Piestany were still coming out. The men told stories about a game they had played as boys.

The most outrageous stories were those about Vladimir Vasiliev. There was something like an unofficial embargo while Russian players became more confident with the language and more comfortable with their North American teammates. They couldn't air secrets from the Soviet era until they were certain that telling tales wouldn't bite them in the ass—until those who'd look bad were out of positions of influence back home. But when they did talk—and to teammates rather than the press—they described Vasiliev not as a coach who sought the best from his team, but rather as a tyrant who pushed them to the breaking point. His approach to the game was more suited to the gulag than the arena, they said. What would pass for emotional or physical abuse in North America was Vasiliev's idea of team-building—that's how the stories went.

The stories fit the stereotypes, of Soviet coaches' absolute power corrupting sport absolutely. If the stories were to be believed, Soviet coaches in all manner of sports practised mind control and threatened to send athletes to Siberia or the salt mines or some other Soviet circle of hell. Soviet coaches as brutal taskmasters; athletes as the powerless victims in reigns of terror. The totalitarian system crushing the individual.

The challenge of Piestany: you have to sort through a lot of rumour, some hearsay and so little testimony of those who were there. Pull out a notebook, hold up a tape recorder and wait while Soviet athletes struggle to remember what must be impossible to forget. It is like the Soviet Union of old, pre-*glasnost*. Silence wasn't just the default mode; it was a preservation instinct.

———

"Sergei Fedorov told me one time that the coach [Vladimir Vasiliev] starved [the players] during the tournament to punish them for losses," Brendan Shanahan says. "Sergei told me that he'd wake them up in the middle of the night . . . that he'd make them go out for runs at 3 a.m."

Shanahan has a well-deserved reputation as hockey's foremost prankster, a born blarneymeister. In old media guides and newspaper stories, he claimed to have worked as a lifeguard in the off-season, played saxophone in a band and put in cameo appearances in an Austin Powers movie. That makes it hard to buy hearsay from a guy who has made a hobby out of pulling the legs of reporters.

But these stories had first surfaced as rumours during the 1987 WJC. Sherry Bassin had heard at the arenas about outrageous punishments for the Soviet teenagers. During the Piestany broadcast, he even alluded to Vasiliev making his players go hungry. "Word of those types of things gets around," Bassin says. "There are no real secrets. Teams stay at the same hotels, eat in the same dining rooms. If no one sees the Soviets eating, you know that they're not getting room service or eating at restaurants in town. No, people around the teams at that tournament knew something was going on."

And years later, players from that Soviet team followed Fedorov to the NHL. Some never discussed Piestany with their North American teammates. "I played with [Vladimir] Malakhov in Montreal and I think that he was one of the guys I fought [in Piestany]," Mike Keane says. "We never talked about the game. It never came up. He didn't talk a lot about anything."

But others told their versions of events. One Canadian NHLer said that he talked with Valeri Zelepukin about Piestany and got the same story as Shanahan's and Bassin's. The player (who asked not to be named so as not to be seen betraying confidences) said Zelepukin told him about a coach getting out of control: "Supposedly this guy [Vasiliev] was all worried about going back to Moscow and was taking it out on the players. It sounded pretty hardcore . . . just the stuff he told me about. It wasn't just bag skates, but practices right after games, runs at night. He didn't say anything about the coach not letting them eat, but that sounds like [the story Zelepukin] told me."

Zelepukin is reticent when contacted directly: no stories of starving or midnight runs or other humiliations. "The discipline on a team goes to the head coach," he says. "Vasiliev always had a reputation of having a strict discipline. All his teams had tough discipline."

The second- and third-hand stories of Vasiliev's "tough discipline" were consistent with history. If Vasiliev had crossed a line with his team, he could have been emulating his former boss with Red Army, Anatoli Tarasov. Tarasov was described as the father of Soviet hockey, but he was an abusive parent. He claimed to be an idealistic sportsman protective of his athletes. In his memoir, *Road to Olympus*,

Tarasov wrote that a coach "has absolutely no right to make ill use of the power bestowed in him" and that a coach must be "100 percent fair and just." Tarasov's former players must have had trouble deciding whether to laugh or cry.

"He was a madman, absolutely ruthless," Robert Edelman says. Tarasov didn't do love and nurture, except on the page. He was tough, but his assistants played good cops to his bad cop.

Yet when Tarasov died, Slava Fetisov offered a sympathetic tribute. "He was a warm, loving human being," Fetisov said. "He truly cared about his players and mankind in general. He pushed his teams to their highest capacity. He was there for them every day."

Tarasov's successor, Viktor Tikhonov, was no less the ruthless despot. Tikhonov looked 100 percent KGB-approved. He was a nightmare to play for, by all accounts. Everyone respected Igor Larionov—everyone except Tikhonov. He let Tikhonov know he was unhappy with his approach all through the '80s. Within a year of Piestany, Larionov aired his complaints, not in the Western press but in the pro-*perestroika* press at home. He called for reform—a more enlightened approach to coaching the team.

Yet Larionov's criticism targeted the hockey establishment in general and Tikhonov himself less specifically. Larionov spoke of the hockey program "treating players like chess pieces."

An odd phenomenon: these two outspoken players were critical of "the system" but guarded—and in Fetisov's case, overly generous—with individuals. They tacitly acknowledged that these weren't necessarily evil men, even if they were men who had done evil things—that in the name of an evil system it's hard to separate what someone wanted to do and what he had to do. It wasn't always forgiveness—it certainly wasn't for Larionov—but something closer to the benefit of the doubt. It's not odd because they said these things or felt this way; it's odd because these sentiments ran so close to those of Sergei Fedorov and Alexander Mogilny about their coach in Piestany, Vladimir Vasiliev.

———

Fedorov keeps it very brief when first asked about Vasiliev and the Soviet team in Piestany. He waves his hand and shakes his head when asked point blank about the stories of starving players or sleep deprivation. "A team like all the other teams," Fedorov says. "A coach like a lot of the other coaches. I was so young that I just played—I didn't think about things, what the coach was like."

It takes a lot of coaxing to get Fedorov to be a little more expansive about the coach. A lot of pressure behind the scenes—that much Fedorov admits. He also admits that Vasiliev had a lot of explaining to do when he went back to Moscow—that much Fedorov says everybody knew, Vasiliev most of all. Fedorov does say that there was more explaining to do back in Moscow because of the brawl against the Canadians, not because of the poor performance of the Soviet juniors earlier in the tournament. Fedorov downplays the idea that Vasiliev punished the Soviet teens—that's how he'd like to leave it. "Vasiliev blamed the players," Fedorov says. "That was the Soviet way if coaches were in trouble . . . blame the players, don't take any blame. That's how you save your job. That's what he did there. Maybe the story was that we didn't send a strong team—that we were rebuilding. That could have become the story during the tournament when we lost games. We went expecting to win. When we lost the first couple of games, that's when the coach says we're rebuilding. He was practising that. That's what he would have to say when he got back to Moscow."

Mogilny at first refuses to talk about Vasiliev. "I have no reason to say bad things about [Vasiliev] or anybody from that time," he says. "[Vasiliev and Gureev] were fine. It doesn't matter anymore. I don't have many memories of him."

Only after much urging is he more forthcoming, though more about the system than the coach himself. In fact, he goes out of his way not to name Vasiliev. "We were not even acknowledged as human beings," Mogilny says. "We were treated like animals—a bunch of horses. That's how it was for many years. We were brought out to play the game and when the game was over we were taken back, like horses to a barn. You shouldn't treat anyone that way, and of course we were unhappy. But it was the life we knew—the only life we knew."

Alexander Semak says that he doesn't doubt the rumours about Vasiliev in Piestany. "He was very controlling with us the year before in Hamilton," Semak says. "I cannot say exactly what he did in Piestany, but it sounds like the same things just taken one step more. But not everything can be blamed to the person—others are approving what he was doing. No one was working alone."

Robert Edelman suggests the reluctance to criticize individuals might not be a prevailing mindset among all those who had lived through the Soviet regime, or those who had prominent places in Soviet sport, but he wasn't surprised. "If that's what [Fedorov and Mogilny] said, you can report it and draw your own conclusions about human nature," Edelman says.

Dr. Catherine Classen describes the naming of names in a public forum as "the most difficult step" for victims of any sort of abuse—even more so for those who were children. It's hard to think of those at age seventeen or eighteen as children, but they should still be thought of as "vulnerable" at that age, according to Dr. Classen, a clinical psychologist specializing in treatment of survivors of abuse. Dr. Classen was given the bare bones of what has circulated about the Soviet juniors' "team-building by ordeal": depriving them of food and sleep, exhausting them, even humiliating them. "It's never easy to come forward with a story of abuse, but it wouldn't be as difficult to come forward [about an institution] as it would to name a perpetrator," Dr. Classen says. "There's a sense of shame that accompanies any reporting of abuse, but naming names [in public] would leave victims feeling most exposed. Often the perpetrators threatened their victims, and even as adults the victims can remain convinced that there will be bad consequences from reporting abuse. The perpetrators understand how to instill fear, and it can be very real for the victims years later."

Conclusions: Fedorov and Mogilny are reluctant to rehash a difficult time and find it difficult to determine what, if anything, Vasiliev did unilaterally. They could be taking a line like the Canadian players who don't want to talk about those who didn't fight—don't talk about it and it didn't happen. They could be sticking to what would be the code in Canadian hockey: what happens in the room stays in the room. They could be worried about how criticizing Vasiliev and others might play back home. And if you have nothing good to say about a dead system, maybe you don't say anything at all. Vasiliev still has friends back in Russia; no sense irritating them. Or Fedorov and Mogilny could be embarrassed by it. It would be hard for someone to come forward all these years later—after the game had been so good to him, bringing him championships and millions—and complain about being treated harshly as a teenager.

Robert Edelman has pored over thousands of pages of documents from the Soviet sports ministry and interviewed dozens of officials, coaches and athletes. He maintains that Soviet coaches in most sports were humane and didn't push their athletes to any physical or emotional brink—for instance, he believes that some Soviet soccer coaches were lax by comparison to others in Europe. But hockey's was a society apart from the other sports, with coaches following the lead of the oppressors behind the national team bench, Tarasov and Tikhonov. Edelman describes the hearsay about Vasiliev—the starving and sleep deprivation of his players—as "plausible." He says the two players could have easily denied the rumours if they weren't true. (More to the point, perhaps, they could have denied them even if they *were* true. "If you look at the words, nothing that [Fedorov and Mogilny say] directly contradicts that story about Vasiliev," Edelman says.

Vasiliev doesn't deny the stories so much as dismiss them as not worth discussing. Gureev doesn't fill in the blanks, either—not quite a denial so much as memory loss.

When Davydov left the bench and his teammates followed him, they were acting out of character—they were doing something that they had never done in hockey, something that they had never seen in their leagues, something they had never seen a Soviet team do before. Perhaps it would have been easier to explain a single player acting on an impulse of a personal sort. An individual aberration. Anything—death of a loved one, a girl breaking his heart, whatever—could account for it. But a collective response . . . on a scale like that. That suggests something that touched all of them.

Some secrets are revealed and some stories verified. This time, though, there can only be suspicions. Maybes. Maybe it comes down to the difference between an open society and a totalitarian one; the former is supposed to have no secrets, the latter protects them by default. Maybe players are more open and truthful sharing their stories with teammates than those who would put them on the page.

———

The members of the 1987 Canadian juniors don't hold back like the Russians—they name the names on their shit list. The ref who let the game spiral out of control—that's unanimous. The international officials who voted them out of the tournament, ripped medals right off their necks, denied them a chance at a gold—that's not going to go away, ever. Dennis McDonald—that's not quite unanimous, but Brendan Shanahan and Stephane Roy are two who think that McDonald didn't support the team the way he should have.

Absent from that list are the names on the Soviet roster. For the Canadian players, disappointment didn't turn into resentment or hatred of Russian players. The fight on the ice knocked some enlightenment into them. They were more broad-minded in the seasons after Piestany than they were before.

The Euros are there to be intimidated: the presumptions, stereotypes and slurs dated back to the Summit Series when Bobby Clarke "intimidated" Valeri Kharlamov with a bone-breaking slash. It gained momentum with the "Chicken Swede" labels attached to the Maple Leafs' Borje Salming and Inge Hammarstrom in the '70s.

Those who played in Piestany were ahead of their time compared to a lot of the rank-and-file NHLers. Those who had played the Soviets in the WJC—whether it was Piestany or Hamilton or Helsinki before that—had seen the future. The Soviets—and others—might be beaten, but they weren't there to be intimidated. As Inge Hammarstrom, the Flyers' scout who worked the 1987 WJC, points out: "If some Soviet players or European players could be intimidated, well, there are some North American players who play scared too. Players are just players—like they are everywhere."

"We thought what a lot of Canadian players thought . . . that you could intimidate the Soviets," Greg Hawgood says. "If you didn't back down, eventually they would back down. Well, they didn't back down in Piestany. We knew that we'd been in a fight. I knew that, for sure. And we came away thinking that these guys are tough and strong.

Sure, maybe some guys will back down—but you can say exactly the same thing about Canadian or American players. The best [of the Russians] weren't soft."

"I think that's true," Fedorov says. "Maybe the Canadian players thought we weren't tough. We were in that fight and we had no idea what to do. We could have been killed. Some of us took beatings. They didn't have to like us, but I think that they respected us."

There were still hard feelings at first when the Soviets arrived in the NHL. Mogilny lived through them. Veteran third- and fourth-liners weren't happy when Mogilny reported to the Sabres' camp. Here was a Soviet kid stealing jobs from red-blooded, gritty Canadians. Some froze him out in the room. Others challenged him on the ice. In his first camp, Mogilny dropped the gloves and showed that he wasn't going to be intimidated—as if someone who had brawled in Piestany, stood up to Soviet authorities and defected before he needed a razor could be rattled. (For his part, Mogilny says he doesn't remember fighting at his first training camp, though newspaper accounts of that camp, and Luce's recollections, confirm it.)

Then the journeymen realized Mogilny wasn't the enemy, any more than Pat LaFontaine was. Mogilny wasn't stealing a place on the lower half of the roster. He was stepping onto the first line. "They got it pretty quick," Don Luce says. "The guys who were threats to their paycheques were their friends who were playing beside them on the fourth line."

"The players who were best towards me were the best players," Mogilny says. "They had nothing to be threatened or jealous about. Pat LaFontaine [who arrived in a 1991 trade] was great towards me all the time. He saw that we had a chance to make each other better and to make the team better. Only very small people are small-minded."

For most of the Canadians who lost their shot at a medal in Piestany, resentment gave way to respect. Looking over at the Soviet bench was more like looking in the mirror than they had ever imagined. "We really thought that [the Soviets] reacted the way we would have," Glen Wesley says. "They ran out there to defend a teammate. They were brave in that way—that surprised a lot of us. They had no idea how to fight, but they showed up. They showed that they were more like us than we ever realized. That's what happened again when the Russian players started to come here."

In the Winnipeg Jets dressing room, Pat Elynuik sat across from Evgeni Davydov, who pulled the thread that eventually unravelled the Canadian juniors' hopes when he was the first to leave the Soviet bench. Elynuik didn't give it a second thought. "He didn't talk very much, but it never came up and I never asked him about it," Elyniuk says. "I don't blame him for it. That's not how I thought about it. He did what he had to do—maybe it was what he was told to do, maybe it was just something he did on his own. Either way, you can't really say that it was gutless or something like that."

Piestany was a watershed moment, a defining moment, but in the end, just a moment. The real proving grind came over the long run. The real acceptance was going to require more than 33 minutes and 53 seconds of hockey and one epic brawl. It was going to require more than Alexander Mogilny dropping the gloves with a veteran at the Sabres' training camp. It would be a day-by-day process and it would take the collective effort of Mogilny and the eight other Soviet players, all national-team veterans, all granted official release, who arrived with various NHL clubs in the fall of '89.

The hard feelings didn't subside quickly. Many, including some of their teammates, thought or even hoped that the Soviets' resolve might wear down under a shower of slashes and elbows and face-washes. In fairness, some did back down, but the real lessons were to be drawn from those who didn't.

Brendan Shanahan told *Sports Illustrated* back in 2000: "A lot of guys, mostly older players and a few fringe guys who felt their jobs were in jeopardy, were really anti-Russian . . . Growing up in Canada and the United States we'd been taught that Russians were the enemy. The 1980 US–USSR Olympic hockey game was more than a game, right? We couldn't understand them; they couldn't understand us. Now they were coming here and taking our jobs in this league?"

The grudges played out on the ice. It wasn't just the guys in the other sweaters.

Shanahan saw it when he broke into the league with New Jersey. Slava Fetisov came over and joined the Devils. Shanahan saw his teammates freeze Fetisov out.

"It wasn't overt," he said. "Maybe it would take a player to spot it. Cold shoulders in the dressing room were the least of it. No, the real freeze-out happened on the ice. It wasn't just the opponents who were looking to beat Fetisov—no, his own teammates were hoping he'd fail. If Fetisov made a mistake, no one else would be covering up for him. Hockey's a game of messages—one team sending a message to another that it won't be intimidated, a coach sending a message to players that less than total effort is unacceptable. Teams are built around every player sending the message to his teammates that he has their backs."

That wasn't the message sent to Fetisov, though. The message to him was, Not only don't we have your back, but watch who you turn your back on in your own dressing room.

Glen Wesley didn't check a player's name or passport when it came to his teammates. Again, as it was with Mogilny's experience in Buffalo, a first-liner warmed up to a Soviet teammate more quickly than a guy who might end up as a Black Ace during a workout, who was a coach's whim away from watching games from the press box.

Wesley didn't see the Russian players' arrival as an a regrettable development—he believed it was a *necessary* one. "Maybe some guys were angry about them taking jobs from Canadian and American players, but the fact is they made the game better," Wesley says. "Whether we liked it or not, the NHL was bigger and it needed more talent and skill or the game was going to suffer. [The Russians] turned out to be like the rest of us—no different. The ones who were ready and willing to contribute were accepted. There were some good guys and some who weren't so good—just like players from anywhere else."

Just as it would be unfair to believe that all Soviets could be intimidated, so too would it be misguided to believe that everyone in the NHL, players and executives, could be enlightened. The notion persisted remarkably, the notion that the players from the former Soviet Union could be intimidated. Long after '72 or the Challenge Cup or Piestany or the Soviets' arrival in '89. It persisted, maybe less broadly and certainly in the face of a lot of evidence that should have put it to rest. Plumbing its psychological foundation is an imprecise and speculative science. Freud's "narcissism of minor difference" would seem to apply. The theory (through a hockey filter): aggressive tendencies can be satisfied and the teams bound together so long as there is someone left to goon. Some NHLers would always see what they wanted to see. They would define their courage by the other guy's cowardice. They would see Mogilny and others as Soviets rather than just other hockey players.

Looking back, Fedorov has a sanguine outlook, in part, he admits, because others did some ice-breaking before he joined the Detroit Red Wings in 1990. "I don't think that there was much anger or hard feelings about that game or my being Russian," Fedorov says. "I was even a bit surprised how I was accepted—other Russian players, too."

Pavel Kostichkin says it went beyond his teammates' acceptance. He says he owes his "survival" to friends he made when he first came to North America. Kostichkin and his wife had never travelled together outside of the USSR. "We spoke only two words of English, yes and no," Kostichkin says. "I was worried about going to the minors, that maybe teammates and people wouldn't be friendly. They were very good to us . . . very supportive. We did not know how to live—how to go to the bank, where to go. We would not have eaten if my teammates did not help us with everything. It was so important for us and I thank them for that."

Mogilny is pessimistic by comparison, which might trace back either to his lifelong outsider status or a tougher, less supportive initiation into the NHL. "If you are Russian when you come here, you are always Russian," he says. "You can be accepted as a player on a team, but you cannot ever be thought of as anything other than a Russian. You can't make yourself into a Canadian or an American. Others won't let you. You can't be a Russian-Canadian or a Russian-American. My children are born here. I make my home here. I'll live the rest of my life here. I've spent most of my [adult life] here. But I've accepted that . . . some type of prejudice . . . some way that people will always look at you. I didn't have much choice."

PART III

WHEN THE LIGHTS DIM:
Fond Memories and a Few Regrets
Twenty Years Later

"SHOW me the child at age seven
and I'll show you a man."

—A Jesuit Maxim

Their Primes and After-lives

There is no history of the Canada–Soviet Union game in the IIHF record books. The federation saved no documents such as the official scoring (so there is no record of shots on goal) or Hans Rønning's report (so there's no shaky penmanship). There is no history of the game, but there's no imagining hockey history without it.

Before the lights went out, the WJC had a niche audience. That Jim Cressman covered the event was a tribute to his enthusiasm for junior hockey; that he was the only member of the print media to attend was a better indicator of the broad public interest in the event. When the tournament was held in Hamilton the year before—and it was cheap and easy to staff—Canadian newspapers had no issue with dedicating coverage to the WJC. Going to Czechoslovakia—even though hotel accommodation could have been had for flophouse rates—was a price that newspapers balked at.

When the lights came back on, the WJC entered another realm. The next year the major Canadian newspapers staffed the tournament in Moscow, and it has gathered momentum ever since. The WJC would be a very different tournament if the IIHF record book were to be believed, if Piestany had really never happened. Without Piestany the WJC might still have become a fixture on the calendar for hockey fans, but it wouldn't have reached the high-profile status so quickly. It gathered even bigger audiences through the seven Canadian championships in eight seasons during the '90s. TSN's largest audience ratings ever were recorded when Canada and Russia played in the final of the 1999 WJC in Winnipeg. Interest reached something approaching critical mass during the NHL's lockout season. With the Canadian team featuring junior phenom Sidney Crosby and with NHL rinks dark, more than 100 journalists, a decent-sized horde at a Stanley Cup, made their way to Grand Forks, North Dakota. Canada ran through the tournament without any significant challenge, evoking the Soviet powerhouses of the first WJCs—never threatened, never relenting.

The video record of the Piestany game can be replayed with the push of a button. It's just as easy to prompt the players to imagine outcomes. To a one, they've thought about the what-ifs. And they've been asked about the what-ifs before. Just as some of them seem more practised in the telling and retelling of old war stories, so too do some seem to offer up more detailed sketches of what might have been. Their speculations say something about Piestany, probably a lot more about themselves.

Some envision everything, as Steve Chiasson said, "falling into place" once more. "There is no doubt in my mind that we were going to win that game by five goals, maybe more," Brendan Shanahan says. "We were pulling away from them. It was all going our way. We had so much momentum. We were playing better and better as the tournament went on."

"We were winning that game and we were going to win it by a lot," Everett Sanipass says. "We knew it and, what's more the Russians knew it. That's why they did what they did."

Others are more cautious in their enthusiasm. "I think we probably would have won," Theoren Fleury says. "But honestly, five goals is an awful lot to win by. I don't know that we would have done it. We would have done enough to get the silver. We probably would have needed the Russian goaltender to be pretty bad to get up by five goals."

"I'd like to think that we were going to win," Dave McLlwain says. "It's easy now to say that we were going to win and win the gold medal. But a lot of things that we didn't expect happened just to get us in position to play for a gold medal."

The one member of the Canadian team who has watched more WJC tournaments than any other—and watched them with a professional's scrutiny—doesn't argue with those who say that Canada was going to rout the Soviets. He does, however, splash cold water on those who would talk this team into greatness. "Compared to the other teams that won [the WJC], we weren't great," Shawn Simpson says. "Let's face it. We were a pretty ordinary [national junior] team. It wasn't a great tournament. We were very lucky to be where we were, and Jimmy Waite deserves more credit than anyone."

Mogilny and Fedorov don't have strong opinions about the hypothetical outcome of the game. It's just foggy history. "It was a game, like other games," Fedorov says. "Anything can happen . . . but our goaltender wasn't very good and the Canadian goaltender was." Fedorov was even more emphatic on that count when advised that the Canadian goaltender in Piestany, Jimmy Waite, was the netminder who stoned the Soviets the next year in Moscow.

One who does have a strong opinion about the game is Hans Rønning. He sees the ice tilting the other way. "I think the Soviets might have won the game if it had finished," he says. "I think they were coming on." (Rønning's interpretation of history might again be self-serving. If the Soviets were en route to a victory, then his lapses would have had no impact on the tournament's gold medal.)

———

Projections are harmless amusements. There's little to learn from them. Walk into any sports bar and you'll hear dozens of similar exercises in fantasy—what would happen if the '27 Yankees played the '75 Reds, if the Canadiens of the '50s played the Canadiens of the '70s. The only difference with projecting Piestany is that the imagining involves two teams that *did* meet. What did happen matters most.

Those who want to write drama or tragedy would claim that the events of Piestany shaped the lives of those who played there and those who were otherwise connected to the unfinished game. That's overstepping. Hyperbole might make a better story, but it's simply not the case.

Whatever these players and coaches were destined to become was in large part determined by the time they arrived in Piestany. In fairness, the players were at the mercy of events far bigger than the games they played. The Soviet juniors had only vague hope of playing in North America, the Canadian juniors had no idea that NHL salaries were going to explode and that some among them would earn tens of millions of dollars in their careers. But these matters of circumstance and fortunes—the stuff of character was die already cast.

Whether the game was halted at 13:53 of the second period or played through to sixty minutes, whether medals, gold, silver or bronze were draped around their necks or not, it was easy to look at the teenagers and project the players and men that they'd become. Circumstances change but the character tends to stay constant.

DAVE McLLWAIN

Ninth-round pick of the Pittsburgh Penguins in 1986, 501 NHL games with Pittsburgh, Winnipeg, the New York Islanders, Buffalo, Toronto and Ottawa. Best NHL season: 25 goals and 26 assists in 81 games for Winnipeg in 1989–90. Also played for the Muskegon Lumberjacks and the Cleveland Lumberjacks in the IHL, Bern in the Swiss league, Landshut EV and, for the last six seasons, the Cologne Sharks in the German league.

It has always been serendipity for Dave McLlwain. Even at nineteen, he had extended his career longer than he imagined it would last. When he played Junior D in Seaforth, he hadn't imagined that the game would take him east of London or west of Sarnia. He hadn't thought about major junior, he hadn't thought about the WJC and he hadn't thought about the NHL draft. He just kept landing on his skates, one happy accident after another. Serendipity fell short of pantheon, the Hall of Fame, All-Star Games or the Stanley Cup. But McLlwain had a respectable NHL career on the strength of two qualities: great skating and get-along good nature. In that game against the Soviets in Piestany, and wherever else he played, McLlwain was one of the fastest skaters, usually the fastest. That made him a great penalty killer. In one season, he scored ten short-handed goals, a Winnipeg Jets team record. Always a team guy, well liked by players, coaches and media. He didn't have great hands and thus was never a great scorer, but at thirty-eight he's still landing on his skates, still earning a living in the German elite league.

"As long as I can skate, I can play," says McLlwain, who racked up more points in Cologne last year, 64 in 51 games, than he had in any previous season there. "I still enjoy the game. I'll play as long as I can. Most players have that attitude, I think. They want to keep on playing and get the most that they can out of the game. If that means going to the minors, they'll do it. If it means going to Europe—well, some situations over here can be really good."

In Piestany, McLlwain seemed to not only play the game but moreover *glory* in it. Some played with desperation and seemed the likeliest to burn out. Others weren't completely invested in the game and seemed the likeliest to drop out. And then a few, McLlwain among them, seemed to enjoy the game on the ice and all that went with it. "Maybe it's not having high expectations or pressure when he was young [that] really allowed him to love the game rather than just play it," Jack McLlwain says of his son.

McLlwain has been reminded of Piestany whenever and wherever he has played. He played in the NHL with Pat Elyniuk and Kerry Huffman, among other Canadian junior alums, and played for Pat Burns in Toronto. He even sat across from Evgeni Davydov in the Winnipeg Jets dressing room. In the German elite league last winter, he met up with Jimmy Waite. "Maybe Piestany comes up every so often. I don't have any big regrets, no hard feelings. It ended up being good for my career—an opportunity I'd never thought I'd get—and I've probably laughed a lot more about it than I ever worried about it."

DAVE LATTA

First-round draft pick of the Quebec Nordiques in 1985. Played one game for the Nordiques in 1986 (no points), ten games in 1987–88 (no points) and 24 games in 1988–89 (4 goals, 8 assists). Played professional for nine more seasons, but never returned to the NHL. Played for the Fredericton Express, the Halifax Citadels, the Canadian national team, the New Haven Nighthawks, the Cincinnati Cyclones, the Manheim Eagles, Bad Toelz EC, the Augsburg Panthers, Peiting EC, the Manchester Storm and finally the Anchorage Aces in the West Coast Hockey League. In his last season, Latta scored 10 goals and 13 assists in 48 games. According to his ex-Kitchener teammate Dave McLlwain, Latta moved back to his hometown, Thunder Bay, after retiring from professional hockey. The NHLPA alumni association did not have a number for him.

GREG HAWGOOD

Drafted in the tenth round by the Boston Bruins in 1986. Played for Boston, Edmonton, Philadelphia, Florida, Pittsburgh, San Jose, Vancouver and, finally, Dallas (two games) in 2001–2002. Also played for the Maine Mariners, the Cape Breton Oilers, the Cleveland Lumberjacks, the Las Vegas Thunder, the Houston Aeros, the Kansas City Blades, the Utah Grizzlies, the Chicago Wolves, Asiago in the Italian league and last season for Tappara Tampere and TPS Turku in the Finnish league. Nineteen professional teams since leaving the Kamloops Blazers. Named the best defenceman in the American Hockey League with Cape Breton and in the International Hockey League with Las Vegas. NHL totals: 60 goals and 164 assists in 474 regular-season games, 2 goals and 8 assists in 42 playoff games.

It looked as if Greg Hawgood would have a long, distinguished NHL career—at least it looked that way in his two trips to the WJC. "Here's a guy who was named the best defenceman at a world junior championship," Theoren Fleury says. "That should be good for a ten- or fifteen-year career in the NHL . . . and when you look at the game he played, the way he handled the puck, the way he could move it around, it was even more reason to think that. He had the type of skill you don't lose when you get older."

Yet Hawgood's struggle at the next level could have been predicted. He was a tenth-round draft pick for a reason: he was considered too short. "A great player in a small package," Dave Draper says. With another two or three inches of height, he might have been a first-rounder—then again, with those two or three inches, maybe Vladimir Konstantinov's head-butt wouldn't have broken Hawgood's nose. The latter hypothetical is as immaterial as the first. Stripped down, what-if becomes as-if. Hawgood was then what he was later: a useful player who was working against physical limits. He would be on the fringes of the NHL for more than a decade. He toured around the minors, spending whole seasons in the American Hockey League, the type of seen-it-all veteran who'd serve as mentor to younger and, yes, bigger prospects. Twenty years after Piestany he signed his first contract with a European club, an elite-league team in Finland, where teams almost inevitably have a smaller, skilled defenceman or two to handle the puck on the big ice surface.

"The Finnish league really suits my game," Hawgood says. "I wanted to go as far as I could for as long as I could in North America before trying Europe, but I've enjoyed my time in Finland. It's hard to leave my family behind in Chicago for months at a time. I was able to come back over the Olympic break this year for a couple of weeks. But it's an opportunity to play and make some decent money. For an older player it's a better living and less of a grind than the minors."

KERRY HUFFMAN

Drafted in the first round, twentieth overall, by the Philadelphia Flyers in 1986. Played for Philadelphia, Quebec and Ottawa in the NHL. Also played with the Hershey Bears, the Las Vegas Thunder and the Grand Rapids Griffins in 1997–99. NHL totals: 37 goals and 108 assists in 401 regular-season games, no points in 11 playoff games.

Huffman went to Piestany on the blue line for the Canadian team at the world championship tournament in the early '90s. "You want to do the right thing for your country, but that hotel we stayed at [in Nitra] had me thinking twice about going over for the worlds." Currently a mortgage broker in the New Jersey area.

PAT ELYNUIK
Drafted in the first round, eighth overall, by the Winnipeg Jets in 1986. Played for Winnipeg, Washington, Tampa Bay and Ottawa. Also played for the Moncton Hawks, the Fort Wayne Komets and the Michigan K-Wings. Last active with the K-Wings in the 1996–97 season, 1 goal in 4 play-off games. Best NHL season: 32 goals and 42 assists in 80 games with Winnipeg in 1989–90. NHL totals: 154 goals in 506 games.

Pat Burns had trouble remembering the name of "the winger from out west." He struggled and eventually mentioned a journeyman of about the same time. "It was Nelson Emerson that played with Dave McLlwain, right?" No, I told him, Pat Elynuik. "He was supposed to have been a big star, but never really made it," Burns said.

Pat Elynuik works in real estate and development in Alberta.

SERGEI SHESTERIKOV
Not drafted. Played in Russia for Gorky Torpedo, Nizhny Novgorod Torpedo and Yaroslavl Torpedo. Last active with Yaroslavl in 1996, failing to record a point in ten games. Best season: 15 goals in 44 games with Nizhny. No other season with more than 10 goals.

ALEXANDER KERCH
Drafted in the third round in 1993, sixtieth overall, by the Edmonton Oilers. Played five games with Edmonton with no goals or assists in 1993–94. Played in 57 games for the Cape Breton Oilers that season, scoring 24 goals and 38 assists in 57 games. Played one regular-season game with the Providence Bruins the next season, recording no points and 15 penalty minutes, and then 4 playoff

games, recording 2 assists. Played in Russia for Dynamo Riga, Riga Paradaugava, and St. Petersburg SKA. Played one season in Finland with Tappara Tampere. Played five seasons in Germany with first-division teams Landsberg EV, Revier Lions and Berlin Capitals. Most recently, Kerch played for Latvia at the 2006 World Championships.

PAVEL KOSTICHKIN

Drafted in the tenth round, 199th overall by Winnipeg in 1988. Played seven seasons for Red Army before joining the Moncton Hawks in the American Hockey League in 1992–93. Scored 16 goals and 18 assists in 65 games in only North American season. Played in the Danish league for eight seasons and in the Finnish league with Espoo for one season. Returned to Russia to play for Krylia and Khimik. Last active with HK Gomel in Belarussian league in 2004–05. Kostichkin played with Evgeni Davydov on Red Army teams that toured North America and played on NHL teams in the early '90s. He did not play for Soviet or Russian teams that went to the world championships and Olympic Games.

Kostichkin believes he could have played in the NHL, but blames only himself for not making it out of the AHL. "I can admit now that I made a mistake," Kostichkin says. "I had an invitation to go to the Chicago [Blackhawks] training camp, but I hurt my knee in Moncton and had surgery. I decided not to go Chicago—I didn't think I was physically ready. I thought I needed a season to get strong again and have my knee heal. So I went to Denmark. That was my mistake. I found out it's hard to come back to the top level when you've played in an easier league. You can't take a season off and start again where you were. Once I went to Europe, I could not go back to North America."

Piestany made a celebrity of Kostichkin briefly. Not in Russia and not in Canada, but during the season he played in Finland. "They had me on Finnish television to talk about the fight," Kostichkin says. "They said I started the fight and got the teams disqualified so I won the gold medal for Finland. It was very funny. I don't think I really started it but for the Finns it was a happy thing so I agreed."

Kostichkin retired from Russian elite league hockey a couple of years ago, and today coaches midget and junior teams in Moscow. "What I learned from the world juniors and my career I try to teach my players," Kostichkin says. "To be a good teammate, to play hard and to do everything you can with the chances that come."

Kostichkin lives in Moscow.

SCOTT METCALFE

Drafted in the first round, twentieth overall by the Edmonton Oilers in 1985. Played for Edmonton (two games) before being traded to Buffalo. Played for the Nova Scotia Oilers, the Rochester Americans, the Knoxville Cherokees, German league teams Duisberg, Weisswasser, the Hanover Scorpions and the Berlin Polar Bears, the Sheffield Steelers (British league) and the Adirondack Ice Hawks (United Hockey League). Last active: Adirondack 2001–02 (three games). Best professional season: 32 goals, 38 assists and 205 penalty minutes in 80 games with Rochester in 1996–97. Rochester Americans' all-time leader in penalty minutes with 1,424 PIM. NHL totals: 1 goal and 2 assists in 19 games.

"I know I'd feel worse about Piestany if I hadn't won a Calder Cup in Rochester in '96," Metcalfe says. "You just want to get a chance to win something once in your career. Fans think it's about money, but winning is always there—that's why guys can play so hard in the playoffs when they're making less money than during the season. I didn't win in junior, and after Piestany I didn't think about having to win. But by the time I played a few years and I was in the AHL, all of a sudden I was thinking, 'Wait . . . when do I get a chance to win?' I remember we were in the final against Portland that year, seventh game in Rochester and maybe people didn't believe that I was as excited—and nervous—as I seemed. When you're twenty-eight, twenty-nine years old, a veteran, y'know, people expect you to be 'professional' about things. Well, I was like a teenager—I was shaking. That seventh game was tied one-all in the third period. We had Steve Shields in goal and Portland had Ron Tugnutt, who was standing on his head. I was trying not to think any negative thoughts. When we won I just felt this huge sense of relief. If Piestany had been the one time I had a chance to win and it had been taken away from me, I would have been pretty sour about it."

Metcalfe scored 6 goals and 8 assists in 19 games in the Americans' Calder Cup post-season. He and his wife and children live in Rochester.

ANDREI SMIRNOV

Not drafted. Played for Krylia Sovetov, Kalinin, Voronezh Buran, Red Army (one season), Tolyatti Lada, Cerepovets Metallurg, Elektrostal Kristall, Nizhny Novogorod Torpedo and Moscow Spartak. Most penalty minutes in a season: 97 with Spartak in 1997–98. Last active: Krylia in 1999.

"Andrei was a good friend," Pavel Kostichkin says. "He was a good player. Today he'd be in the NHL. But he was a defenceman who did not score—a very safe player, consistent and strong, but not a powerplay defenceman. Fifteen years ago you had to be a top-two defenceman to go to the NHL, and Andrei was not that type of player. He was a very good Russian elite league player.

"One day five or six years ago, Andrei was changing a tire on the highway and he was hit by another car. He died right away. He was the first player on one of my teams who had died. It was a very sad day for many of us. They had a ceremony [a moment of silence] at Elite league games after that. He was the type of player who would still be playing today [if not for the accident], someone who could play until he was forty."

Who ganged up with Smirnov in the assault on Stephane Roy? Why did they beat Roy so viciously? The answers died with Andrei Smirnov on the soft shoulder of a highway outside of Moscow.

DMITRI TSYGUROV

Not drafted for the NHL. Played in Kazan and Sverdlovsk in Russia. Last active with Amrbi-Piotta in the Swiss league in 1997.

STEPHANE ROY

Drafted in the third round in 1985 by the Minnesota North Stars. Played for Minnesota, the Kalamazoo Wings, the Halifax Citadels, Olten (Swiss league), the Memphis RiverKings, the Anchorage Aces, the Quebec Aces, the Macon Whoopee, the Abilene Aviators, Point Rouge Grand Portneuf and Riviere-du-Loup Promutuel. Last active: Riviere-du-Loup in 2001–02. NHL totals: one goal in 12 games.

In his three seasons with the Canadian national team, Roy never had a chance to play against Andrei Smirnov, one of two players who double-teamed him in Piestany. Smirnov did not play for Soviet or Russian national teams. Roy is currently a businessman in Quebec City.

LUKE RICHARDSON

Drafted in the first round, seventh overall by the Toronto Maple Leafs in 1987. Played for Toronto, Edmonton, Philadelphia and Columbus. NHL totals: 33 goals and 156 assists in 1,312 games, no goals and 8 assists in 69 playoff games.

Richardson made more of a splash on the ice in Piestany during the bench-clearing brawl than he did in the 34 minutes of play leading up to it. Richardson looked like he might develop into a player. He looked like he was carved out of marble, a big physical specimen. But he spent a lot of his career, if not most of it, as a fifth or sixth D. No help on the power play. A stay-at-home defenceman not long on mobility, but more than capable of meting out justice. The Toronto Maple Leafs acquired him in a misbegotten and ultimately thwarted push for the 2006 playoffs.

Luke Richardson signed with the Tampa Bay Lightning for the 2006-07 season.

CHRIS JOSEPH

Drafted in the first round, fifth overall by the Pittsburgh Penguins in 1987. Played for Pittsburgh, Edmonton, Tampa Bay, Vancouver, Philadelphia, Phoenix and Atlanta. Also played for the Nova Scotia Oilers, the Cape Breton Oilers, the Philadelphia Phantoms, the Cincinnati Cyclones, TPS Turku (Finnish league), the Mannheim Eagles (German league) and Milan (Italian league). Last active: Milan in 2006. NHL totals: 39 goals and 112 assists in 151 games, 3 goals and 4 assists in 31 playoff games.

YVON CORRIVEAU

Drafted in the first round, nineteenth overall, by the Washington Capitals in 1985. Played for Washington, San Jose and Hartford. Also played for the Binghampton Whalers, the Baltimore Skipjacks, the Springfield Indians, the Minnesota Moose, the Detroit Vipers, the Berlin Polar Bears, the Berlin Capitals and Berlin Preussen SC (German league). Last active: Berlin Preussen SC in 2005. Best NHL season: 12 goals in 38 games with Hartford in 1991–92. NHL totals: 48 goals and 40 assists in 280 games, 5 goals and 7 assists in 29 playoff games.

The Washington Capitals had a number on file for Corriveau, but it was out of service. A public-relations staffer with the Caps said that he believed Corriveau was living in Conneticut.

VALERI IVANNIKOV

Not drafted. Played for Chelyabinsk Traktor, Central Red Army (two games in 1988), Lenigrad Red Army and St. Petersburg. Last active with St. Petersburg in 2003.

JIMMY WAITE

Drafted in the first round, eighth overall, by the Chicago Blackhawks in 1987. Played for Chicago, San Jose and Phoenix. Also played for the Saginaw Hawks, the Indianapolis Ice, the Hershey Bears, the Springfield Falcons, the Utah Grizzlies, the St. John's Maple Leafs, the Essen Mosquitoes, Iserlohn Roosters and Inglostadt ERC (German league). Last active: Inglostadt in 2006. Best NHL season: .913 save percentage in 17 games with Phoenix in 1997–98. Last NHL season: Phoenix in 1998–99. NHL totals: 28 wins, 34 losses and 11 ties with 4 shutouts in 106 games.

Jimmy Waite was the least talked-about of any of the players in the Canadian lineup before the 1987 WJC. The seventeen-year-old goaltender was supposed to have been just along for the ride, the backup to Shawn Simpson. Of five goaltenders who vied for positions on the Canadian under-20 team, Waite was the longest of longshots. Waite ended up as the player the team rode into contention for the gold medal. Based on his performance at the 1987 WJC, NHL scouts thought he looked like the game's next great goaltender, another Patrick Roy. The Blackhawks saw enough to break with NHL orthodoxy and select him in the first round, eighth overall. "He was a can't-miss goaltender," Sherry Bassin says. "The thing is, he missed. I still wonder how."

Waite doesn't wonder. He says he didn't appreciate how few opportunities a player gets to prove himself. If he had, he would have been more worried about his first trips to Chicago's training camps.

"I was in the worst possible place at the worst possible time," he says. "When I was in Chicago, the Blackhawks had Ed Belfour breaking in. The guy trying to beat him out was Dominik Hasek. Two Hall of Famers. That was 'all' that was between me and the starter's job. A year in the minors and then two and pretty soon people either forgot about me or just thought I was a career backup. Now I know that window doesn't open wide, and doesn't stay open long. I'm not the only guy with that story. That's just hockey."

It seems like the 1987 WJC revealed something about Waite that was never again tapped, not by the Hawks, not by the other teams that gave him a look. But consider how different things were for Waite by the time he arrived in Chicago. At seventeen, he had an opportunity presented to him when nothing had been expected of him, when even he didn't think he would play. By the time he reported to the Blackhawks he was expected to play, to start, to become one of the best goaltenders in the game. To step in when someone steps aside is one thing; to beat out someone (in Waite's case, two emerging Hall of Famers) was another thing entirely.

"Would things have turned out differently for me if I had been an undrafted free agent like Ed Belfour was?" Waite says. "Maybe. For sure I wouldn't have signed with Chicago. I played my best when I was proving myself at the world juniors. But I started to think that my problem wasn't performance when I started out in Chicago—I think I played well enough to play for almost anybody . . . or at least anyone else."

ALEXANDER GALCHENIUK
Undrafted. Played for Minsk Dynamo, Moscow Dynamo, the Milwaukee Admirals (1992–94), the Berlin Polar Bears

(German league), the Madison Monsters (1995–97), the Michigan K-Wings (1996–98), with Pat Elynuik the first season), Milan Saima, Omsk Avangard, Asiago HC (Italian league), Sierre (2001–2002 Swiss league), Milan (Italian league) and St. Petersburg SKA (with Alexander Kerch, Valeri Ivannikov and former Calder Trophy winner Sergei Makarov). Last active: St. Petersburg in 2002–2003. Also played roller hockey for the Philadelphia Bulldogs in 1994.

DMITRI MEDVEDEV
Undrafted. Minsk Dynamo in 1984–90.

IGOR MONAENKOV
Undrafted. Played for Vladimir Vasiliev with Khimik for ten years. Last reported to be playing with Metallurg Serov in 2000.

VADIM MUSATOV
Undrafted. Played for Elektrostal Kristall. Last reported to be playing with Elektrostal in 2000. No significant international experience after the 1987 WJC.

SERGEI OSIPOV
Undrafted. Played for Sverdlovsk Automobilist, Red Army (scored 7 goals in 43 games over two seasons), the Atlanta Knights (6 games in 1992) and Magnitogorsk Metallurg. Last reported to be playing with Magnitogorsk in 2004 (twelfth season with the club).

VALERI POPOV
Undrafted. Played four seasons with Chelyabinsk Traktor (6 goals in 57 games).

ANTON ZAGORODNY
Undrafted. Played three seasons with Saratov Kristall and two seasons with Svedlovsk. Scored 29 goals in five seasons.

January 1987 looked like the worst time to skate onto the scene as a top Soviet hockey prospect. If an NHL team had been able to land one of the Soviets at that moment, it would have risked a public-relations disaster. Fact is, though, most NHL teams were far more concerned with talent than politics (though Harold Ballard's Maple Leafs would have been an exception).

Relations with Canada weren't exactly "diplomatic" or "normalized" when the Soviet Hammer and Sickle was lowered and the Russian tri-colour was raised. The Russian elite leagues resented the NHL for raiding its best young talent, disputed or maybe even extorted transfer fees and tried to bind players with laughably unfair contracts. But soon after Piestany, and certainly by the fall of 1989, when the first significant wave of Russian talent washed up on North American shores, the relationship was transformed— metaphors for war were out, metaphors for commerce were in. A war zone was turned into a marketplace. Political ideology was not as important as supply and demand. The Russians had talent the NHL needed. Therefore, the NHL had millions to spread between the players, their Russian league teams and the national federation. Previously there had been a lot of chest-thumping about who was best and who was right; by the '90s, the noise you heard was largely negotiation over prices.

Several of the players from that '87 Soviet junior team were objects caught in the haggling. But many of the other Soviet juniors weren't good enough. Some of them weren't good enough to stick around in their home leagues.

"The Soviet talent pool was like the Canadian one," Igor Kuperman says. "The only difference is that the bottom third of the Canadian roster would be given every chance to succeed by NHL teams who had signed contracts. They would have to prove they weren't players before teams gave up and cut their losses. The bottom third of the Soviet roster were probably players no better, no worse, but they only had one chance. If they didn't prove they were players very fast, they would be lucky to land a job in the [national] elite league."

BERT TEMPLETON
Second in the Canadian major junior ranks in career wins.

NORTH BAY
Sandy Templeton doesn't have a scrapbook to show visitors, nothing that offers a clear, complete, chronological look at her late husband's hockey career. She has some souvenirs, some clippings, some photographs, not organized, stuff from uncertain sources, stuff that can't be organized without him. "It was something that we always put off," she says. "After a while we just said it was something we were going to get around to after we got back to North Bay . . . when his career was over. But Bert never had a chance."

Bert Templeton's final souvenirs were gathered over three seasons with the Sudbury Wolves. Sudbury seemed like a good place for him to land at the end of his career. A classic junior-hockey town, Sudbury had a history of turning out players, an old barn where all kinds of pro stars have skated, a fan base where Inco workers and miners shoot the breeze in standing room. The Wolves are the only show in town. They matter. Bert Templeton wouldn't have fit if he had landed in one of the big cities.

Burt Templeton saw what might have been while he was in Sudbury. He had seen the outpouring of affection and the spotlight shining when Brian Kilrea, coach of the Ottawa 67's, won his one-thousandth game. Kilrea's landmark win came over Templeton's Wolves in what turned out to be the last game these men coached against each other. Kilrea gets inducted into the Hockey Hall of Fame. As Red Buttons used to say, Templeton "didn't even get a dinner" for all those wins with lesser talent.

And it didn't matter. Bert Templeton had done it long enough and well enough not to be wrapped up in talk about "legacy" and "history." There was a reason the scrapbook was never organized. He coached—that's what he did, and Sudbury fit. It was his comfort zone. "It was coming home for Bert," Sandy Templeton says. "I think he would have liked to stayed on in Sudbury and coached for at least another five years, maybe more."

A good fit went bad in three seasons. The team fired Templeton in 2002 after a Sudbury player claimed Templeton had physically assaulted him. That might have been the old way (or even Viktor Tikhonov's way), but it wasn't going to fly in 2002. Not when junior hockey was competing with U.S. colleges for talent. Not when junior hockey was trying to forge a progressive image. Not when teams were worried about matters of legal liability. Not when coaches were at the mercy of agents. Jim Cressman notes, correctly, that Templeton "changed with the times," even as far back as Piestany. But somewhere along the way the coach had reached a point where he could change no more—and the game kept right on changing without him. He was a good coach, maybe a great coach, in his time, but that time had passed. He had made concessions to the times, but never mellowed with them.

It was never easy for Bert Templeton, and his involuntary retirement was like the rest of his life. Controversy stalked him to his death-bed. In the eighteen months he had left, he was embroiled in a court battle with the Wolves, who fought him over money and benefits owed on the last year of his contract. The Wolves managed to make Templeton a more sympathetic figure outside of hockey than he had ever been inside it. The team contended that it shouldn't be completely on the hook for salary and medical benefits because Templeton wasn't doing enough to find another job, even though he had been diagnosed with advanced renal cancer. The parties reached on out-of-court settlement.

"I called him in the summer before he died," Dave McLlwain says. "Just before I went off to Europe to play. I felt like I owed him and I wanted to thank him. I don't know if I would have had a career without him. I'm playing twenty years later, and it was because he believed in me and gave me a chance. He was a tough guy and a tough coach but I think he really cared about his players, more than most of them and everyone else ever knew."

"I stayed in touch with him right up to the last few weeks," Pat Burns says. "I told him that I learned stuff from him. Not technical stuff—motivating stuff I used the rest of my career. He fought right to the end."

Bert Templeton died in December 2003. It wouldn't be accurate to say that he had died peacefully. He broke his back in a fall and was paralyzed from the waist down.

The team he had coached all those years was gone by the time he made it back to North Bay. The franchise had been Templeton's as much as it was North Bay's. "Bert made the North Bay franchise," Centennials' play-by-play man Pete Handley says. By the time Templeton made it back to North Bay, others had unmade the franchise. The team always struggled to make ends meet, and it lost money after Bert Templeton moved on. The team was sold and moved to Saginaw, Michigan, after the 2002 season. It was probably a good thing for Bert Templeton. He loved hockey, and he loved North Bay and wanted the best for the town. It tore him up not to be coaching, and it would have torn him up if a team had been playing in town, if players had been sitting on the bench that he used to stand behind. All the hockey he could stand was the stuff from better days: the scattered clippings, some photographs not yet placed in an album, phone calls from players like Dave McLlwain, games on television.

Sandy Templeton is a religious woman. On her phone message, she tells callers to "have a blessed day." There are more symbols of faith than hockey trophies around her house. Her late husband's absence is marked by his presence in photos with her, not by team photos. She keeps in a closet one souvenir that reveals something about her husband: the navy jacket he wore in Piestany, when the lights went out. The jacket is ripped at the sleeve and the seam in the back.

"He ripped it fighting to keep the players back," she says.

PAT BURNS

Five hundred, forty-three wins with Montreal, Toronto, Boston and New Jersey. Burns also has won three Jack Adams Awards as NHL coach of the year.

The summer after Piestany, Burns was hired by the Montreal Canadiens to coach their American Hockey League affiliate in Sherbrooke. "I wasn't worried about that fight having any effect on my coaching career," Burns says. "I don't know what other people might have thought about it, but hockey people knew what happened and that we were powerless to stop [the fight] from happening."

Pat Burns coached the New Jersey Devils to a Stanley Cup victory in 2003. In the spring of 2004, he stepped down from the Devils' bench to undergo treatment for cancer. Two years later, Burns was cautiously optimistic about returning to the NHL: "The cancer is in remission and I'm feeling better than I have in a long time."

VLADIMIR VASILIEV

He's a hard man to chase down. He spends most of his days in retirement out at his *dacha*. He returns to Moscow only occasionally. He's enjoying retirement more than Bert Templeton ever did. He remains the outrageous character who chewed out reporters in Hamilton.

The title of Tarasov's memoirs is *Road to Olympus*.

These are different times. Vasiliev's book is titled *Play Hockey and Make a Million Dollars*. It sounds like a book that might be sold on a late-night infomercial, but Vasiliev says it's an account of his hockey life: playing the game for the Soviet Wings, learning the game from Tarasov and others, working with famous players, coaching in Germany after the fall of the USSR and, finally, working with NHL stars at the world championships and World Cup in 1996. He claims that one hockey organization ordered 1,000 copies of his book. He claims the first print run of 10,000 copies sold overnight, that he only has a couple of personal copies left.

Vasiliev wants and needs no tears. He describes himself as "a self-satisfied person." He doesn't second-guess himself—you're shopping in the wrong place if you're looking for self-doubt. Dennis McDonald spent the rest of his life rehashing Piestany but Vasiliev makes it sound like he never looked in his rear-view mirror.

Sixty-five now, he works as a coaching consultant for several clubs just outside Moscow—Khimik still, but also Electrostal and Vitiaz, lesser clubs in the Russian Superleague and those trying to play their way in. He won't write off getting behind the bench again. "I would still like to go to a team and coach directly," he says. "Perhaps this can happen next year." He's just another case that proves that all retirements from coaching are involuntary.

Vasiliev makes it sound like the demise of the old Soviet hockey program has left a hole in his life. "We've lost some of our former greatness," he says. "But Slava Fetisov is the Minister of Sports, and he is our hope. He understands the game. He is a well-respected individual in Russia, and he is doing his best to help get us back to where we were in the past. Things are better now than they were ten years ago."

Perhaps not coincidentally, that was the period when Vasiliev coached the Russian team to an off-the-podium finish at the World Cup of Hockey.

Vasiliev makes no connection between Piestany and the declining fortunes of Russian hockey, and maybe these are dots that don't connect. Yes, the Soviet and Russian teams won just three world junior titles over the next fifteen years—a development unthinkable after the USSR teams' ownership of early under-20 tournaments. It's only fair to Vasiliev, who probably doesn't deserve a forgiving reading, and the Russians, who do, to note that the Russian program didn't necessarily have to go into decline for the rest of the world to catch up.

VALENTIN GUREEV
Gureev is retired and lives in Moscow.

WALLY TATOMIR
Tatomir has worked as the trainer for the Carolina Hurricanes for several seasons, including their Stanley Cup championship season of 2005–06. After winning Game Seven against the Edmonton Oilers, the Hurricanes passed the trophy around. When it was passed to Tatomir, he dropped it, dislodging the bowl. Before the Hurricanes players could take the Cup home it had to return to Toronto for repairs.

VLADIMIR KONSTANTINOV
Drafted in the eleventh round by the Detroit Red Wings in 1989. Played seven seasons for Red Army, six seasons for Detroit. NHL totals: 47 goals and 127 assists in 446 games, 5 goals and 14 assists in 82 playoff games.

DETROIT
Vladimir Konstantinov can't tell his story. He can only nod and wave. He's wheeled into the Joe Louis Arena, his routine for games on Friday or Saturday nights, his routine during the nine years since he played his last game. He can't stand and cheer. He is bound by a wheelchair. Tragedy has

robbed him of any chance to tell his own story of the years after Piestany: a great athlete whose gifts, and almost life, were taken from him.

He struggles to say a few words. He doesn't need to say anything to make it clear that there's little quality to his life, only the quality of his care. He looks little like the player on the hockey card, little like the all-star defence-man who raised the Stanley Cup. He looks smaller. He has little muscle tone. His nickname used to mislead. Gramps. Now it's cruelly accurate. He is old before his time.

———

In this rink, ten seasons after Piestany, Vladimir Konstantinov was a hero. He achieved heights few ever know. He delivered a crushing bodycheck to Dale Hawerchuk. If Hawerchuk had any doubt about his decision to retire before that Stanley Cup final, he had none after that play in Game Four. It wasn't the hardest check that Konstantinov delivered during that Stanley Cup final. No, that was a hit laid on Trent Klatt earlier in the series. It was, however, the last memorable moment in the hockey career of Vladimir Konstantinov. Yes, he raised the Stanley Cup after the Red Wings' 2–1 victory over the Philadelphia Flyers. He took his turn skating around the rink. He posed in the team photo. It seemed the perfect ending to a season in which the media and the public really noticed his gifts. He would have a seat reserved for him at the NHL Awards in Toronto, where he would be one of three finalists for the Norris Trophy.

Konstantinov didn't say much in the dressing room after the victory. Reporters chased other stories after the Wings' first Stanley Cup win in more than forty years. They went elsewhere for colour. The cameras were trained on the better-known names in the Detroit lineup. You couldn't have caught Konstantinov spraying Slava

Fetisov with champagne. Or walking around with a big stogie. Nothing was going to be that memorable with Konstantinov. No clowning beside the Cup. He made no impression on those in the champions' room, no impression, nothing except that he was smaller than you imagined after watching those hits that sucked the oxygen out of Hawerchuk and Klatt. Don Wittman mentioned that Konstantinov was six-feet-four and well over 200 pounds on that broadcast from Piestany. If you had stood beside Konstantinov in the dressing room, you would have realized that those measurements must have been taken while Konstantinov was wearing his equipment. It was clear in the dressing room, in his stocking feet, that he wasn't even six feet and his build was more like a tennis player's than that of Scott Stevens or other hard-hitting defencemen.

———

"Vladi has a hard life," Jim Devallano says. "He had one way of dealing with all his challenges. He worked hard. He never backed down. He out-toughed other players and his problems." Many of the details of Konstantinov's life don't fit on his hockey card. Playing in Murmansk in the brutal cold, growing up the son of a sailor, watching his father walk out the door for weeks or months—these events shaped his character and his game. He called on all his strength in Piestany. He had to call on all his strength when he battled cancer in the early '90s. Piestany and cancer didn't break him—he came through all of the challenges tougher. But he never imagined how much he would have to summon his strength, never imagined that there was something he wouldn't be able to overcome.

Konstantinov can't tell his story, so Igor Larionov must. Larionov first played with Konstantinov on the CSKA team in the mid-'80s, when Larionov was already an Olympic gold medallist. Kostantinov was a centre at that time. "On Soviet teams, young players were expected to work hard and say little," Larionov says. "What impressed me about Vladi, even as a young player, was his resilience . . . his toughness. He had a great work ethic. He didn't say much—he wasn't supposed to. But after a while I knew that this was his nature. He wasn't somebody who would ever talk a lot in the dressing room, or even when players would get together away from the rink. He always seemed older than [his years]. When other players were single and enjoying their status, Vladi was married. He and his wife Irina had a daughter [soon after].

"I don't remember much about Vladi going to play at the world junior tournament," Larionov says. "It seemed like a great step up for him. We didn't see the games on television and we didn't see the game against Canada. What we heard after was that [the Soviet hockey establishment] was very unhappy with the team. But Vladi didn't talk about it—he was still a young player. He wasn't supposed to speak up."

Larionov says that Konstantinov wasn't like Mogilny or Fedorov in the late '80s. Mogilny had seen the horizon. Fedorov aspired to it. Konstantinov had his comfort zone. "Vladi was like players when I started playing; we didn't think about playing in the NHL," Larionov says. "We thought about the life that we had under that terrible government. We had a better life than most, maybe better than anybody [other than] those in control of the country. The next generation of players heard that the NHL teams were scouting them and drafting them. For Vladi and the others on CSKA—Sergei Fedorov, Alexander Mogilny and Pavel Bure—the NHL started to look more real to them."

If Konstantinov realized that a world of possibilities was out there for him a little later than the others, it took the world even longer to appreciate his potential. Konstantinov was a steal in the eleventh round. Earlier picks produced two future first-team all-stars and major trophy winners in Nicklas Lidstrom and Sergei Fedorov. Detroit's two scouts in Piestany, Christer Rockstram and Neil Smith, pushed the Wings' brass to draft those players. Their talent made the team's longshot chances to sign them a risk worth taking.

Konstantinov had a tougher transition than Fedorov or Mogilny when he arrived in North America. He didn't irritate just opponents. No, even his teammates took exception to his game. He got into shoving matches and fights during practices. A stick-swinging once in '93. A scrap with Steve Chiasson another time. "I'm not sure they knew about that connection [from Piestany] when they fought, but I'm sure they put it together," Jim Devellano says. What became clear to Mogilny's teammates in Buffalo in one training camp—that he wasn't stealing a third- or fourth-liner's job—took several seasons to hit home with Konstantinov's teammates in Detroit. His talent, value and potential were easier to miss. He was, after all, a ninth-rounder. He was pretty far down on the list of the Russians by the time the NHL got around to drafting them.

———

"Scotty Bowman knew what he wanted to do with the five-man Russian unit," Larionov says. "He brought me in to work with the young forwards [Fedorov and Vyacheslav Kozlov] and he brought [Slava] Fetisov in to work with Vladi. Maybe it was easier for Vladi to make a transition to the North American game. Sergei was a great talent and already playing at a high level, but Vladi's physical play made him a natural fit. And Vladi was only starting to play up to his promise when we won the Cup in 1997. Nik Lidstrom won Norris trophies and was a first-team all-star later on. But Vladi was ahead of Nik in 1997. Vladi was a second-team all-star that year and he was coming off a torn Achilles tendon, [but] Nik hadn't made an all-star team yet.

They came into the league at the same time. No doubt Vladi was going to get better."

Konstantinov's contract was going to run out over the summer of '97, a one-year deal he had signed in lieu of a long-term pact before the World Cup, a gamble that should have paid off with a career season. That was the plan. It didn't work out that way.

Just a couple of nights after Konstantinov skated around with the Stanley Cup, Larionov was supposed to go out with the defenceman, Fetisov and the Detroit's masseur, Sergei Mnatsakanov. "They had rented a stretch limousine to celebrate," Larionov says. "I was going to go, but instead I stayed home with my daughters. They wanted to go swimming. I decided to stay in. Late at night, Stevie [Yzerman] called me at home. He said there had been a car crash, and he asked me to call their wives . . . Slava, Sergie . . . and Vladi. I didn't know the extent of the injuries. I had no idea. I went to the hospital. Almost right away I knew that these were serious injuries."

In the days ahead, though, celebration of the Stanley Cup would give way to pall and cheers to prayers.

———

Vladimir Konstantinov's stall was turned into a shrine. His sweater still hung there after the final game of the Wings' second consecutive run to the Stanley Cup. His skates, his pads, other equipment were all in place, as if he were ready to play. Nothing was removed. Only one thing was added: an oval stone on which the word PEACE is carved.

"In the beginning we had hopes for a miracle," Larionov says. "We hoped that Vladi was going to be able to come back and play. There was talk about radical treatments, experimental work in other countries. And he was always such a tough guy. We hoped it was just one more thing that he was going to beat. But after months, during the season, his improvement slowed or stopped. We understood that he could come back to the arena, but not to the line-up. It never distracted us. It focused us."

Intentional or not, the Wings honoured Konstantinov by *not* replacing him. In effect, they declared him irreplaceable. There were additions to the line-up. The Wings traded for Dmitri Mironov, who underwhelmed, and journeyman Jamie Macoun, who exceeded limited expectations. Mostly, though, those who had played beside Konstantinov found ways to raise their game and do more. Nik Lidstrom had a breakthrough season. Larry Murphy and Bob Rouse squeezed everything possible out of their games. The loss of a player of Konstantinov's quality for an entire season should have killed any chance of a championship. Instead, the Wings found something inspirational in that empty locker.

———

Igor Larionov retired at age forty-two in the spring of 2004. Former teammates and other stars whose lives he had touched received invitations to a farewell game in Moscow in December, some relief during the NHL lockout. Larionov wished that Konstantinov could attend, but he wasn't going to be able to. "Vladi would still have been playing," Larionov says. "He will always be in our thoughts . . . in our hearts. He should have played so many more seasons, and he should have enjoyed life so much more."

Inspirational stories always have the potential for tragedy. That was a theme of Vladimir Konstantinov's life. The Stanley Cup victories transcended tragedy only momentarily. Ten years after his accident, twenty years after Piestany, Konstantinov is wheeled to games by friends, by Wings officials and by a nurse and her husband, a couple whom Konstantinov lives with in Ann Arbor. His wife,

Irina, is absent. They made it to Detroit—against all odds. She stayed with him for several years after the accident, but ten years passed and she's gone from his side. There's no asking Larionov or other Red Wings players or officials about it. It's a sore point. The toughest man in Piestany became the toughest man in the NHL, however briefly. He's going to have to prove his toughness by going it alone. Back in the Soviet Union, Irina had read *Wheels*; she had read about fast cars and millionaires; she had read about Detroit. She then lived the life depicted on those pages. If Vladimir Konstantinov knows where that battered copy of *Wheels* is, he can't say. Vladimir Konstantinov applies the brakes to his wheelchair. His secrets from that game in Piestany will remain untold. He has memories, but no stories.

STEVE CHIASSON

Third-round draft pick of the Detroit Red Wings in 1985. Played with Detroit, Calgary and Hartford/Carolina. Last active with Carolina in the the first round of the playoffs in 1999: 1 goal and 1 assist in 6 games. Played 23 games with Adirondack in the AHL in 1987–88. NHL totals: 93 goals, 305 assists and 1,107 penalty minutes in 751 games.

Steve Chiasson was killed when he drove his truck off the road after a party at the end of the Carolina Hurricanes' season. He was going almost twenty miles an hour over the speed limit. He wasn't wearing a seat belt. His blood alcohol level was three times the legal limit. At his funeral, some said that his drinking that night was an exception. "He was not a guy who lived real hard," said Kevin Dineen, a teammate and roommate. Many knew it was not an exception for him. Many knew but didn't dare talk about Chiasson's drinking—how he had been charged with drunk driving in Detroit right out of junior, how he had gone to Alcoholics Anonymous meetings with Bob Probert and other Red Wings teammates at Jim Devellano's urging. "It didn't make him a bad guy," Devellano says. "He was a good guy who had a problem. He did play hard off the ice and people might not think it's the right thing to say, but it's the truth. Steve knew he had a problem, and he started to address it [while in Detroit]. But then he decided to continue playing hard." A few beers after a game, on a flight, late at night at a teammate's house; in this case, at Gary Roberts' house. No different than that bus ride from the arena in Piestany to the airport.

In Piestany, a game was played and didn't end. In Carolina, a cab was called and didn't come.

Everything fell into place in Piestany, and then fell apart. Everything fell into place for Steve Chiasson in his hockey life, and then fell apart when he fought off teammates who wanted to take away his keys.

Ex-teammates are guarded when talking about Steve Chiasson. They're protecting his wife and three children by not going into details. They're honouring him with their reticence. "Steve didn't speak just to be heard," Dineen says. "When he spoke, he had something to say."

Says his teammate in Piestany and in the last game Chiasson ever played, Glen Wesley: "Steve was just a professional hockey player."

GLEN WESLEY
Drafted in the first round, third overall, by the Boston Bruins. Played for Boston, Hartford, Carolina and Toronto. Played in two Stanley Cup finals in Boston and two in Carolina. Posted a plus-minus of +18 in the 2005–06 season with Carolina. NHL totals: 124 goals and 382 assists in 1,247 games, 15 goals and 35 assists in 144 playoff games (not counting 2006).

Glen Wesley is a professional hockey player, one who has maintained a remarkably high quality of play throughout a long career.

The best indicator of that quality is the fact that the

Hartford Whalers traded three first-round picks to the Bruins to acquire the native of Red Deer, Alberta, early in his career.

No player active in the 2006 post-season had logged more playoff games without winning the Stanley Cup. He had taken a regular shift with Boston in two Stanley Cup finals when he could barely grow a faint blonde moustache. He had been the lead defenceman on a Carolina team that was routed by the Red Wings in 2002 final. Yet somehow Wesley had flown under the media radar for almost two decades. He had never received as much attention as he did going into the Hurricanes' appearance in the 2006 final against the Edmonton Oilers.

"When I went to the Bruins as a nineteen-year-old we went to the Stanley Cup final," Wesley said early in Carolina's 2005-06 season. "Back then I was sure everything was going to come together ... just a matter of time. I didn't appreciate how many guys never get a chance to play in a final, never mind winning. I've been close in the NHL and I was close in junior [to the Memorial Cup]. I have mixed feelings about the world juniors. It's a different thing than the Stanley Cup and the Memorial Cup— because the team is together only a few weeks and not for a season or even a few seasons. [The world juniors] just seemed to be over so quickly that we didn't even know what hit us. And the mixed feelings have something to do with the unfairness of what happened. I don't know how I'll look back on it when my career is over. I'm proud of what I've done over the years—I try to keep that in perspective. But I don't think I'd feel satisfied to have a world junior gold medal and not a Stanley Cup ring. I know how hard it is to be so close, and it was really so much harder with the Stanley Cup."

Wesley has gone about his career with a quiet dignity. He was never a colourful quote like Shanahan or Fleury. So it seemed strange that he made news in the 2006 final by making noise in the Hurricanes' dressing room. With his team down 3-1 at home in the first game of the series, Wesley stood up in the dressing room during the second intermission and, as one commentator put it, "peeled the paint off the walls."

Maybe Wesley sensed that another chance, a last chance, was slipping by. You'd want to believe the outburst had a role in Carolina's third-period rally to win Game One, and in the Hurricane's seven-game victory over the Oilers. A few weeks later, Wesley re-signed with the Hurricanes for another season, probably not his last.

VALERI ZELEPUKIN

Drafted in the eleventh round, 221st overall, by the New Jersey Devils in 1990. Played for New Jersey, Edmonton, Philadelphia and Chicago. Also played for Voskresensk Khimki, Kalinin, Red Army, the Utica Devils, the Norfolk Admirals, Kazan Ak-Bars, St. Petersburg and Mytishi Khimik. Best season: 26 goals and 31 assists in 82 games, five goals and two assists in 20 playoff games with New Jersey in 1993–94. NHL totals: 117 goals and 177 assists in 595 games and 13 goals and 13 assists in 85 playoff games.

Zelepukin was a good soldier in Konstantinov's mould but eventually broke rank. He was kicked off the Soviet team heading for the 1991 Canada Cup because he refused to sign a contract that would bind him to Khimik and the Elite League. The Devils were able to negotiate his release because they had already brought Slava Fetisov and Alexei Kasatonov to the NHL.

"I don't feel like a foriengner here." He said when he was greeted by Fetisov and Kasatonov on his arrival in the Devils' dressing room. "To play with them in the NHL is a big dream come true for me."

Zelepukin's first seasons in New Jersey were his best. His play invited comparisons to Jaromir Jagr's. If famous events turned out just a little differently he might have been remembered for scoring the most famous goal in Devils history. With less than eight seconds remaining in regulation Zelepukin scored a goal that sent the seventh game of the 1994 Eastern Conference final against the Rangers into overtime. New York ended up famously winning that game on a goal by Stephane Matteau in double overtime and even more famously winning the Stanley Cup that spring. That's the story of Zelepukin's career; just on the fringe of brilliance.

When the Devils won their first Stanley Cup the next spring, Zelepukin was a supporting player. Injuries limited his role. He went from emerging prospect to role player in just a couple of seasons.

Zelepukin didn't want to discuss what went on behind the scenes with the Soviet team in Piestany. He was no more forthcoming in his NHL playing days. When it came out that the families of several NHL players had been threatened and extorted in Russia, Zelepukin was once asked if it came as a surprise to him. "I knew about these things," he said. "But what can be said that helps?"

VLADIMIR MALAKHOV

A tenth-round draft pick of the New York Islanders in 1989. Played for Moscow Spartak, Red Army (with Evgeni Davydov), the Unified team (with Davydov), the Capital District Islanders (3 games, 2 goals), the New York Islanders, the Montreal Canadiens, the New Jersey Devils, the New York Rangers, the Philadelphia Flyers and, finally, the New Jersey Devils.

Malakhov won a gold medal with the Unified team in 1992, and had his name engraved on the Stanley Cup with the New Jersey Devils in 2000. These enviable highlights aside, he's one of the most enigmatic and underachieving players of his time. The encyclopedic *Ultimate Hockey* gave Malakhov the award for "Most Unpredictable Career" of the 1990s. Even into his mid-thirties, teams looked at him as they might have at a prospect: They waited for him to get his act together. They're not waiting anymore—it's not that he at last realized his potential, just that he retired in the middle of the 2005–2006 season. Malakhov left millions on the table—the story of his career. He didn't completely waste his talent, but he certainly didn't make the most of it. Malakhov didn't explain his decision. There was no tear-filled press conference. Just a press release and an empty locker. A fitting end to a curious career.

The New Jersey Devils signed Malakhov to a fat contract during the summer of 2005. Money was tight all over the NHL, the new salary cap ushering in a new austerity. So the Devils' signing of Malakhov seemed a desperate attempt to fill the hole left by the departure of their Norris Trophy–winning defenceman Scott Niedermayer as a free agent. The signing seemed all the more curious because the Devils had to urge, if not beg, Malakhov to accept an overly generous contract—he seemed reluctant to come back to the NHL after the lockout. As if he was tired of waiting for himself to get it together, too.

With some, you can measure how their games grew as time passed. Malakhov is a different story. What you saw in Piestany was what he would always be: a guy who played without a compass or a map, with brain locked, with iron hands. As a scout once told me: "He might have fewer real instincts for the game than any talented player in the league. He never developed any with experience. Just on size and skating, he could look like a Norris Trophy defenceman. Based on his worst moments you just think that he can't play at all." Harsh stuff, yet it rings true.

His defining early-career moment: Carrying the puck in his own end, looking down the left wing for an open man, waiting for a play to unfold when he shold have been unfolding it, just watching Dave Latta skate up to him on a casual forecheck, looking like he was hypnotized as Latta raps him across the gloves, standing frozen as Latta skates away with the puck and scores on Ivannikov.

Representative vignette from mid career: Carrying the puck in his own end in the opening minute of a game, looking across the ice to make a pass to his blueline partner, half-assing the play like it's a practice or pick-up game, just watching Pat LaFontaine float in for token pressure, looking like a zombie when the puck hits the tape of LaFontaine's stick and ends up in the net.

The former was Piestany; the latter was the 1996 World Cup semi-final, a 5–2 loss to the U.S. A lot of things had changed; Malakhov playing for Russia rather than the Soviet Union, the crowd in Ottawa cheered the Russians rather than the Americans, Malakhov's club team was down the road in Montreal. Some things stayed the same: Vladimir Vasiliev was behind the Russian bench, Fedorov and Mogilny were in the Russian line-up and, yes, Malakhov looked hopeless coughing up the puck for a spirit-crushing goal.

MIKE KEANE
Undrafted. Played with the Montreal Canadiens, the Colorado Avalanche, the New York Rangers, the Dallas Stars and the St Louis Blues. Also played for the Sherbrooke Canadiens and Manitoba Moose. Best NHL season: 15 goals and 45 assists in 77 games, 2 goals and 13 assists in 19 games in 1992–93. NHL totals: 168 goals and 302 assists in 1,161 games.

HAMILTON
There it was in the program, a journeyman's vitals: *Manitoba Moose. No. 12. Mike Keane. GP 34. G-A-P 1–5-6. PIM 44.* The thought has to occur to casual fans who buys a ticket to Copps Coliseum for the Bulldogs–Moose game: Is this the same Mike Keane? Or a cousin? Or, well, a son? This is that Mike Keane, one and the same. He was

original article, one of only eight men to win Stanley Cups with three different teams, and certainly the only one among them to be playing in the American Hockey League at age thirty-eight.

Mike Keane's presence in the Moose's lineup is creating unusual circumstances: playing against teams coached by former teammates or rivals. This night is more unusual. Keane was once captain of the Montreal Canadiens; the top prospects in the Bulldogs' lineup are in the Canadiens' system already, young players who dream of making it to Montreal someday. Most of Keane's Manitoba teammates have yet to spend a full season in an NHL lineup and, at best, have been called up for a few dozen games over the years. Keane has played in 220 NHL *playoff* games.

There is hardly any room for biographical notes on his hockey card—not when they have to list stats for his career, season by season, going back to his debut in junior, one game with the long-gone Winnipeg franchise in the WHL in 1983–84. In signing on with the Moose in the fall of 2005, he returned to play for a team in his hometown after twenty-one years away.

The consensus among scouts working the AHL is that Keane signed on with the Moose as a favour for the Vancouver Canucks, the team he played for in 2003–2004, before the NHL lockout. A favour that the Canucks might repay with a position as coach or general manager with the Moose or an executive position with the big club. Not an empty gesture, though. Not going through the motions, they said. One scout: "He probably had something that he just had to get out of his system. He wanted to end it on his terms . . . the lockout didn't let him do that. And it just looks like he still wants to play."

"It's good for me, the only place that I would have played for this year," he says. "I get to bring my wife . . ."

Yes, Tami, that girl from Moose Jaw who already had a boyfriend, who was showered with gifts from the player with the Warriors, who was the subject of discussions in the bunks in Piestany.

" . . . and kids home to be around my folks. It's a chance for them to see each other daily. It's something that I owed them after so many years of living away."

The stats line isn't the best indicator of the state of Keane's game all these years after Piestany. It never was.

Describing his role required a contradiction in terms: "High-quality utility player," "elite complementary player," "talismanic leader."

He was a great fighter who gave up fighting—at the advice of Pat Burns, who coached Keane in the only season that either would spend in the AHL. "I remember he lost one of his fights bad and I told him, 'Keaner, these are men, and at the next level you can't go in with the heavy-weights,'" Burns says. Burns told Keane that there was a lot more he could offer—and a lot more that he could get out of the game—if he kept his gloves on. And so for twenty years he has done just that. Mostly. Keane picked his spots. Whenever Keane fought, it was memorable. And none of his professional scraps was more stirring than his fight with New Jersey's Bill Guerin at the Forum one Saturday night. "One of the greatest fights of all time," Theoren Fleury says. "Toe-to-toe for what seemed like five minutes. Keaner was like an old dog who wanted to show that he can still hunt—that was his attitude when he dropped the gloves."

Stripped down to shorts, Keane still looks like an athlete, like a young—okay, *younger*—man. Three percent body fat at most.

"If I didn't think that I had something to contribute, here or within the NHL, I would have just retired," he says. "I'm hoping that a team sees me when the playoffs get closer and will sign me."

His young teammates want reporters to ask Keane about an incident in a game the previous night. Kris

Newberry, a rookie with the Toronto Marlies, the Maple
Leafs' AHL affiliate, trying to make his bones or get anybody's attention, challenged Keane to drop his gloves.
"Mike sort of had this look on his face, like 'You're kidding,'" one of his teammates says. "Then it was like,
'Okay, whatever.' And Mike beat the shit out of him. We
were killing ourselves. They were practically pouring the
kid into the penalty box and we're like, 'Rookie, now you
know. Keane's a leftie.'"

As of late June of 2006, Keane was still considering
playing a second season with the Moose.

STEVE NEMETH

Drafted in the tenth round by the New York Rangers in
1985. Played for the Rangers. Also played for the Colorado
Rangers, the Canadian national team, Krefeld (German
league), the Sheffield Steelers and the Kingston Hawks
(British league) and Tacoma (West Coast league). Best season: 92 goals in 25 games with the Sheffield Steelers in
1991–92. NHL totals: 12 games, 2 goals, no assists, 2
penalty minutes.

In 1999, after several seasons playing in the British pro
league, Nemeth notified the Kingston Hawks of his retirement. He was offered a job with the post office in Calgary.

"I can't believe that a guy that skated as well as
Nemeth didn't make it in the league," Pat Burns says.

PIERRE TURGEON

Drafted first overall by the Buffalo Sabres in 1987. Played
for Buffalo, New York, Montreal, St. Louis, Dallas and
Colorado. Best NHL season; 58 goals and 74 assists in 83
games with the New York Islanders. NHL totals: 511 goals
and 809 assists in 1,277 games, 35 goals and 60 assists in
104 playoff games.

Turgeon was a touted prospect who was supposed to
star but didn't. Outshone by the feral Fleury, outworked by

the overachieving McLlwain, and outplayed by Dave Latta, Steve Nemeth and other forwards who wouldn't make much of a dent in the NHL. The few scouts who had reservations about Turgeon put this down to a failure of character—mettle fatigue in the rough going. Looking back on his career after Piestany, more would see it that way.

Turgeon was the captain of the Montreal Canadiens when the club played its last game at the Forum. On that night, Hall of Famers lined the ice and against the backdrop of heroes, Turgeon never looked more than an imposter. It looked as though a young Rocket Richard would have burned a hole in Turgeon with a glance. For that matter it looked like the Rocket circa 1996 could have done a number on him. Ovations rocked the arena and hockey fans knew they were in on history: not just the last game at the Forum but this never-to-be-reconvened quorum of legends. While memories danced in the minds of the honoured *Habitants* and fans alike, Pierre Turgeon held aloft a torch and seemed to be focused on one thought: *don't burn myself.*

Months later, the Montreal media was deep-frying him daily, and Turgeon didn't defend himself. He tolerated the abuse meekly, just as he did years before, when he was with the Islanders and Washington's Dale Hunter steam-rolled him.

Turgeon has heard two decades of criticisms. The same thing over and over again, in Piestany and through 1,200 NHL games. If only he played with more passion. If only he cared more. He had the talent of those Hall of Famers in Montreal, but five clubs let him pack his bags and go. Turgeon takes issue with these knocks—they're enough to make him almost angry. "I think that a lot of people have been wrong about me," he says. "I'm not a fighter, but maybe because I'm not people underestimate me—they think that I'm not tough. Hockey is a tough game whether you fight or not. Skill and scoring is my game. For me, being tough means playing hard in the corners and going to the front of the net. People will say that a skilled player isn't tough enough [but] they don't criticize a tougher player by saying that he [could] score more or pass better."

Turgeon admits that there's one hole in his resumé that keeps him holding on into his late thirties. "I've never won anywhere yet," Turgeon says. "Some people have [labelled me] a loser, but I don't think that is fair. I think that a winner is someone who thinks [that] winning matters. I could have walked away from the game. I could have retired after the lockout. I'm playing now because I want to win. And because I want to win, I have to accept a role. Not the first line. Eleven, twelve, thirteen minutes a game, that's what I expect to play."

———

Look again at Al Strachan's column. "Whether the attitude is right or wrong, the fact remains that any youngster who stayed on the bench in Czechoslovakia would have never been allowed to forget it *and would have seriously jeopardized his NHL future.*"

Strachan had it half-right about turning the other cheek—or, in a less flattering light, turning your back on teammates. Yes, a player wouldn't be allowed to forget it. No, it wouldn't seriously jeopardize his playing career. Six months after Turgeon vanished in the heat of battle, the Sabres picked him first overall in the draft, ahead of talented, willing warriors like Brendan Shanahan and Glen Wesley. Piestany jeopardized his reputation inside the dressing room, but talent trumps everywhere else.

"What he was then, he always was," says Everett Sanipass, who was traded to Turgeon's Quebec League team in a push for the playoffs in the spring of '87. "He was soft. Gutless. He scored goals, but I bet his teammates didn't have any time for him, wherever he played. I guarantee it."

Not all teammates are so outspoken. Getting the truth requires that names be withheld. Candour requires anonymity.

A former Canadiens star says that his old team's problems in the mid-'90s started with Turgeon, the most skilled player in the lineup at the time. "You're never going to win," he said, "when your captain has balls the size of snow peas."

Word about Turgeon's phlegmatic personality was all over the league. Others saw the blankness that disconcerted reporter Jim Kelley. But talent is talent. General managers believed they could light a fire under him. Or that they could suffer Turgeon's softness to add skill to their rosters. Until proven wrong.

One story made the rounds a few years back. The Dallas Stars had locked up Turgeon to a long-term big-coin contract. He was pulling in a $6 million salary—but when the playoffs rolled around and the Stars faced elimination, Turgeon was a healthy scratch. That, on its own, would have been an indictment. But at the end of the season, Stars general manager Doug Armstrong called Turgeon into his office to discuss this untenable situation. "What situation? What's the problem?" Turgeon asked.

These stories prompt knowing looks and shrugs from Turgeon's former NHL teammates. Just as he didn't jump in to help out in the brawl in Piestany, nobody races in to defend him from criticism all these years later. Nobody will jump in to defend him if he gets beaten up in print.

Turgeon thought about retiring during the NHL lockout. He signed with Colorado in the summer of 2005 after the Avalanche lost Peter Forsberg to Philadelphia as a free agent. The Avalanche gave Turgeon a chance to win for the first time in his career. In some games during the playoffs, he was listed as a healthy scratch.

PETER POMOELL
Pomoell is a vice-president of a Helsinki banking institution and heads the Finnish on-ice officials' association.

HANS RØNNING
Rønning is a kindergarten teacher in Sandifjord, Norway. "I take the children skating during the winter," he says.

SERGEI FEDOROV
Drafted in 1989 in the fourth round by the Detroit Red Wings. Played for Red Army (1986–90), Detroit Red Wings (1990–2003), the Anaheim Mighty Ducks (2003–2005) and the Columbus Blue Jackets (2005–2006). Best NHL season: 56 goals and 64 assists with the Hart and Selke trophies in 1993–94. Three Stanley Cups. Career totals at the end of the 2005–2006 season: 443 goals and 620 assists in 1,055 regular-season games, 50 goals and 113 asssists in 162 playoff games.

CALGARY
He had seen greatness and played in Stanley Cup finals. Late in his career, Sergei Fedorov is seeing the other side of the game. He has played for Stanley Cups. Now he's playing games that barely matter. Anaheim traded him to a struggling Columbus team in mid-season. At one time that would have been billed as a score for the Blue Jackets. Instead, Anaheim was credited with a successful salary dump. For the first time in his career, Fedorov is playing for a team that has nothing to play for—*for months*. His numbers at the end of the season will be those of a journeyman rather than a former Hart Trophy winner: 12 goals in 62 games.

Fedorov and his teammates are in Calgary for a game in early February, and after the morning skate reporters descend on Rick Nash, the Blue Jackets' franchise player and a member of the Canadian team headed to the

Olympics in a few days. Fedorov is ignored in the dressing room.

"Everyone changes, and I've changed," Fedorov says.
"Things change, and I've changed with them. That game in
Piestany was a long, long time ago. I remember a lot more
about playing the world juniors in Moscow or winning [the
WJC] in Anchorage the next year with Alex Mogilny and
Pavel Bure. But I couldn't have imagined how life was going
to turn out when I was a young man. And for a lot of years
I think I didn't appreciate how good I had things—I should
have been more grateful than I was. But I'm grateful now.
I'm older and I'm smarter."

Fedorov rarely sounded so reflective in his days in
Detroit. Then, he didn't seem passionate enough to be truly
angry about his lot, just resentful. He had respect but not
the love. He was dissatisfied with being considered No. 1 in
the NHL (winning the Hart Trophy) but No. 2 in Detroit,
never winning over the fans, Wings management or his
teammates as Wings captain Steve Yzerman had. Fans wearing Yzerman's No. 19 filled the stands at Joe Louis Arena.
The Wings executives were looking at tying Yzerman up for
life. Eyes in the dressing room were trained on Yzerman.
Yet Fedorov was arguably the best player in the game. He
wasn't satisfied with the millions he made. "Of all the
Russians, Sergei became a capitalist faster than the rest,"
Jim Devallano says. "He didn't think he was appreciated."
Mirror image: No. 91 with Detroit, Yzerman's number
reversed.

But as Sergei Fedorov and Bob Dylan say, things have
changed. It's not that Fedorov has fallen to earth: he's making $6 million this season, and the season after that. It's
simply easier to see his career in perspective from one end
of it rather than from its middle.

"For years I didn't talk much, and the fact is I didn't
trust people," Fedorov says. "It was language, in part, but
I know some of it was cultural. I kept things in. A lot of

people think I was a jerk. I was. Now I understand that you don't have to be a jerk. You only get what you give. If you're good, you get good back. When I was traded, I could have been a jerk, but I want to see the positive in everything. I get a chance to help build something. I've had a chance before to win and carry the Stanley Cup—but not with a team that gets better like we have a chance to."

Fedorov isn't a completely open book. He skates around questions about Anna Kournikova. Tabloid burn is just one of the reasons for his "no-comments." According to those close to him, Fedorov was genuinely wounded by the breakup with Kournikova, long-time girlfriend and stealthy bride. But otherwise, almost anything is fair game.

This is what he says about Piestany: "I was overwhelmed. My eyes were as big as pucks. I didn't know what hit me—not the fight, just being in that tournament, playing with older players. There wasn't anything political [in the Canadian game], not for me. Just two teams, just hockey. I didn't think anything more about it—that came later. By the time of Anchorage and the national team—after that, yeah, I thought about North America, but just about playing there. The idea that we hated Canadians, that was never true. We hated some other people—ones that we had to work with—but I think you have to know someone to hate them. The Canadians, we couldn't hate them for being Canadians. Maybe something that happens on the ice can make you think a guy is a jerk. But we were players, and they were players. We had to respect them just for that. And when I got to know a guy like Brendan Shanahan from that team, that proved it."

———

The game against Calgary: Fedorov's game is still there in flashes. It hasn't abandoned him. Every once in a while his skates churn and he passes people on the glide. Columbus wins in a shootout, an extra point that barely slows the team's fall from the playoff race. After the game, the reporters again descend on the Blue Jackets' dressing room and again walk by Fedorov to get to Nash's stall. Fedorov peels off his equipment. "Been there," he says as the light from a television camera hits Nash like a bun warmer. "I don't envy him. But I wish I were that young again."

BRENDAN SHANAHAN

Drafted in the first round, second overall, by the New Jersey Devils in 1987. Played with New Jersey, St. Louis, Hartford and Detroit. Also played with Duesseldorf (German league) during the NHL lockout in 2004 (5 goals in 3 games). Best season: 52 goals and 50 assists in 1993–94. NHL totals: 598 goals and 634 assists in 1,350 games, 53 goals and 66 asssists in 157 playoff games.

DETROIT

It's an off day in mid-season at Joe Louis Arena and coach Mike Babock lets his two over-40 superstars, Steve Yzerman and Chris Chelios, skip practice. Thus Brendan Shanahan, three-time Stanley Cup champion, 600-goal scorer, Olympic gold medallist, assumes the role of voice of experience.

Shanahan isn't labouring in the Red Wings practice. It only looks that way. He was never the fastest skater in the league. Or on his team. Or on his line, for that matter. It was true at nineteen, and twenty-one, and twenty-seven, and it's true here at thirty-seven and for however long he chooses to hang on in the game. It looks as if he can hang on for a couple more seasons. Skating laps in practice, he could teach Dale Earnhardt Jr. about the art and physics of drafting. And it serves him well. He'll score forty goals in 2005–2006, which put him ahead of a lot of high-tempo, hard-curving younger stars.

After practice, Shanahan sits at his stall like Kofi

Annan at the head of the General Assembly. If anyone pipes up, he fires off verbal shots like an emcee at a Friars' Club roast. Those he insults probably take some consolation in the fact that they're being abused not only by one of the game's premier cut-ups, but also a guy whom, yes, a lot of his teammates grew up watching. Shots from a guy who played in a game they are too young to remember: "That game in the juniors where they turned the lights out—or something," says Wings forward Dan Cleary, parked a few stalls down from Shanahan.

———

Brendan Shanahan had called it "our history." He had taken a prominent place in it. Go back to the pressurized moments for Canada in international hockey in recent times and you'll find Brendan Shanahan. On the ice in Piestany when the lights went out. On the ice in Montreal when Canada faced the U.S. in the final of the 1996 World Cup. And, most famously, on the ice in Nagano when Dominik Hasek stoned five Canadians in the shoot-out that decided the 1998 Olympic semi-final. Theoren Fleury was in Nagano too and, like Shanahan, he was picked for the shoot-out. Fleury's position wasn't quite as pressured-filled as Shanahan's, though. Fleury shot first, a chance to contribute. Shanahan shot last with Canada needing a goal to keep hopes of Olympic gold alive. Before dawn millions of Canadians watched Hasek anticipate a deke by Shanahan. They saw Shanahan sag before he even finished the move, knowing that he was toast.

A lot of athletes have psychologically cracked when they've failed in big games. Donnie Moore, a relief pitcher with the California Angels, committed suicide not long after giving up a homer that cost his team a shot at the World Series. The Buffalo Bills' Scott Norwood became a recluse after going "wide right" on a field goal attempt with the Super Bowl on the line. Others simply withdraw and grow bitter. Not Brendan Shanahan.

A few months after Nagano I sat down with Shanahan in a pub in Detroit. He was nursing a back injury and nursing a pop. I asked him about Nagano. I asked him if he thought much about the reaction back in Canada when Hasek didn't bite on the deke.

"So do they hate me in Canada? Can I go back there?" he said.

Shanahan did his best to look wounded, but then cracked up. "Life goes on," he said, making it sound like he had lipped out a four-footer on the 18th hole of a club tournament. He wasn't exactly casual. He admitted that Nagano made him angry, but not sad, and certainly not clinically depressed. "Is that going to make me crawl under the covers, crawl up in the fetal position, and suck my thumb?" he said. "People who think that don't know me. I'd be a suck if I just folded my tent and sulked."

Shanahan told me that he never thought of it as a weight or burden to be in that shootout. "I was picked out of a lot of players to play in the Olympics," he said. "When they were calling out who was going to be in the shootout, I was hoping I was in it and I was hoping that I was going to be shooting fifth, with a chance to win the game."

Not exactly as it turned out. He was shooting fifth, needing a goal just to keep Canada in it.

When I asked Shanahan about Nagano, he compared it to Piestany. He said Piestany prepared him for the fall-out from Nagano. In fact he made Piestany sound far worse than the '98 Olympics. "We were sleeping on the floor in Vienna [and didn't know] we were a national disgrace," he said. "But I didn't ever second-guess myself."

———

Since that dissection of Piestany and Nagano, Brendan

Shanahan has added two Stanley Cup rings to his collection and an Olympic gold from Salt Lake City. Piestany is growing smaller and fainter in a rear-view mirror that Shanahan only occasionally checks. "I would be lying to if I said I had regrets about not being able to go to Moscow [in 1988] for another shot at the world juniors," he says. "I was in the NHL. That meant a lot more to me at eighteen or nineteen. That was the goal that I played for. That's what I dreamed about. I can't say that I feel like something is missing from my career or my life [because of Piestany]. I have my wife and children. I've had a long career. I can't complain about anything that happened along the way."

And since Nagano Shanahan has added a wife and three children, including two infant twins. The perpetual boy (his nickname was Big, after the Tom Hanks film) has given way to the harried husband and father. And in the Wings' dressing room, in Yzerman's and Chelios's absence, he's at the very least a big brother if not a father figure.

———

Wally Tatomir worked for the Hartford Whalers when Shanahan played there in the mid-'80s. He says that Brendan Shanahan "was a born leader even at eighteen." He says that Shanahan has been "a leader of any dressing room he walked into."

He's a lot more than that. Shanahan has become a presence in every dressing room in the league.

The NHL brought in new rules to open up the game in the fall of 2005, part of its damage-control program after management's lockout forced the cancellation of the 2004–2005 season. League executives radically rewrote the game's rule book. Gone were the goaltenders' Michelin Man–like pads. Passes across two lines, previously whistled as offside, were opening the game up. League officials limited goaltenders' ability to handle the puck, moved the blue line to create space in the offensive zone, and, most controversially, instructed referees to strictly enforce rules penalizing players for hooking and holding away from the puck. The league wanted more scoring. The league wanted a game that emphasized speed. The rules implemented were drawn up to reward speed and skill and expose brawny, slow-moving rule-breakers. The rules seemed to reward those who aren't made in Shanahan's template and punish the real article, Shanahan himself.

Sports leagues have rewritten rules because of athletes' performances. Wilt Chamberlain scored 100 points against the Knicks and the NBA widened the key. Bob Gibson posted an earned-run average of 1.12 and Major League Baseball lowered the mound. The NHL's makeover had nothing to do with Shanahan's performance on the ice, nothing to do with the hundreds goals he had scored, nothing to do with Detroit's continued success with wise, crafty and, yes, sometimes rules-bending museum pieces. No, it traces back to an initiative Shanahan undertook off the ice.

The NHL and its players' association were staring each other down in collective bargaining sessions in the fall of 2004. The season hung in the balance. The sports pages were cluttered with a thousand points of negotiation. Lawyers from the respective sides took turns playing the spin game. Ultimatums and final offers preceded other ultimatums, other final offers. The fans' patience and loyalty was being ground into dust. One story was mostly missed in this morass: Brendan Shanahan, a known name but a guy without any official position or portfolio, extended invitations to Toronto for a summit meeting on hockey's future. The guest list included players, coaches, general managers and even owners. Few envisioned that it would have much of an effect on the game. Some accused Shanahan of self-promotion of the worst sort. Of being a publicity junkie. A guy preparing to make the jump into the media after his playing days. He was a magnet for mud. A traitor. A phony.

"A lot of people told me that, with the collective bargaining and the lockout, this was the wrong time to do something like this," Shanahan says. "I thought it was absolutely the right time—even the only time—to do it."

Shanahan's status as a veteran player, a three-time Stanley Cup winner, an Olympic gold medallist and a certain Hall of Famer ensured that his calls would be returned. Still, he was shocked by the RSVPs. "I thought maybe the league would tell its people to stay away," he says. "But [Philadelphia Flyers owner] Ed Snider came in, and Bob Gainey [the general manager of the Montreal Canadiens] played a huge role. Bob commanded everybody's respect because he's a Hall of Famer as a player. He just gave the whole thing a sort of seriousness and authority."

Shanahan didn't rewrite the rule book. He did spur a dialogue, though. Months later, the NHL GMs gathered in Toronto for a series of games featuring minor leaguers and collegians, trials for new rules.

Some are chosen. Some nominate themselves. Some are led. Some lead. "'Why me?' . . . that's what some people ask," Shanahan says. "I say, 'Why not me?' I felt that I had the ability and opportunity to make a difference. It's a game I love, and has given me everything I have. I wasn't going to wait. I wanted to give back to the game."

Leadership consists of many things, including acting first, acting on principles, accepting and even seeking responsibility and, yes, hearing that little voice inside your head. That's how Shanahan became a leader in dressing rooms he had never entered, not just in the NHL but throughout hockey.

———

He was thinking outside the box even in Piestany. He was a teenager who didn't just play but also wrote a ghosted column. He was in the game, but could also see the game—sort of an out-of-body, or at least off-the-ice, experience.

Ten years after Piestany, he was invoking history, talking about being raised in the lore of the Summit Series; twenty years after Piestany he was making history, shaping history with the rule changes.

Ten years after Piestany, he was talking about being an example to young kids and playing the game with respect for the other guys; twenty years after Piestany, he was showing the good that comes with everyone—players and management—working together with that same respect.

———

It might seem as if his opening the discussion about improving the game is Shanahan's biggest joke ever, a joke on an almost cosmic scale for fans of the sport: just as he gets out, he makes it a harder game for those who follow him. It might even seem like a great cosmic joke on himself. A ponderous skater has a hand in making hockey a game that goes to the swiftest. The guy who was stoned in the shootout at the 1998 Olympics sets in motion events that lead the NHL to establish shootouts as tiebreakers.

When these ironies are pointed out to Shanahan, he sees them as proof of the absence of a personal agenda. "I don't think that anyone can accuse me of self-interest in all this," he says. "I was opening myself up to a lot of criticism. It could have been really embarrassing if nobody came to the discussions—and I thought about that. And I didn't need change to keep playing the game. I was doing just fine under the old rules. You could make a case that a lot of the new rules don't help my game out at all."

Shanahan didn't necessarily make friends with his push for a new brand of hockey. The rules have prompted criticism in the Red Wings' dressing room. Team captain Steve Yzerman has perhaps been the league's most outspoken critic of the its look. It's Yzerman's day off—seniority and captaincy has their privileges—so Shanahan has the floor of the dressing room and the podium.

Shanahan says he's happy enough with the idea that he might be remembered more for the push for new rules than highlight-reel goals. "Players and officials are adjusting to the new rules. It's going to take seasons. It'll get down to the grassroots. Eventually it will be the only game young players ever played, and the game will be better for it. And eventually I won't even be remembered for having [had] anything to do with it."

He says all this heartwarming stuff with a straight face that no one can trust. He says he kept on punching in the dark, knowing that no one would know the difference.

He says he played pranks and practical jokes to cope with pressure, but that old newscast feature when the lights went out, the one with Donal, Rosaleen and his three older brothers, even it was a joke and he wasn't there. "Thing is," he says, "only two of those guys were my brothers. My other brother had a game that day, so they went out and got one of their friends to play him."

Brian Shanahan confirms the prank. "Our brother Sean was away when the reporter from the station called," he says. "It was just me and Danny. A bunch of us had been watching the game at a friend's house, having a few beers. My mother had been taping the game and [the CBLT] reporter wanted our reaction to Brendan's team getting thrown out. So we got a friend, Mark Coyne, to come over. As soon as the cameras came on we were fooling around—talking over each other, shouting at the TV."

———

In July 2006, word came that Brendan Shanahan's act was going to open on Broadway; he signed as a free agent with the New York Rangers. At some point he and his brothers will be placing a For Sale sign on the Brooklyn Bridge.

EVGENI DAVYDOV

Selected by the Winnipeg Jets in the twelfth round of the 1989 draft. Played for Winnipeg, Florida and Ottawa. Also played for Chelyabinsk Traktor, Red Army, the Unified team (1992 Olympic champions), the San Diego Gulls, the Chicago Wolves, Amiens (French league), Brynas IF (Swedish league), Zug (Swiss league), Kazan Ak-Bars, Karpat (Finnish league), Berlin Capitals, Krylja Sovetov, Milan (Italian league, 2002–2003). Best performances: Red Army (17 goals in 44 games), Winnipeg Jets in the 1992 playoffs (joined the team in the last month of the season, 2 goals and 2 assists in 7 playoff games) and 1992–93 (28 goals in 79 games).

Tim Campbell visited a hotel in downtown Winnipeg where a touring Soviet team was staying the winter after the Jets drafted Davydov. The *Winnipeg Free Press* reporter figured that the team would be off limits to the press—that he might have to go through a coach or manager to finesse a two-minute interview of stony *da*s and *nyet*s. Just as he was about to enter the lobby, Campbell spotted Davydov. Leaving the hotel. By himself. Walking out into the street. With a newspaper.

"What are you doing?" Campbell asked.

"I'm going to look for an apartment," Davydov told him.

He didn't sign a lease that day—in retrospect, it's surprising that he didn't. And those who know him expect that he at least looked.

"Gene wasn't like other Russian players . . . he wasn't like other players at all," Campbell says. "He was a happy-go-lucky guy, carefree, not the serious or reserved type that you might expect of a Soviet or Russian player coming to North America for the first time."

It went beyond Campbell's first impression. Take the name: not Evgeni, but Gene. The change in name wasn't a matter of convenience for sportswriters and teammates. No, when Davydov arrived in Winnipeg, he let everyone know that he wanted to be called Gene. Other players cling to their language, try to import their culture, move warily in an unfamiliar society. Gene Davydov wanted to become a Canadian, a North American, a NHLer. He wanted it all, and he wanted it overnight. He wanted to move ahead so quickly that he shed the past as if it would weigh him down.

"Davydov wasn't a serious person," says Igor Kuperman, a scout who worked Eastern Europe for the Winnipeg Jets. "He wasn't emotionally ready to come and play in the toughest league. And he wasn't ready for the freedom. He was used to being told what to do—others prepared him to play. He didn't know how to prepare himself to play or to live. He loved the idea of independence, but it wasn't something that really helped him, at least as a player."

His stats line suggests that he had an outstanding rookie season. But Craig Hizinger, who worked in the Jets' front office, says the numbers flatter Davydov. "He scored 22 goals in his first 40 games and did nothing in the second half. And he only played one end of the rink. He was the softest player we had—one of the softest I've ever seen."

He was the type of player who makes his teammates burn. Willing to do the glory stuff, unwilling to take on the dirty work. Skating away from any trouble he might land in, skating away even faster from any trouble his teammates had got into. He was the type of player who makes his teammates burn, but somehow Gene Davydov didn't. Somehow he was hard not to like.

"When Gene walked into a room, everyone smiled," Eddie Olcyzk says. The veteran Olcyzk was assigned to be Davydov's roommate and bristles at those who knock Gene. "There are all kinds of players—it's not fair to say what type of player Gene should or shouldn't have been. He was a good guy and a good teammate."

Gene was comic relief. And he didn't change. "He made the same mistakes over and over again," Hizinger says. "On the ice and off. Gene would come to the bench all the time and spray himself in the face with Gatorade. He never got the idea that the clear-topped bottles had water in them and the coloured ones [had] Gatorade—even though someone told him in Russian. He just didn't look."

So how does it jibe, the fact that Evgeni Davydov, soon to be Gene, was the first off the bench at Piestany? Those who believe in a great conspiracy would have to believe that the planners picked a cross-eyed gunman. "Gene would be at the bottom of the list of players who would be picked to send out to fight," Craig Hizinger says. "But he'd be right at the top of the list of players who would do something impulsively in a game—who would do something completely out of character."

Kuperman knew Davydov best of all, knew his history, knew his character. He also knew the other principals involved. He says that other players may have been sent by Vasiliev over the boards, but refused to go—they could refuse because after the tournament they were going back to their club teams and wouldn't have to deal with Vasiliev again. Kuperman says that Soviet officials wouldn't have held them accountable for insubordination. "He'd go to the fight on the ice if it meant avoiding a worse fight somewhere else," Kuperman says. "He probably went on the ice because he wanted to avoid a fight with the coach. Almost for sure, he didn't go on the ice with the intention of hurting anybody."

Davydov takes no offence to the pokes and jokes from those who know him from his early playing days and his brief stint in the NHL. He wishes he was remembered for winning an Olympic gold medal and finds it funny that his name is connected to a hockey fight.

"Piestany was my first and last hockey fight," Davydov says over the phone from Moscow while his wife tries to stop the crying of their young daughter. "I haven't talked about it in years. When I was in the NHL, I know that there were players [from the Canadian juniors] who were on my teams in Winnipeg and Ottawa but we never talked about the fight. That's okay. I don't think hockey players in a dressing room worry about history. And nobody who I played against ever tried to start a fight with me [to get revenge]. That was a good thing about the NHL—they have players like Tie Domi who do that job. It's not a job I am good at."

Davydov seems neither proud nor ashamed of the game in Piestany and his role in it. He seems amused that anyone remembers it, never mind that someone would want to interview him about it. "On our team we didn't know that it would be a famous game," Davydov says. "We didn't know that there would be television [in Canada]. To us it was just a game, that's all. Today, it is history . . . behind us."

These days history is frequently on the ice with history. He plays recreationally with recently retired players who wore CCCP on their sweaters and won world championships and Olympic gold. "In Moscow we call it the NHL … the Night Hockey League," Davydov says. "All friends, no fights. We're all too old."

ALEXANDER MOGILNY
Drafted in the fifth round, eighty-ninth overall, by the Buffalo Sabres in 1988. Played for Buffalo, Vancouver, New Jersey and Toronto. Also played for Red Army, the Soviet national team (1988 Olympics), Moscow Spartak (1 assist in 1 game during the 1994 lockout) and the Albany River Rats. Best NHL season: 76 goals and 51 assists in 77 games, and 7 goals in 7 playoff games with Buffalo in 1993–94. Best NHL playoffs: 5 goals and 11 assists in 25 games with New Jersey (Stanley Cup champions in 2000). Statistics

when sent down from the New Jersey Devils to the Albany River Rats in December 2005; 12 goals and 13 assists in 34 games. NHL totals: 472 goals and 559 assists in 990 games, 39 goals and 47 assists in 124 playoff games.

ALBANY

It's hard to watch someone like Mike Keane, with his three Stanley Cup rings, finish up in the minors. It's impossible to imagine a former first-team all-star riding the buses at the end of his career. But there was a certain symmetry to Mike Keane returning for a season with his hometown team at the end of his career. Alexander Mogilny and the Albany River Rats, though . . . well, there's something fitting about it, but you have to look harder.

Alexander Mogilny's hair is close-cropped, which hides the grey. There's no hiding his talent, though. Not even in Albany. Not even during a practice in mid-winter. He does something practically every time he touches the puck that gives away the fact that he has played at a much higher level. He'll do something that a career minor leaguer wouldn't even think of. Talent, though, isn't the issue. Never has been. He was the New Jersey Devils' second-leading scorer when general manager Lou Lamoriello assigned him to the team's American Hockey League affiliate a few weeks earlier. Lamoriello dispatched him to the minors because he was displeased with Mogilny's play, his attitude or the team's return on the dollar. Maybe all three. When Lamoriello signed Mogilny to a two-year $7-million contract, it didn't seem to fit into the redefined NHL marketplace, especially since Mogilny was coming off major hip surgeries. Dubious when announced, disastrous for the Devils now. Mogilny's contract made him untradeable— the Devils couldn't even waive him because if another team claimed him, New Jersey would be on the hook for half of his salary, and that amount would count against their salary cap.

"There is the game and there is the business of the game," Mogilvy says. "I'm here [because of] the business of the game. There is not much that I can do about it."

It's an unusually direct statement for Mogilny, whose musings often read like Russian postmodern literature. Or maybe clues to a cryptic crossword.

Others have done damage control on his behalf. Devils teammate Sergei Brylin told reporters that the dispute between Mogilny and Lamoriello traced back to a language problem, a misunderstanding, something lost in translation. Some would grab hold of that lifeline. Not Mogilny. No use claiming that, not when he had no trouble with the language of his contract.

Some would dissemble. Some would say there's still hope when there obviously is not. Some would talk about injuries or trades opening up a roster spot, all the industry shoptalk. Not Mogilny. No shoptalk when a metaphor is available.

"There is no road to New Jersey for me," Mogilny says.

Too cute. Mogilny has just parked his car after the drive in from, yes, New Jersey. There's a road to and from New Jersey, just no spot in the Devils' parking lot. He commutes a couple of hours each way a few times a week to be with his family.

———

Mogilny's reputation has evolved over the years: first, a problem child, then a mercenary and later an enigma. The truth is, he has always defied easy categorization. He might be the most inscrutable player of his generation.

Consider this anecdote: Mogilny hurt a hip when in Toronto. Reporters pressed him about time spent out of the lineup. They wanted to hear how hard it was to watch his teammates carry on without him. They wanted to connect psychic pain to physical pain. He volunteered that it was hard to come to the arena for games and feel powerless to contribute. He was asked: Is it tough when you're at home and you think about the team having to play without you?

"When I'm not at the arena, I never think about hockey," he said with a straight face.

It got a huge laugh even though he kept a straight face. His whole life was shaped by something he never thinks about. Earning millions at a job that he leaves at the office. Not thinking about a game Shanahan *rethought* in his spare time.

No one among the reporters huddled around him knew whether Mogilny was kidding or not. No one could know the lot of the original defector. No one could empathize with the conflict, the torment, the inner turmoil. He left the Soviet Union behind, and it ceased to be. He came to North America, and he continued to be a Russian in his heart. He walked into a dressing room full of strangers as a teenager, speaking a different language, owning a gold medal earned playing for a country that he could no longer even visit. He started playing in a city that he couldn't have found on a map.

"Of course there were times I was misunderstood," he says. "That's the language barrier. It's also a cultural difference. I've always thought of myself as a Russian, not a Russian-American or Russian-Canadian."

Mogilny wasn't just the first. He's also the last. It's a different player who comes from Russia now, he says. A different player with different values.

"Now the Russian game is much more for the individual player," Mogilny says. "Maybe people thought I was selfish. I don't think I ever was. I tried to score when I was in Buffalo. I tried to score everywhere I played. But I always thought of the team. Maybe some people [outside the game] didn't see it that way, but it's true. It still is. Robbie Ftorek [the River Rats' coach] will tell me to look to score—sometimes I'll make the pass just because that is what feels good to me . . . that is the game I learned to play, the team in front of the player."

He was once thought of as a prime example of the spoiled athlete, and yet he balks at the idea that his minor-league assignment is a hardship, that his career deserves a more dignified denouement.

"I can't feel bitter," he says. "Things are much harder for other people. I see it when I go home. I see it here. I say that I never have lived in straight lines, and I don't even like straight lines. I have never been afraid of change. I like to change. I had to change when I came to North America. I had to change when I came here. When hockey is finished for me, I'll have to change again. When it's over, there is just one change I want to make. I want to go some place sunny. Whether it was in Khabarovsk or Moscow or one of the NHL cities I played, I never had a chance to live someplace sunny and warm."

How his career will end is not clear. He's sure that New Jersey will buy out the last year of his contract over the summer. (That way, his salary won't count against the Devils' salary cap.) Maybe a team will offer him a contract—after all, talent remains scarce and the new NHL is made to measure for the Alex Mogilny who scored 76 goals in a season. But maybe that offer won't come, or won't pay enough to justify the risk of another more serious, or even crippling, hip injury. Maybe the non-straight line will end in Albany.

The suggestion that his hockey career started as a straight line cracks his straight face. "The funny thing is . . . I cannot say who told the sports academy—the national program—about me all those years ago." "I travelled 5,000 miles to Moscow with 100 rubles in my pocket, and when I got to the sports academy they weren't expecting me. I couldn't tell them who it was who told me to come. I travelled 5,000 miles and I never asked who did this for me. I've never found out. It just happened. The big mystery."

It's just one of many mysteries. Another is his role in Piestany. He should know who was the second Soviet player to leave the bench. After all, he was sitting beside the first, Evgeni Davydov. Maybe he saw that second player go. Or maybe it was Mogilny himself.

The idea that he's that mystery man is too tough to fathom for those who have trashed him in the press or booed him from the stands or wished him out of their dressing room. The famously phlegmatic Mogilny . . . it seems completely out of character. The instigator in Piestany couldn't have been a player who was best known as a pure scorer, who stood accused of floating, who was regarded as something less than a team guy . . . could it?

The question is asked point-blank: "Could you have been the second player off the bench with Davydov?"

Leave out anything that might point in this direction, anything that might support this suspicion. The fact that he was sitting next to Davydov, his linemate. The fact that, floater image aside, he was suspended for ten games the next season for fighting in a league game—the only player suspended in an incident that league officials described as vicious. The fact that Canadian players didn't recognize the player who jumped the bench with Davydov, and that many, perhaps most, of the Canadian players are surprised when I tell them Mogilny was on that Soviet team.

Leave out the suppositions, anything that might fit. The idea that a seventeen-year-old starting to find his way around competition at that level would have simply followed the lead of a veteran player reflexively. The possibility that he skated by the Canadian bench so fast that no one got his number.

Again, only a cryptic clue where a clear answer would straighten out the line, a non-answer that only leads to more questions: "It was a long time ago," he says. "I don't want to guess. There are some things that you never know.

It's one thing that makes life amusing . . . you laugh at life, life laughs at you."

———

Cue the brawl once more. Press play. Don't look at the start of the fight. Look at what comes after. Mogilny, Number 8, a bushy head of hair, skates by the Soviet bench. Vasiliev is yelling at him. He's motioning with his hands, palms upturned—international sign language for "what were you doing?" The Soviet trainer is yelling at him. The trainer is bent over the boards, impassioned in his hand movements, finger to forehead—international sign language for "what the hell were you thinking?" Mogilny shrugs. He offers his own bit of sign language. He holds his fists chest high out in front of him, the backs of his hands upward, parallel to the ice. Then he turns his fists 90 degrees, the backs of his hands out, perpendicular to the ice. It is the international sign language for "breaking up." They could be asking him why he didn't fight more—but if he was third off the bench, as he would claim, that would hardly seem to be a problem. They could be asking him what he was thinking when he left the bench—which would only be a question if Vasiliev didn't send players over the boards, if no one opened the gate for them.

Press pause. Close the notebook. The second man off the Soviet bench is one of those things that makes life amusing.

THEOREN FLEURY
Drafted in the eighth round, 166th overall, by Calgary in 1987. Played for Calgary, Colorado, New York and Chicago. Also played for the Salt Lake Golden Eagles, the Horse Lake Thunder and the Belfast Giants. First NHL season: 14 goals and 20 assists in 36 games, 5 goals and 6

assists in 22 playoff games and a Stanley Cup. Best season: 51 goals and 53 assists in 79 games in 1990–91. Last season: 23 goals and 58 assists with 274 PIM in 38 games with Belfast. NHL totals: 455 goals and 633 assists in 1,084 games, 34 goals and 45 assists in 77 games.

BELFAST

The tales of Theo Fleury's tragic waste have become as much a fixture in newspapers as the crosswords and weather forecasts—without the solutions or predictions. Everyone knows after the first paragraph where it's going. His comeuppance and comedownance. Hanging on, not letting go. Staying in a child's game when everyone else is coaxing him into adulthood.

That's the story they like to write about Theoren Fleury. That's the story they've been writing about him since 2002. Sort of a continuous prose loop, a few details changing here and there. Chicago substituted for New York. British hockey league substituted for Senior hockey league in Alberta. Take your pick from a list of substances. Sort out whether he's in for treatment, whether he's in or out of the program, whether he's re-instated or suspended indefinitely, whether he's trying to get back or has made his peace with never playing in the NHL again.

Theoren Fleury's is the story they like to write whenever they get a chance. Rod Serling wrote it as *Requiem for a Heavyweight*. Reporters are junkies for the downward spiral. They shovel on the pathos.

Cue the interview from the first intermission in Piestany. Theoren Fleury squeezes in a call-out to his friends and family and the people in Russell, Manitoba. Fred Walker has to cut him off or he'd talk right into the second period.

Press stop. Look at the video from Piestany. Look at Fred Walker interviewing Fleury in the first intermission. If you Google "Russell, Manitoba," each hit is a Theoren

Fleury reference. He didn't just put Russell on the map, he put it on the Internet.

—

Coming up on the twentieth anniversary of Piestany, Theoren Fleury is playing for the Belfast Giants. Only in Belfast might he be considered a giant. "The people here love him," says Giants owner Jim Yaworski, a Calgary businessman who's diversifying a portfolio heavy in high tech. "They love his attitude. They know he's genuine and they know he likes it here."

Coming up on two decades in the spotlight, Theoren Fleury is packing up his equipment in the Giants' dressing room at their home rink, the Odyssey, which would be a perfect title for his memoir.

Pour him a coffee after practice and Fleury will pour his story out onto the pages of a notebook or into an open mike. Other days he'll offer up other stories. This time it's about his state of mind and his personal history. This time he rebuts those who claim hockey was his ruin. This time he claims that his self-destructive tendencies are in check. Tenuously.

He starts by saying he'd be "dead without hockey." It's hard to doubt that. He has cheated death. Even with the game, even with the financial security it has provided. He has cheated death a bunch of times in just those four years since Salt Lake.

On and off booze. Drinking with homeless drunks on street corners in New York. Bouncing around crack houses to get a vicarious buzz. Drawn to the low life like a moth to a flame.

He probably can't even remember the worst of it. He lived it and survived it in body, but had no memory of it just hours later. Stories are hard. Scenes stick in the memory, but not how he got there, and not how he got out.

"Life is really good here," he says. "I know more about myself than I ever did before. I've peeled back the onion more than ever. I've worked at it and it's great for me to get away from some of the bad stuff. Coming here was great for me and my fiancée. On off days we can go to Paris or Rome for the day. My son came out here, twenty years old, not a hockey player, a *poker* player, a pro. Unbelievable . . ."

Hard to imagine any son of Fleury having a poker face. Theoren Fleury wore his emotions like a Shriner's fez. Concealed? Couldn't if he tried.

" . . . and things with my parents have never been better. It wasn't always easy but they did one good thing, one really important thing, for me growing up. When I wanted to play hockey—when I told them that's what I dreamed of—they never stood in my way. Never. They never tried to talk me out of it—y'know, never tried talking 'sense' into me. They left me to chase my dream. I brought them here a few weeks ago. I had a couple of free days. I took them to the Vatican—front seats to see the Pope. I bought them front seats. All the troubles my parents had, the one thing that got them through it was faith. As strange as it sounds, that was something that was really important to them . . ."

It's hard to imagine someone so relentlessly positive ever being so self-destructive. It's hard to imagine anyone so happy living and playing on the dark side. But there is that. Danger. He suffered from colitis—that might account for part of it. He suffered from substance abuse problems—whatever label you want to attach: abuse, addiction, whatever, it matters not. He raged on the ice—he only ever managed to play by force of iron will, and that will became more volatile with fatigue. And there's a dark side because they just won't let him forget.

The Chicago Blackhawks, who signed him and too readily kicked him to the curb.

The NHL executives, the Hawks' enablers (for want of another word), who voided Fleury's contract and thus picked millions from his pocket because of its vague substance abuse policy.

The bastard fans on the road, even in this British league, who heckle him and harass him with a conscienceless loathing that would shame a guard at Abu Ghraib.

A coincidence in scheduling. Belfast has a game against Cardiff at the very same hour that Canada will be playing the Russians at the Olympics in Turin.

"You know, I want to be there," he says about the Games in Turin. "It might sound strange, but I really want to be there at the Olympics . . . and I even think I could help. What I always knew, and maybe other guys didn't, is that you have to step up—be in the moment, y'know—because you're measured by what you do when you're needed most. I'm proud of the way I played in those games.

"That's what I tell the guys in the dressing room. I still get to be in the dressing room and hang out with guys. There's no replacing that, and when it's over I'll miss that. I tell them that you never know when you're going to get a chance to win again."

Winning and losing: the pathos-shovellers write the story of a man drowning in a toxic whirlpool of booze and drugs. That storyline almost makes winning and losing beside the point. But look at Fleury's life through that filter—winning made everything shine in the brightest light and losing reduced it to opaque darkness.

"I don't know what would have happened if Piestany had been it. That's the message that I tell guys, the younger guys. You never know when you're going to get a chance to win again. You never know *if* you'll get a chance to win again. I consider myself so lucky that I was able to go back with that team to Moscow. I know that there were a lot of guys who didn't, and a lot of guys who never knew what it was like to win a championship: juniors, Olympics, Stanley Cup, whatever. I can't be sour about Piestany or the things that happened to me [in recent years]. I got a second chance to win in Moscow—you can't imagine the experience. [At] twenty, I'm playing in the Stanley Cup final, winning a Cup. How lucky is that."

Lucky. *Lucky.*

"I prided myself on the way I played in the biggest games. That's what mattered most to me. In Nagano, I was the first guy to go in the shootout against Dominik Hasek, and you don't know how hard I took it when I missed. *You can't know.* I've thought about this long and hard, and I think everything started to go off the rails for me after that. The World Cup, that was a team thing, something that just came down to one game, one day. But [in] Nagano *I* missed. I had a chance for us to win and I missed. I think that's when I really started to get out of control . . . [when] it started to come apart. It could have been so different if I had scored. I consider myself lucky that I was able to hang on to play in Salt Lake—I hung on, but barely. But I'm even proud [of] how I played there. It was like Piestany and Moscow. Life isn't about second chances a lot of the time. All the trouble I've had, all the things I've put myself through and put people close to me through, and I've had second chances. My marriage broke up, but I've got a new girl and we're getting married this summer. It's my second chance again. I think I've got a real chance at being happy."

Happy. *Happy.* Hung on barely. *Barely.*

———

The Belfast Giants have a chance to clinch the British league's regular-season title. They've dominated the league all season long. This game against the Cardiff Devils is the Giants' last chance to claim the title in front of the home fans. But the Giants lie down like Gulliver among the Lilliputians, and Cardiff jumps to a two-goal lead. Fleury's mood becomes surly. And surlier. First, it's a little stickplay. Then it's f-bombs and threats for the ref. The Belfast fans love it. It escalates. A double-minor. A ten-minute misconduct. A stream of profanity. A thrown stick. A slamming of the penalty box gate. Fourteen minutes to contemplate what he's doing, where he is.

Turn on the television in the press box at the Odyssey. Find the feed of the Olympic hockey game. The Canadian Olympic team is losing to the Russians 1–0.

Look at the Canadian Olympians who weren't there in Salt Lake, and some who were. You can't tell how desperate the situation is in Turin, maybe because the players don't find the situation desperate at all. The 2006 Olympians play hard, just not hard enough. They're skilled, but they don't have the edge. They've had it easier than Theoren Fleury ever did. They were never passed over in an NHL draft. They never had to listen to people telling them they'd never make it. They don't approach the line that Fleury had to learn not to cross. They don't approach the line that Fleury couldn't help but cross in Piestany . . .

Turn off the television.

. . . not even in this minor league, Giant steps down from the NHL. Fleury rages in the postgame press conference in front of the red-faced league officials he targets. Taking it all in: Jim Yaworski, the owner who convinced Fleury to come here and who convinced Fleury to try to coax Mike Keane to come with him. "I won't be coming back here, because of how I've been treated on and off the ice," Fleury says. "And if any NHL players tell me they're thinking of coming to this league, I'll tell them not to go within 500 feet of Heathrow Airport. That was the worst officiating I have ever seen in my career, and all it does is harm the league and turn people off from coming to watch the game."

The moods of Theoren Fleury change like television channels. He is happy. He's lucky. *Happy. Lucky.* Just hours before, he was happy and lucky to be in Belfast and now . . . Now he might only consider himself lucky to have been in Salt Lake and not Turin. Or maybe he believes that he could have helped them against the Russians tonight. Maybe this meltdown in Belfast is a sympathetic reaction; maybe he *knows* the Olympic teams needs help. In Piestany, Fleury has beautiful moments and outrageous ones, often in the same shift. Even twenty years later there's no knowing if the next minute will be sublime or scandalous, happy or tortured. That's between Theoren Fleury and his many Theoren Fleuries.

FRED WALKER
Walker retired from the CBC in 1995. He lives in Etobicoke.

EVERETT SANIPASS
Drafted in the first round, fourteenth overall, by the Chicago Blackhawks. Played for Chicago and Quebec. Also played for the Saginaw Hawks, the Indianapolis Ice and the Halifax Citadels. Last active: Halifax in 1992–93. Best season: goals and 12 assists with 126 PIM and 2 goals in 2 playoff games with Chicago in 1987–88. NHL totals: 25 goals and 34 assists with 358 PIM in 164 games, 2 goals in 5 playoff games.

Usually NHL clubs have a comprehensive list of contact numbers for their alumni. Nobody in the Chicago organization had a number for Everett Sanipass. A PR person said that they've never had a request to talk to him in all the years since he played the game.

Scouts who hear every rumble, who have every tale stored in something like computer memory, chuckled at the mention of his name. They started telling stories. Hard to sort out the fact-based tales from the apocryphal ones. One scout tells the story of Sanipass being sent down by the Blackhawks to their farm club in Indianapolis. An afternoon's drive. It took him four days to report. Another said Sanipass wanted to go home one year when hunting season started—or maybe he *did* go home and the team didn't know till he left. Knowing where he was these days, though—no, they hadn't a clue. Best guess was New Brunswick. Said one scout: "Here was a tough kid who was physically mature enough but just not emotionally ready to play in the NHL. He was a man on the ice, but a complete innocent away from it—not even close to being able to handle the big city. He was a disaster waiting to happen. The good news, I guess, is that he was able to walk away from the game. It could have gone real bad." Other scouts said a lot worse. Attached epithets to his name. Made jokes about his playing for a team that had his face on the sweater. Stuff straight out of a dressing room.

There were dozens of Sanipasses listed. It's a common name out on the Mi'kmaq reserve. No listing under Everett, though. None under E. Sanipass. Calls to the Sanipasses listed. They've heard of him, know he must be related to them, but just don't know where he is. All that's left is to go to the place where his story started.

ELSIPOQTOQ FIRST NATION (formerly BIG COVE), NEW BRUNSWICK

You have to get directions from the kids who play on the pond where Everett Sanipass learned hockey. Sanipass lives a five-minute walk from that pond.

He has a baby in his arms. "Second kid with the woman I'm in a relationship with," he says.

Sani~~pass is the~~ one player in the Canadian junior lineup who ~~ended~~ up furthest from the game. His playing career was done more than ten years ago. It's been fifteen years since he played in the NHL.

"I get out and play on that pond every once [in] a

while," he says. "Mostly I play in a men's league and I get out with an all-star team that plays in charity games around the province and in Nova Scotia."

Sanipass suffered an ankle injury early in his career. He never lived up to the promise that he showed in flashes in that Piestany game. He says the injury was bad luck. He says it was bad timing otherwise. He doesn't blame the brevity of his career on racism but, he says, "there's still racism . . . lots of it . . . in the game."

"There was always something racist in hockey wherever I played," he says. "It was tough in the Quebec league. The fans are really on you, shouting racist things. At the next level, it was there too. Some things I could hear, some things you just know."

Sanipass says he just accepted it. Tried to be better than it. Tried not to react in a way that would have pleased those who threw slurs his way. He had hopes that when hockey was over, he'd leave racism behind. He figured that hockey was behind the times. That the rest of society had it right. That he was going to leave racism behind when he gave up the pro game.

"I didn't realize that nothing had changed—nothing— until I ran for office as a Conservative candidate in an election. When I was wearing the maple leaf and playing for Canada, these people were cheering me. I was playing for my country . . . for their country. But when I went around knocking on doors, I had a lot of [them] slammed in my face, and a lot of people said some horrible things. I wanted to win, but maybe it was for the best. I don't think that I would have been happy doing that stuff."

Sanipass says that broke his spirit, at least about living and working off the reserve. He knew where he felt comfortable. He knew where he didn't. He went home, as close to home as he could. Only when he went home did he understand how uncomfortable life off the reserve had made him.

"I don't like crowded places," he says. "I get all jumpy. They scare me. I don't know what it is. My girlfriend says that it might be panic attacks or anxiety attacks. Maybe that's what it is. I don't know. No matter what it is, I don't even like going to the mall. I don't like going downtown or anything like that. Even when we're going around and playing in those charity games . . . at least they're in smaller arenas. But I remember just shaking when I went to play at the Chicago Stadium that first time. It's been a long time. I don't know if it was easier or worse playing in front of 20,000. I was uncomfortable in something like that too, though. Maybe if you have something like that now, a team would try to help you, but not then."

Cue Everett Sanipass's interview with Fred Walker.

"Everett Sanipass, you were the first one involved in that fracas on the other side of the ice. What happened?"

"A bit too aggressive," he says. "They been on us all through the game. I don't think . . . I think we took a bit too much. I was gonna settle it down a bit. I wasn't expecting for the other guys to do it. I really didn't expect that at all. . . . They were stickin' us and everyt'ing."

Hit pause. His lip almost quivers in the still frame.

Hit stop.

"I don't know if Piestany had anything to really do with it. And I don't know if that fear had anything to do with fighting like [I did in] Piestany. What I do know is that after it happened I was one frightened kid who never [had] been around a bunch of people, and I knew that there was gonna be a bunch of people wanting to talk to me when I got back to Canada. I loved to play, but if I didn't have to talk to anybody that would have been fine with me. It's not like there were crowds of people wherever I went but, yeah, when we got off the plane coming back from [the tournament] there was a crowd of reporters and cameras and I was scared big time. And even at that party when I came home from Piestany—a crowded place, people looking at me—I was never so scared fighting as I was in a crowd."

VADIM PRIVALOV
Undrafted. Played for Leningrad (3 games) and Khimik (10 games). Last active with Khimik in 1988–89.

None of the players, coaches or officials contacted for this story knew of Vadim Privalov's whereabouts.

SHAWN SIMPSON
Drafted in the third round, sixtieth overall, by the Washington Capitals in 1986. Played three seasons (35 games) for the Baltimore Skipjacks.

PIESTANY
Shawn Simpson is back at Zimny Stadion in Piestany again, this time for an anonymous pro tournament rather than a world championship. It's a game between the Slovaks and the Swiss, not the Soviets and the Canadians. This time it's in a seat in the stands, not on the bench. This time it's a rental car in the parking lot, not a team bus. This time he's heading back to a four-star hotel in Bratislava, not a rock-hard bunk in a tiny room in Trencin. This time he's sporting a shaved dome, not a strawberry-blond mullet.

"There've been changes everywhere. There have been changes in hockey with all the East Europeans coming in. Changes in the country here—now it's Slovakia, not Czechoslovakia. Changes in the town here—it looks a lot better than it did back when we played here. But this rink looks exactly like it did back in '87."

A few things have changed in the years since the 1987 WJC. There were no real concession stands at the rink— just some bad black coffee. Now the arena has a sports bar, owned by Jaromir Jagr, beside the main entrance. Some things have stayed the same. The same crappy ice. The same crappy ice-making system. The same peeling paint job at the rink. The same simple scoreboard that showed 13:53. The same lights that were turned out.

"Right there at centre ice," Simpson says. "I can't remember the name of the guy I fought. I can't remember if I ever knew it."

Press play. Freeze on a frame of the fight between the backup goaltenders. "Privalov 20" across the back of the Soviet's sweater. *Hit pause.*

Vadim Privalov's numbers as they show up on a hockey database: 28 games in the Soviet elite league. Most of them with Vladimir Vasiliev in Khimik, a few with Leningrad . . . and only a few after that season when Simpson fought him in Piestany.

Simpson looks at one line in Privalov's stats.

Privalov . . . Khimik . . . 1986–87 . . . 5 games . . . GAA 6.66.

"That's a bad sign," Simpson says.

He has no memory of Privalov. He could have been sitting beside him and he wouldn't have known it. "I fought the guy, but, you know, I never saw him stop a puck. I didn't even really get a good look at his face. Hard to recognize him . . . he spent a lot of that fight with his sweater pulled over his head."

Centre ice. That's where Simpson and Privalov fought. That's where their lives intersected. And one other thing that they never suspected: that there wouldn't be much more after that brawl, after they rolled around on the ice. They would keep on playing, but if Simpson thought that his career ended too quickly, he can take some cold consolation at least in lasting longer than Privalov. And he can count himself luckier than Privalov, because he landed a job in the game. Vasiliev says that he has no idea where Privalov is, what he's doing. "One of the guys who fell off the face of the earth," Vasiliev says.

"I lasted about as long as [Privalov] did," Simpson says. Simpson played more games and posted better numbers than Privalov, but within about three seasons of that game in Piestany, his playing career was over. He didn't even have a chance to announce his retirement at age twenty-two. Hockey can move so fast you can't keep up. Sometimes it's moving up fast. Sometimes it's moving out fast. Simpson's was the sadder option, the latter one.

"I went back to the Soo," he says. "And I played a couple of seasons with the Capitals' farm team in Baltimore. But then the Caps traded for Mike Liut and sent Bob Mason down. So I was the third man in a two-man system. Only an injury to one of the regulars was going to change things. Nobody got injured. So while I was with the team I went up to the broadcast booth and tried doing some colour commentary for our games. Right away, I knew it was something I liked to do. I worked in Baltimore and in Washington, and then [Capitals executives] David Poile and Jack Button had me double up . . . do some pro scouting while I was doing the broadcasts. I was scouting at twenty-four. Pretty soon I was doing scouting full time. I have ever since."

Simpson was the only Canadian who didn't play in that '87 game against the Soviets. He wore the Maple Leaf and watched. He is watching this game at the same rink nearly twenty years later. He's carrying a clipboard with a Maple Leafs logo. A couple of years ago, he moved from the Washington organization to Toronto's.

When he sat on the bench, he watched players who would go on to greatness. He watched others who would go on to the NHL or would carve out careers playing in other leagues. Back then, he understood that a career could end in a blink. He was reminded of that by coaches all along the way. That anyone in the game is just a play away from the end. So, *carpe diem*. And *sic transit gloria*. He just never imagined it would be him.

He became a scout—he went from goalkeeper to one of the keepers of the game. He never imagined that the misfortune of a career-ending injury was going to visit his previously charmed life. Now he divides young players into those destined for greatness, those destined for pro careers of a lesser sort and those who will be out of the game in only a few seasons.

Kerry Huffman made it back to Piestany once, for the world championships in '92. But no one else from that Canadian team other than Shawn Simpson ever made it back, and Simpson haunts the place like a ghost. He's been coming back once or twice a year for ten years now. Almost two dozen times over that period, he figures, sometimes for a week at a time.

"I'm not bitter, and I hope none of what I say will be taken that way," he says. "We didn't get the gold medals here, but we got medals from Mr. Ballard and we got a lot of support from fans back in Canada. That's not anything to be bitter about. I don't look back on that as a bad time. That was one of the great experiences of my life . . . being around a great group of guys even if it was only a for a few weeks. And I'm not bitter about where I am now. I love my life and my work. This is how it's meant to be. I consider myself lucky. It's not hard to come back. I really look forward to it. You know, there's not a day goes by when I'm in Canada or even in Europe that someone doesn't ask me about that game. And they always remember my fight with that guy . . ."

Privalov.

". . . the funny thing is, I put a DVD of that game on the other day for my son Shane. And I didn't feel comfortable, not with the type of hockey we played. Then, when it came to the brawl, I wanted to turn it off. For years, the fight was good for a lot of laughs when we'd get together and have a beer in a bar. I'm not saying that I would do anything different. I don't think that I could have. I'm proud of playing for Canada, but I don't know about all the things that happened at that tournament. This arena didn't change, but I think the way I look at what happened here has changed."

—

Hit play one last time. Look for something that, all these years later, would cause Shawn Simpson to have a change of heart. Look for something that was good for a laugh years before, but not suitable for family viewing now. The two goaltenders roll around the ice. Simpson pulls the sweater over Privalov's head. Privalov blindly gets his fingers into Simpson's mask. No punches seriously land. Nothing that would hurt as much as a puck. Something close to a playfight in the middle of the brawl. Maybe it would be embarrassing to show a kid. There has to be something else though. Something else that is less than heroic. There has to be something else to explain Simpson's turn from smile to wince, from pride to ambivalence.

Press review. Go back to the moment when the benches clear. Look at the far-left edge of the screen, centre ice. Look at centre ice. Try to determine who lands the first punch in the playfight between the backup goaltenders. Privalov is the one Soviet who doesn't leave the bench right away. Simpson jumps the Canadian bench. Simpson is over the boards almost immediately. Maybe it's frustration in not being able to contribute in the way he had hoped. Maybe it's just part of being with the team. Simpson skates to centre ice. A Canadian teammate—there's no making out his number—is hammering a Soviet player—his number not clear, either. You can only make out that it's Simpson because of the goaltender's equipment. Simpson starts swinging. He throws right hands over the top. Minimum number: eight. Damage: could have been worse if the blocker wasn't so awkward. Mental image: a lobster throwing right claws. Simpson has his back to Stephane Roy, who is getting double-teamed. He can't see it. The two

Soviets are doing a lot more damage than Simpson can. Simpson slaps at the Soviet player with his blocker. Four, five, six shots. Then Privalov skates in from the bench and grabs Simpson. Again, you can't make out Privalov's number, just the goaltending equipment. Privalov grabs Simpson and drags him away. Privalov does for his double-teamed teammate what a couple of players destined for the NHL didn't do for Stephane Roy.

Press stop.

———

Shawn Simpson went to the dressing room with his teammates, knowing he was the only one who didn't get into the game against the Soviets. He never suspected that he'd be the only one in the room who'd never play in the NHL, the only one who'd never make it out of the minors. The Canadian players talked about being ready for the game to restart, about the game picking up again. And then, it was like they "were never here." For Simpson, it must feel like the game never ended, like he never left. "Practically every day someone asks me about it," he says.

EPILOGUE—VANCOUVER
The Abyss and the Sign-Man at the Brink

The reunion game has been played a few nights ago. They have toasted each other. They have renewed friendships and relived their greatest friendships. And most of the alumni of the 1982 and 1985 Canadian junior teams who made it to Vancouver for the reunion have made their way home. They weren't sticking around in Vancouver for the 2006 WJC final, a showdown between two teams that had advanced undefeated on opposite sides of the draw, the defending champion Canadians and the Russians, silver medallists the year before.

On the basis of those brief thumbnails, it looks as if the Canadians will enter the game as favourites—even more so after you factor in home-ice advantage, 18,000 fans at GM Place and the standard North American ice surface. Memories of the 2005 WJC were are fresh, too. It would have been hard to forget a Canadian team that rolled over all of its opponents that previous winter, a run that included a 6–1 rout of a Russian team led by phenom Alexander Ovechkin. And here, in Vancouver, Canadian fans take some assurance in the fact that the coach of the 2005 gold medallists, Brent Sutter is again behind the bench.

Yet many pro scouts and insiders believe Canada is in trouble with the Russians. In fact, they consider the Russians something just less than a lock to win.

The U.S. team arrived at the tournament as the smart choice, not least because the two highest-ranked juniors eligible for the 2006 draft—forward Phil Kessel and defenceman Erik Johnson—were wearing the Stars and Stripes. The Canadians beat the U.S. 3–2 in the opening round, but that score is deceiving—the Americans needed a victory to secure the top spot on their side of the draw, and with the score 2–2, they pulled their goaltender in the last minute.

The semifinal between the Russians and the Americans could hardly have been more one-sided. It looked like men versus boys, the Russians being men and being led by Evgeni Malkin, the second overall pick in the 2004 draft, a large and smooth-skating forward who weeks later would suit up for Russia at the Turin Olympics. The Russians put on an imperious skills exhibition against the U.S., winning as they pleased and causing a nervous buzz among Canadian fans. The Russians didn't just look good. They looked *too* good.

Prior to 2005, the Russians had been too good for the Canadians at the WJC since 1998. Just slightly too good, it should be pointed out. In 1998, in Finland, the Russians beat Canada 2–1 in overtime in the quarter final. In 1999, in Winnipeg, the Russians beat the home team 3–2 in overtime in the gold-medal game. In 2000, in Sweden, the Russians ushered in the new millennium with a 3–2 victory over the Canadians in the semifinal. In 2001, in Moscow, the Russians defeated Canada 3–1 in an opening-round game highlighted by Ilya Kovalchuk's showboating after an empty-net breakaway goal. In the Czech Republic in 2002, Canada managed to beat the Russians in the opening round—but it was a different story in the final, a 5–4

Russian victory. Then, in 2003, the Russians—including a precocious seventeen-year-old Alexander Ovechkin—taunted the Canadians after beating them 3–2 in Halifax. With a shot at medals on the line, the Russian juniors registered five consecutive one-goal victories over Canadian teams.

The 2006 Canadian juniors look eminently beatable, as if they might lose to Russia by more than one goal. This Canadian squad hardly compares to the team from the previous WJC. The 2005 roster featured Sidney Crosby, the player Wayne Gretzky nominated as the likeliest candidate to break his scoring records; Patrice Bergeron, who had taken a regular shift with the Boston Bruins the season before; and Dion Phaneuf, who would have taken a regular shift on the Calgary Flames but for the NHL lockout. In 2005, every line seemed to have a player who was ready to step into—or in Bergeron's case, *back* into—an NHL line-up. In contrast, NHL scouts think the 2006 Canadian team is not even two lines deep in elite talent and has no one even remotely in Crosby's and Bergeron's league.

Canada's best player in Vancouver is a centre named Steve Downie, an eighteen-year-old whose life has been marked by tragedy and whose recent career was blotted by controversy. Tragedy: at age eight, Downie saw his father die in a car accident—young Downie had been a passenger in the car. And he had serious hearing loss—no hearing in his right ear, limited hearing in his left. Controversy: Downie had been captain of the Windsor Spitfires at the start of the season, but was suspended after a hazing inci-dent—with possible racial overtones—and a vicious brawl during practice with a rookie teammate, Akim Aliu. Downie is fierce and tough, perhaps the only question being whether he is too fierce and too tough. He plays with an edge, but only at the risk of going over the edge. With his hard life and hard game, he evokes no one more than Theoren Fleury.

Downie never looks more like Fleury than on the first shift of the final against Russia. He takes a fifty-foot run at Russian defenceman Denis Bodorov, who is chasing down the puck in his own end. The referee, an American named Brian Thul, raises his arm immediately. Charging. Thirty-six seconds into the game, the Canadians are not only in against a team that looks bigger and more skilled but are now killing a penalty without their best player and against Malkin, considered the best player outside the NHL. The buzz around GM Place is pure dread. It is going to be tough enough to compete with the Russians on any terms. Without discipline, it looks impossible.

———

Downie's reckless play evokes the Canada-Russia game in Hradec Kralove in the Czech Republic four years earlier. Downie is a tough kid, but not nearly as tough as a Canadian centre named Brian Sutherby. And if Downie thinks he is in a tough spot, it isn't nearly as tough as Sutherby's on that day four years earlier.

Sutherby felt worse than Everett Sanipass did after the brawl in Piestany. Worse than any player on the 1987 squad did after the disqualification. Worse than any player on any Canadian team that ever lost to the Russians at the WJC. Sutherby was fighting back tears. He was trembling. He struggled to speak. He couldn't look reporters in the eye.

It looked as if he had just walked out of the dressing room after the worst defeat of his life, a loss he had to take complete blame for, a moment that would follow him for the rest of his life. Yet Sutherby's Canadian team had won an opening-round game against the Russians. In fact, the Canadians had impressively prevailed with a 5–2 victory. They had never looked threatened by the Russians. And yet Sutherby looked not just humbled but disgraced.

Never let anyone suggest that it's easy to turn the other cheek. It wasn't for Brian Sutherby. Not when it was his cheek, covered in saliva. Everyone had seen it. In the final minute of the game, Alexander Svitov spat in Sutherby's face. And everybody waited for it. A response in kind. Gloves dropping. Punches thrown. Sweet vengeance. Piestany *redux*. Anything.

Or almost anything. What they didn't expect was Brian Sutherby showing discipline as part of his resolve. He looked at the ref and made his case. He glared at Svitov and uttered threats of payback. And then he skated away. "It was the hardest thing I ever had to do, not to do something right there. That would never happen in the Western Hockey League. You'd have to be held accountable."

Svitov's spitting in Sutherby's face ranked as the most inflammatory act in the history of the world junior tournament since Davydov jumped over the boards and skated into the fray at Piestany fifteen years earlier.

Don Cherry claimed that the Canadian juniors had covered themselves with glory in Piestany, doing what they had to do. Maybe so. But it was a far harder thing for Brian Sutherby to fight back impulses rather than start thowing punches. It wasn't a matter of Sutherby lacking the stuff to take on his tormentor. In fact, Sutherby had a black belt in tac kwon do and a tough-guy rep with the Moose Jaw Warriors.

It was a measure of Sutherby's commitment to the Canadian program that he would accept momentary humiliation for the collective good. It was a measure of the Canadian program that its coaches could *sell* that message to nineteen-year-olds, a tough audience. Getting them to fight is often easy. Getting them not to fight, far harder.

Sutherby had a chance to hold Svitov "accountable" a few nights later when Canada met up with the Russians in the final. It was one of the few times a Canadian team cheered the return of a Russian player from a suspension in time for a final.

It was a frustrating night for Sutherby. The run of the play wouldn't give him a chance to line up Svitov. Sutherby couldn't risk taking even a minor penalty. Not when he scored in the first period to make the game 3–1 for Canada. Not in the third period when Canada was down 5–4. Not in the last minute, or in the last ten seconds, when a Russian knocked the net off the magnets.

None of that takes anything away from Sutherby's decision in that opening-round game. Sutherby is the embodiment of the message the Hockey Canada delivers to its players: as much as you want to hold someone accountable, you are first accountable to your team and to your country.

———

It looks like Steve Downie didn't get that message. It looks like he lacks Brian Sutherby's self-control.

Then a funny thing happens. The Canadians kill the penalty—Brent Sutter would later say that teams "always kill that penalty." It looks like a bad penalty if you go by the book—the book that says you should never take a penalty 200 feet from your own net, especially in a scoreless game. In Sutter's book, though, it's a good penalty. It establishes the emotional level he wants his team to play at. It imparts a message to his teammates: play with my edge. It imparts a message to their opponents: it's a long night, so keep your head up.

Downie scores the opening goal, and it turns out to be the game winner in a shockingly one-sided Canadian victory: 5–0. The five-goal margin matches that of the 2005 Canadian juggernaut of Crosby, Bergeron, Phaneuf and the others. And, yes, a 5–0 victory would have given the 1987 Canadians the gold medals they thought they had deserved.

There may be many parallels between the Canadian teams in Piestany and Vancouver. Certainly, the story of goaltender Justin Pogge reads a lot like that of Jimmy Waite—not just that he stars but that, at the start of the season, few expected him to backstop the Canadian juniors. Jimmy Waite, though, couldn't say much about it—he didn't see the 2006 tournament, and he doesn't know Pogge.

The one parallel that jumps out all game long is the one you draw between Fleury and Downie. They are too valuable and too skilled to ever be labelled "pests"—that designation is reserved for the Sean Averys of the game, the guys more likely to win a war of words than a battle of skills. No, Fleury and Downie both bring a pest's attitude to a first-liner's game.

A vignette: with Canada up 4–0, a Russian defenceman and goaltender Anton Khudobin mugs Canadian forward Benoit Pouliot after a whistle. When referee Thul and his linesmen break up a minor skirmish—one that the Russians can't turn into something more—Downie rubs it in. He takes off a glove, holds up four fingers, and points to the scoreboard for Khubodin's benefit. Strictly drive-by diplomacy. Downie looks the very image of a young Theoren Fleury.

I ask Mike Keane about Downie a couple of days later. I ask him to compare his former junior linemate and the Canadian teenager. Keane, who has watched some of the 2006 WJC, balks. He seems deeply offended. "Theoren was an amazing talent," Keane says. "No comparison."

And maybe it's true. Theoren Fleury was an amazing talent, a one-of-a-kind player, no one else like him in his prime. Maybe it's true that there's no comparison on talent. Even though Downie wasn't passed over in his first year of draft eligibility like Fleury was. Even though Downie's selection at the draft didn't produce snickers like Fleury's did. Even though Downie was a first-rounder in an era when more than just North Americans and the occasional Scandinavian were on most teams' draft lists. Downie has done some amazing things in junior—he led a seemingly overmatched Windsor squad to a playoff series victory over a Soo Greyhounds team led by Jeff Carter, who was still in junior only because of the cancellation of the NHL season.

But maybe other worthwhile comparisons could be made, comparisons about different players and different times. Compare their circumstances in Piestany and Vancouver, respectively.

Piestany and Vancouver: these were the biggest games of Fleury's and Downie's lives. They both scored goals. They both got under the skin of the other team. But Fleury crossed a line that Downie only toes. The same can be said of their teams. The Canadian juniors in Piestany ran Soviets at every turn, and didn't mind playing cheap— whether it was a facewash, a kendo-like bit of stickwork, or in at least one case, a jock-high slapshot after a whistle. The Canadians in Vancouver take the body at every opportunity, but they never take cheap shots. They play with discipline—even their loosest cannon, Downie.

———

It might be the most hackneyed of clichés in sportswriting: the turning point. Sometimes there are points when things are indisputably won or lost: a first-round, one-punch knock-out, a clinching putt in a golf tournament. But a game of hockey is the sum of a thousand little pieces—thousands, really. Twelve moving pieces in motion simultaneously. Goals. Saves. Hits. Bounces. Injuries. Each and every one of them in a game might represent, as Jim Sandlak said at the reunion just days before the gold-medal game in Vancouver, "the line beween winning and losing," which can be "a real fine line so many times."

So, naming a turning point in a game as complicated as hockey is dubious stuff. It's even more dubious when that game was played in Piestany on the fourth of January back in 1987. What was the turning point on that day? What set in motion events that took that game to the brink and beyond? It's like trying to name the turning point of a perfect storm. The first low-pressure system? Or the second or third? A change in wind direction? There's no saying. You might as well say it was the first drop of rain to fall. And leave it at that. Maybe the only way to go is to go outside the box, as another cliché has it. And it's far outside the box to suggest that a turning point is not a moment of high drama. It's even further outside the box to suggest that a game turned in its first minute.

Submitted for your consideration: turning points in the WJC games in Piestany and Vancouver, ones that weren't much discussed at the time. Again, you'll find parallels between them.

Vancouver: The game's first shift. A few commentators suggest that the tone of the game is set by Steve Downie's hit on Borodov. Perhaps. But watching that shift and that play, I think of the referee making a very tough call in a very tough situation, a call against the home team and against the home team's hero in front of a huge arena packed to the rafters. The difficulty of that call is compounded by events at the tournament—the American team was booed by the Vancouver fans during their games, which might have had more to do with a few mouthy U.S. juniors than Canada's strained relations with the Bush administration. A call against a Canadian team less than a minute in, the first time body hit body, could look like payback or sour grapes. But it isn't. It's a tough call, but not a bad one. It serves Thul well—he establishes control of the game. It serves the Canadians just as well— they have to exercise self-control.

Piestany: The game's first shift. The drop of the puck. Hans Rønning didn't call Shesterikov for elbowing McLlwain, didn't call McLlwain for retaliating with a cross-check on Shesterikov, didn't call Popov for slashing Elynuik and seconds later kneeing him, didn't call Chiasson for interference or charging or cross-checking an unsuspecting Soviet fifty feet from the puck. It was hard to find Rønning in the first minute—at least until he was knocked flying by a Canadian defenceman. On the broadcast from Piestany, play-by-play man Don Wittman described the sequence as "some good bumping early in this game." Later, Wittman described it to me as "unbelievably tough out there." In the stands in Piestany, Josef Kuboda, head of Piestany's local organizing committee and a former international linesman, had a sinking feeling about the referee too shaken to hold a cigarette before the game, too rattled to blow the whistle once the game started. Kuboda was in the same row of seats as Gunter Sabetzki and he watched the IIHF president's expression turn from self-satisfaction to embarrassment. "It was like a game between children played on a pond—like there was no referee at all, which is fine with children but not young men and not with so much at stake," Kuboda told me. Could the game in Piestany have been finished? Perhaps. Could the brawl have been avoided? Perhaps. Would the game have turned out differently if Rønning had sent players to the penalty box on that first shift and thereafter until he had control of the game? Likely. Would the game have been less memorable and less infamous if the whistle had been handed to someone other than an overmatched referee too proud to ask for his linesmen's help? Definitely.

If you have any doubt, find the broadcast of the game. *Cue the opening face-off. Press play.*

INDEX